Antonio Balzani

THINKING FREELY

an endless journey

Questo libro è stato realizzato con StreetLib Write
https://writeapp.io

Indice dei contenuti

ANTONIO BALZANI 3

an endless journey 5

FREEDOM OF THOUGHT 11

ANTONIO BALZANI

THINKING FREELY

AN ENDLESS JOURNEY

To my children,
to my wife,
to my friends,
remembering them with gratitude.

Thinking freely: an endless journey

A book you should and can read forwards or backwards starting at each end. Always a new beginning, and never an end.

*Reading allows us to live many lives
and each time to confront and
challenge the discussion even with yourself!*

I dreamed I was making, or had to make a will. Since I've hardly anything of material value to leave I decided I'd make a kind of spiritual
will; I would leave you myself.

Here is a suggestion for anyone who is about to read my diary: it is a
diary and doesn't follow either a logical or chronological line of
thought; the reader is authorized and even encouraged to use and
evaluate, investigate, challenge or approve, every sentence, every re-
mark, every thought: totally outside the context it is found.
Much further on, there is an analysis of nature – as I know and interpret it – during simplification, it took hold of me: like with cherries,
one definition lead to another: where and when does one stop?
You don't need to read everything that follows; you can grasp the
ideas here and there, as with all books it is best to read from beginning to end and then if you want, jump around.
I've had these thoughts, expressed them, as far as I'm concerned
they are my treasures: any way you use them will never change my
reality, therefore make of them what you can.

FREEDOM OF THOUGHT

Have you ever wanted to write a diary? Maybe occasionally I've also wanted to, but I've never been able to. A journal is a chronological account, methodical, about events that have happened, impressions. I've never been methodical but I'm a good observer and an independent thinker. I explain thoughts, based on random ideas, a landscape, a situation, a spoken or heard phrase, which hopefully suddenly arises after years, when the brain, all on its own, decides to provide the links, maybe when traveling by car, when the attention is mostly automatic, for most of the time, roughly like between waking and sleeping. Well, I decided that every now and again I'd concentrate and randomly jot down some of these thoughts, as they came up and, in the end, create an introspective diary that sweeps across everything that passes through and determines life.
What I've written and reordered to create, the diary, if not only because it will also be read by others and not only by me?

I go over my thoughts again hoping they'll still be useful to someone.

In the end, just a little before anyone else might read it, I'll read it again and maybe I'll try to put it in some sort of order although I'll leave the option open to the readers to discuss the wherewith all and stimulate them to think about everything, because life is a series of things, and only idiots could think it is something simple and straightforward.

I had to collect and identify the essential points, simplifying and expressing them as food for thought for those who are reading, never falsifying or completely ignoring the truths that lie behind them.

A good summary is abstracted from reality, a synthesis that suggests touching on as many aspects as possible in the breadth of the topics involved.

I hope you can read these thoughts from anywhere in the text, and always find a beginning and not an end, because these are thoughts, they arrive, disappear, reappear change and start again as freely as chaos that seeks order to exist and be, in eternity.

When someone gives you what he or she is able to, they've already given too much! Be content, therefore, be grateful for what you've received anyway; don't ask for more than what, in any case, you know you cannot have.

New ideas always advance, but not because they are necessarily better, just because the old die.
It's natural that the elderly are supplanted, replaced by the young; the important thing is that they, the old, understand this and give them something to do, not to obstruct them but to select and train the best, the finest young people who will replace them.

Ideas run through my head.

Choose your, your c...onsequences!
Always think positively but be prepared to face the worst.

It would be nice to know for certain what we're going to do, whatever it is.

A good and useful question to ask, and one to ask the person you're talking to, would be: why are you here now? But it would also be good to ask: how do you justify your existence?

Life does not need justification, and that's it!

I'd like to know if, in serious difficulty, would it be worth being helped. If, in the final moment, I'd intend to die and stop living or would I want to be helped at all costs to get out alive at any price and condition!

A discussion foresees that certain people at least believe in some certainties or truths or fixed points; without this foundation there is no reason for or chance of discussion and debate.

It isn't worth the trouble arguing with anyone who is not up to the argument, or isn't willing to compare their ideas and views with yours and thus possibly to modify them, at least a little.

I believe it is for this reason that knowingly the state, directed always and in any case by financial oligarchies, also if publicly expressed as different forms of government, ranging from dictatorial regimes to the more shamelessly democratic, changing over time, as far as possible the programs and conditions uphold the ignorance of most of the population, the same instruction is given but the provision of a culture is carefully avoided, a concrete knowledge or a capacity for analysis that permits the development of autonomous and free thought. This is also needed for the advancement and stabilization of the results of progress.

The possibility of comparison and the ensuing innovation that comes with it is, and must be, reserved for the few who develop, steal and seek it, constructing, fighting fiercely and investing much time.

The ignorant and foolish are excellent products for the composition of a nation of consumers, able to be indoctrinated, persuaded, willing to take charge of the induced needs of consumer and subliminal demands, which are gradually imposed by development strategists, in

exchange for a few trite demagogic and populist slogans.
I know you're not ignorant, and I also know you're not imbeciles.
It's not worth arguing with the ignorant, since they ignore, precisely, they are so full of certainties and so arrogant about defending their narrow viewpoint with their fanatical enthusiasm they seek nothing else but victory, which is the very antithesis of animated discussion, since this necessarily changes over time, the ideas of those who argue acknowledging or questioning a few certainties or views expressed by each, including you, always introducing new ideas to be studied.

Ideas change, must change over time otherwise, if yours have solidified and have become unvarying, then you have become one of the ignorant, and our exchange, your reading, ends here.

I still think you're not stupid since the only impossible thing to do in the world, the entire universe, is to explain to a fool that he is one. If he were able to understand this he would not be a fool. If you can understand this, you can't possibly be one.

A diary should be read or re-read after time has passed; totally passed and when only at the point of death but only when you are no longer able to do so. I shall therefore start with the phrase I'd like to be my epitaph, written in large letters on my grave in the cemetery at Bardi: *I don't know if my life had any sense or if I managed to make a mark, but I did the best I could!*

I try to remember how I felt as a child: I can't.

With time memories about facts fade, so that history becomes legend and then the legend becomes a myth. Nothing we like or don't is, or may be, destined to last unchanged for a long time, let alone forever, let alone the 'love' of the young.

Why, why, why?
There are so many whys, so few answers and so little time to search
for them, so few certainties!

I consider myself a European citizen, of cultural origins and education
Italian, something I'm fiercely proud about. I don't know what the homeland is and would like to be treated exactly like a French, English,
German, Spaniard, Romanian; the only difference between them arises from the skills and qualities that originate in my being Italian.

I observe, I don't think, don't presume, don't believe: take note!

To believe is to assume and analyze based on logic; logic is based on
unproven assumptions, is subjective, doesn't lead anywhere but where we want to go.

Science fiction is the art of reconstruction based on the logic, of un-
proved premises that however permit you to construct real worlds
that are developed according to the desired model. False worlds and
liars but they are fiercely credible and often predictive.

I never believe in anything!
Tomorrow will be another new day!

At this point I feel I have a duty to introduce myself and I'll list a few
sayings I've adopted, where I recognize myself, and that describe who
I am symbolically or at least who I believe I am.

Nothing is normal in nature: you are normal, me too!
Like the mammal the duck-billed platypus, beaver tail, rat body, capable of varying its metabolism, from 200 to 10 heart beats so it can

stay underwater, armed with poison, with its eyes closed it can detect the electrical currents linked to the life of its prey. A freak of nature, a set of possibilities.

Normality is bullshit! It's unnatural, does not exist ... fortunately!!! I repeat and emphasize this for the skeptics, the certified, conformists, minors! And that everyone is seeking finding and playing their own game!

Quote: *you see who it belongs to, that's easy. Brevi cito clare rare est: a brief explanation is rare.* I'm always seeking this basic quality.

What follows is the summary of my pragmatic and profound thought on how things should be in general and especially in Italy where people wake up in the morning and start thinking: what should we prohibit today?
More whores and fewer pains in the ass! And that everyone pays taxes.

And then: *Saint Madonnina please pray for everyone and that we will also be among them!* This was the prayer my mother always recited. This is a simple prayer, complete and kind.
Quando quenta boegna! The diphthong oe is pronounced as in the French a very closed o. It is a quotation in the dialect used in my home town Bardi and it means exactly: "when you must you must!" *Work as hard as you must, enjoy as much as you can!*

My favorite animal, one that I believe most represents me is the eagle: strong, independent, free, it chooses where and how to move, acting out of necessity and by choice. Darts through the heavens and surveys the world. Few things are fundamentally important to it but these are critical. It is so free and independent that although it loves company it is happy, most of the time, to be in isolated places. If you don't bother it, if you haven't threatened it, you have nothing to fear, but woe to you if ...

And now for the last: *Time is short. How many emotions are wasted!*

Every New Year: many wishes to all; also this has past, in some way. Certainly the next will be great ... wonderful ... marvelous ... inimitable ... worth remembering. All your dreams and desires will be realized; good will defeat evil, taxes will be reduced and love will triumph.

I work with the environment and pollution, mediating between the interests of the production facility and the residents' right to enjoy the environment they live in; safety and prevention, and the continuing education of adults and adolescents: for company workers or teaching integrated science in high school. For years I've also been the National President of the Board of Arbitration (AIAS), the Italian Association of Safety and the Environment, which is the guarantor of the code of ethics, of respectful behavior in counteracting the different professional needs that often result in unpleasant personal situations.

The old adage is valid for everyone always: *be optimistic because if today is not serene, tomorrow will be! And if it is not serene resign yourself!* The important thing is to be able to say it without stuttering, without the tongue rolling over on itself. Sometimes it needs to be repeated many, many times.

Venice: I hate it but in fact it only needs a ray of sunshine to transform the city, because the walls of the old city, which appear so gloomy and gray in the rain, become a festive and dazzling white. Excessive!

... A landscape in Cornwall impressed me: among the pretentious stone houses with a narrow garden, an old building that was at least a couple of centuries old, typical expensive country estate of the good

old days, with the gardener's cottage, out buildings, stables, the chicken coop, an outside spiral staircase with six steps flanked by a stone balustrade with antique torch-holders or actual pot-holders in wrought iron. It reminded me of my grandparents' small wooden villa where I was born. My grandparents' house was surrounded by a wall around the garden and outside we could only see the first floor, balconies full of purple flowers, red tile roof, the umbrella of a fig and hazelnut tree over a bench. Gooseberries surrounded a well, which had been planted there to keep children out of danger. On the edge of the courtyard abandoned tools and a plow.
The house in Cornwall was inhabited. A wisp of smoke rising vertically from a chimney. In the distance yellow flowering brambles flanked the narrow lanes, (here is the tangle of brambles found in fairytales; if you haven't seen them you can't imagine them) a bell tower and farms; the wind and drifting clouds. At times gray, bright blue and green in the sunbeams; the scent of the sea, nothing more.

The greatest danger for everyone with the consequential health risk, with undeniably lethal results over time, is the simple act of living! All else are only the costly side effects.

What everyone forgets today is now common knowledge since men and women have existed; to the time when man was only an expendable tool for the survival of the woman and the species depended on them. Women have their cycle; during the cycle they become terribly intrusive; they are nervous, sensitive, suffer, cry, have unjustified sudden mood swings, they pick the first one who comes into range or for normally trivial reasons or easily solvable; contest and bear upon the quiet daily life of the men creating a notable disturbance. They can't do anything, they are women and are like that, during that time hormones matter more than conscious control. From the time women ruled and governed, the wisdom and knowledge of the problem prevented women from suffering the stress of coexistence during their period, permitting them to rest, care for themselves, and prevented them from being ridiculed, humiliated or offended; they were ceremonially removed from the group, more or less isolated, with no guilt or deceit, preserving themselves and the family from 'abnormal' interference.

Then came the long period when women ruled but men commanded; unfortunately a time when hypocrisy and religion was in the service of male power, when violence against the weakest and their exploitation was elevated to a system. Filling it with false motivations – from witchcraft, to contamination, to the impurity that brutalized the very idea of femininity – the same isolation was now decreed.

Today, at least for us, fortunately all this has past; effective equality of roles, if not complete from the socio-economic viewpoint, is total at least from the point of view of the person, understood as a human being; the extension of this equality, intensely won back outside the walls of the home, moved from the family to civil society, creating social upheaval and new preconditions for confusion.

No one today questions the right and duty of women to fully participate on a par with men in everyday life; their right and duty to surmount, for themselves, the highest social outcome possible; their right to have the best chance of competing with men, a competition they often excel at in areas where men are in short supply, there is ample confirmation. Notwithstanding, this state of affairs has led to women and only them, of having the only possibility of conscious control of their 'period'; it has provided them symptomatic drugs but has taken away the chance of getting away, for a moment at least, from the social scene. The result is a situation of periodic conflict and stress, for all, since women are in conflict with their difficult to control essence, men with the periods of uncertainty and indetermination caused by female instability.

It wouldn't be anything if there were one, but multiplied by millions of women in our society means a constant state of conflict and stress since all are forced to fight to overcome acute moments with minimal damage.

It has come to be defined as *a lack of communication* and is measured statistically, in the name of a principle, false and artfully slurred: men and women are equal! A bogus and demographic totem appropriately reduced to the synthesis that has marked social evolution for two centuries, until the global financial power took note, quietly, that the emancipation of women and the protection of children renders them, economically, far more than any male-dominated economy. Statistically one to three times at the least, in fact if two people are working in a family it is likely there will be two incomes but they will also

need two cars, two sets of insurance, a maid or nanny or caregiver, kindergartens, amenities and specialty shops, changes in nutrition, etc. A woman working (almost twice that outside the home) induces the creation of at least three other jobs and generates a more stable economy.
Of course it isn't sustainable, true and possible that men and women, males and females are equal, fortunately.
The complete slogan should have been: *Men and women, males and females, are equally and on an equal basis human beings.*
Any publicity, you can however check this, announces such a simplistic principle could only lead to a peaceful sharing and not to a fanatical struggle and clash of passions, it would not therefore bring results and in short profits ... and thus ...

The time of the dance hall ... The party in full swing, colored lights music, beautiful women and interesting characters, girls with a great desire to laugh and with few inhibitions....

And the night club ... in the scene that promises everything there is something tragic about her: the controlled sadness and displayed with skills acquired over time, the feeling anything but reprehensible that the soul ... I'll never be able to pay taxes and help my parents or children!!!

He coveted and courted, the powerful official, the successful business man, the professional, the worker on a business trip, the director of the tax office, perhaps rich or makes it seem so, has spent and chatted has drunk a lot, feels powerful and satisfied but it is three in the morning, unhappily he looks at her, sighs, takes the glass from the table, empties it in one gulp and murmurs: excuse me Miss... I have to go to sleep...

The time of the paparazzi scoops, and interceptions... he, the Knight ... made merry!
The journalist, who has not yet left the phone for a moment while he

takes possession of that last word, walks up the hotel stairs with heavy steps. Tomorrow there will be a front-page scoop ...

The time of the wine bar, I remember Elvira, who was always leaning on the cash register at the wine bar in the village we went to spend the evening, to drink a glass of wine, play cards, talk of the principle world systems, of politics, women, eating a sandwich with raw pesto or *cicciolata* and gorgonzola: an ageless woman. Her smile was wise, measured, as her cheerfulness was never misplaced. She was strong but not fat, not tall. Beautiful long reddish hair framed her always slightly flushed face, all together pink. Efficient, she didn't miss a thing, but didn't act: looked at you, just you, a long time. That wise calm look, those regular features apparently without character, did not inspire joy but boredom yet, I remember her still only for that: an icon.

Da Onorato, was a place where time stood still. The owner had a long beard and a silk cream-colored scarf, stained with sweat; he went stubbornly from the kitchen to the cafe not listening to the chattering and the continuous demands of the customers, old men playing the card games scopone or tresette beside a group of prattling girls, glancing right and left, scruffy college boys and laborers, sitting side by side on the benches around the large wooden tables. And everyone, but absolutely everyone, smoked and an aromatic mist hung constantly in the air, present at every hour of the day. In the background music from a jukebox.

I remember Anna at Marina di Carrara: there was something murky, vaguely morbid, that attracted boys like me, teenagers always in search of adventure, eager to win her confidence. There was something attractive about her and yet her breasts were almost flat, a body not made to awaken the senses. Boys always surrounded her, but I don't remember anyone there.

Beyond the beach, towards Lerici, the terrain becomes steeper. Per-

pendicular rocks, crowned with pines overhanging the sea, they meet
the wind, carrying the smell of resin and salt everywhere. Since then I
have liked the sea in October and March, but not after June, when
the tourists arrive in droves.

When I was a student at Carrara they called me Parma because they
heard I doubled the s and then after, later identified me like that in
other places as well, but with some doubt, because they felt the Ligu-
rian accent was not right. It was probably true. In Emilia no one would
have been able to identify me, even after 45 years, as a Parmigiano,
someone from Parma.

*U dialettu l'è drento de mei cumme u castelu che l'è sta a prima côssa c'ô
vistu dopo iöci de me mare* . The dialect is inside me like the castle I
first saw after my mother's eyes. Even if I don't agree with the use of
graphic characters that have nothing to do with the read language.

Bardi, the town of my origins and of my childhood, only now I realize
how important ones childhood is throughout life: as time goes by I
feel my roots calling me and they increasingly remind me of where I
came from. I left, like many if not everyone, a long time ago but now
more than ever I feel Bardigiano.
Dialect is like the blood that binds a family, close and diluted blood;
our parents taught us to speak Italian so we could get ahead and the
dialect doesn't come spontaneously, but it is part of our being. Although it has become buried by living in other places and with other
languages and dialects that enter our ears every day.

*U dialettu l'è cumme u sangue che liga na famijia. Gh'è cui de sangue
striccu e cui de sangue longu ma tutti ien ligà* . Dialect is like the blood
that binds a family, there are those of close blood and distant blood
but all are connected.

A duck hunting scene on the beach in Cinquale: it was October, a beautiful day after all, the sun still warmed while it was necessary to dress warmly; every day I went to the beach to chat with a couple of friends I noticed a strange formation of men lined up on the dock about ten meters apart. They were armed with guns, waiting without moving, obviously hunters. Suddenly, one started to shoot and then another and yet another, all together; it seemed to be a new year. They were shooting the ducks coming from the sea in huge forma-tions. Evidently tired, they dragged themselves in flight; they rested on the water riding near the shore and were greeted by hundreds of gunshots. They were torn down as they arrived. The dogs, dozens of dogs, threw themselves into the water and went back and forth brin-ging the birds to their respective owners. A dog was hit as it approa-ched the prey.

Two hunters quarreled violently finishing by shooting at the feet in the sand over possession of a bird that had fallen between them – it's mine, I hit it – so close they can't be identified. A real cold-blooded slaughter of creatures no longer able to continue their flight: from being dead tired to dead. A dreadful sight that made me hate hunting. Also another occasion contributed, when I went with a friend to hunt migrating birds: they'd brought five hundred shots and the same number for each of the companions; they carried back about two hundred mounds of feathers filled with pellets which then finished up with polenta and flasks of wine. As there were not enough birds for everyone tins had been placed among the trees, objects, and they'd fired all the shots provided. I didn't want to try!
Returning to the beach, a nice episode lessened the horrible impact. Every so often a bird that reached higher than the others was struck again in flight and ended up falling along the waterfront where many people were walking. I remember an old man, but I was young, maybe he was just elderly or simply a mature man in a dark coat: the duck fell a few feet from him, without even stopping he bent down to pick it up, slipped it under his coat and continued, undaunted, on his walk. Such was the excitement that no one apparently noticed. I remem-ber this episode with great pleasure and I always start to smile.

The flooring was gray, the marble of the tables a raw white with blue

and green veins. The bar where we spent most of our evenings. Through the yellow glass, I glimpsed the bright clock on the tower of the
old city that marked ten minutes to seven. We were playing *boccette*
like billards without the sticks; we drank a soda, smoked Nazionali ci-
garettes.
It was school time; it was winter. The beach was as gray as the sea
and the sky and the buildings, the bathing stalls were without glass,
the same plants. Everything was wet. Piles of sand on the beach waiting for March to be spread out and clumps of seaweed and whitened sticks, twigs and charred objects; who knows why there is always
charred debris.
In summer, everything became cheerful colored, painted and transformed by humans and by the sun, but in the rain, with the roar of
the surf and the mud, everything was desolate and depressing, maybe even a little sinister.
Looking up into the distance, on top of the Monte Marcello cliffs, the
bones of a hotel or perhaps rather an unfinished hotel of the future,
with truncated walls, of a raw gray and the windows closed with
boards and cardboard. .

Men were standing near the harbor, others sitting on the walls. Boats
resting. Four sailors were playing cards, two men on their feet nearby
commenting and arguing.

In the evening – especially in spring, when the air opens up, at the
end of March, April – we walked the sea road in groups of four or five,
happily chatting: we went to visit the hookers. They were our age or a
little older, there were many, were cold and chatted happily, waiting
for a customer. One went, one came back.
Traffic and people: really a lot, especially in the early evening. There
were the wine bars, restaurants and dance halls, bars, there were
girls, and the ice cream parlors opened, sometimes the small markets. We walked because we needed to feel immersed in the crowd, including the group: who knows ....
Gradually as the night progressed, the air cooled, the breeze became
ever more filled with the scent of seaweed and iodine, there were
fewer people and the silence increased, it was almost intimate.

I remember Gina ... It was summer, perhaps the month of June. Maybe she was anemic or was ill or drugged; she began shooting heroin in that period.
Unwell. Very feminine, very sweet and always extremely sad, but capable of exploding into sudden contagious laughter. She was like a shadow in the full summer sun, a shadow that everyone sought. She had a guy she was madly in love with. A bad type who we didn't like and he didn't like us. Older than us, he was always surrounded by young men with a swaggering air and the little kids thronged around them.

A windy day, blowing strongly in from the sea: the wind entered the streets; occasionally pieces of paper fluttered close to the ground among the swirls of dust and sand. I was lost to her. She was a beautiful girl in the most popular and vulgar term, an animal. The only one I remember after 50 years, I still remember her name, surname and address: *L.P. Via M.A. La Spezia* .
At times suddenly I turned to look at her, mussed up light hair but I made it look as though I was looking at the horizon, I didn't want her to know.
You could have sworn that no I couldn't care less for my companion; it was what I wanted: I assumed.
She talked and talked, and I didn't answer. There wasn't a single word I was able to say, that I felt like saying; I was intimidated, silenced, but she interpreted my silence as she wanted.
A clock chime struck one, and we parted to go home.
On the landing outside the front door to the house, suddenly, she took hold of my neck and kissed me with surprising aggressiveness. Good night! Then she shot into the house, leaving me startled ...
The moment had passed and I hadn't understood. A month later school finished and I never saw here again.
In my fogged mind she seemed to promise much more than friendship ... And at the same time she threatened to take that away also, if I didn't do something ...
Techniques: today I know that, even if unintentionally carried out, we are dealing with techniques, techniques established in human rela-

tionships selected to obtain uncertainty, aimed at obtaining an objective.

It is common knowledge that in general men are always happy to provide an explanation and though, particularly if they've been asked by young and beautiful women who are having difficulty in understanding, tormented by physical desire, a desire stimulated or tormented by stolen kisses and furtive flirtations. It is also the method used by all information services, more or less secret, since the world began. The only difference from case to case is in defining the objective and mostly that of whom, for example to obtain political consensus.

Someone in the crowd shouts out a question for senator B., he doesn't understand one word, but replies condescendingly, "Tell me … I'm listening to you!" The crowd applauses … good technique!

Therefore … for whom … which … since … therefore … afterwards … we'll pay more taxes, because they are necessary!

Each point of view examines the same situation in different ways, coming to different conclusions and if not supported by rational pragmatism requiring comparison, often resulting in contrasting actions with no chance of gain for any of the factions.
Only those who scientifically and pragmatically plan for the results they seek to achieve, regardless of the emotions therefore with no disregard for the viewpoints and the departure, generate actions to obtain an absolute advancement.

The meeting was over: Naples, trade congress, and everyone left after six hours of being in a darkened room with projected slides, words and partial or incomplete questions and answers; we went out quite tired and tense, some angry, onto the hotel's seafront terrace.
I walked away to light up a cigar and smoke it in peace without having to talk to anyone; after a few puffs I began to look around.

Who knows why but they all seemed more relaxed. Maybe it was because of the time spent with beauty, the sky seemed freshly washed,
blue a little pale, vibrant; sparkling light clouds; the horizon was wider,
almost as if it had not existed before; the sea was absolutely calm,
glistening with small points like colored flags.

Emotions faded memories, milestones of our lives.

It was a meadow in late July near Marinella: finally she had decided to
give me pleasure. With an attitude of concentration, completely absent, I faced the flood of sensations without participating, no effort of
reflection: I limited myself to observing everything slowly, thoughtfully,
trying to relive the scene with a steady delay, to perceive. Gradually
an unstoppable excitement grew in me mirrored in her face, controlled by her determination.

Eternal recurrence of the situation:
We must do something ... It's a revolution!
The two opposing groups invade the streets around City Hall in the
places of power; they break the shop windows belonging to their fa-
thers, uncles, relatives, friends or strangers.
They don't realize that after the elation, euphoria, after the effects of
adrenaline, if all goes well, they'll only have to repair the damage, generating consumer needs, financial difficulties, gains in the insurance
system. My 1968, and then ... and then again.

The demonstration resulted in violence ... finally they'd given those little communist shits a lesson... it was time, well, well ... shit! Ugly ba-
stards, fascists, shits ... you'll pay for your violence ... servants of the
state ...
On closer inspection the point was not what these protesters were
asking but who these demonstrators were; all dressed the same all
committed to shouting the same slogans, each party in opposition
depending on the party they belonged to.
Privileged children, young men from the upper class; I remember a

friend who was the son of a pharmacist, and several years later he
became the Socialist mayor of a small town that led to the Bussola
(the famous nightclub in Versilia in 1968) a concoction of cobblesto-
nes on the evening the stones were thrown: the car was a Porsche.
Much to our amusement he was very angry, when during the demonstration the guys overturned his car.
Young men protesting with the arrogance of children against the system that had given them the comforts and certainties they enjoyed
and the opportunity to express themselves. Imbued with the philosophy of Marx, Engels and Mao Tse Tung. Young men who knew little or
nothing about communism, of dictatorship, fascism, the horrors and
suffering that one or the other system have widely distributed in one
or other of the various countries because their parents didn't talk willingly and made them study to make them different. None of them
had known anything about the war that is now celebrated and no longer feared.

Our state, perhaps all countries, devours its young.
We boys were shouting and screaming, but the old anarchist who had
lived through the war, the real revolution and its effects the real ones,
saw it differently, he felt this state was in danger of being devoured
by its young.
He the old anarchist, teacher of life that spent his time in the sun in
the little sheltered square near the school, was as furious as anyone
and even more than the others because he had first hand experience in Italy of being labeled as an anarchist, he emigrated to Cuba
where he was labeled a fascist and again fled to Chile to be held up
as a communist. Anyway he was persecuted because he believed the
state should serve the people and not vice versa, and he'd said this,
both here and there. According to him these spoiled rich brats didn't
realize they were the important people, their behavior, their decisions, their actions and not the interests of the establishment or the
opposition for whom they acted unknowingly, like pawns. He had to listen to these young Europeans, singing the praises of Castro and of
Che, Benito and Peron and Hitler, or Mao, to the Greek colonels to
Stalin or Lenin, and so on and so forth as statesmen ... dreamers ...
idealists ... as heroes ... as points of reference. Not as murderers,
thieves, scoundrels, hungry for power. According to him these young

people were led by false prophets, corrupt men, ambitious, grandiose interests of pawns having the sole objective of obtaining their own advantage and used every means, advertising, newspapers, songs, or force, violence; all directed towards obtaining only the immediate goal of constant profit.

He was generally angry with the protesters, both sides. Because they threatened the social status that had been so laboriously achieved, its peace, its future now finally defined and programmed; they had to be eliminated! He was an artist, a sculptor, had done work that had been successful. For years he drew on copies of the same work. He allowed himself to be a new form of fanaticism, conservative, with respect to his experience and to both sides. He hit anyone at the demonstration; he was arrested and ended up in jail again.

Many years have passed, and his words, our long conversations, always return to mind clear and fresh.

Anger, always and in any case only the anger, an end in itself, unites and involves, always motivating, always unprovoked!

The Black Block (considered to be anarchists): the pure pleasure of action without thinking about it, pure emotion. An uncontrollable fury, to throw oneself into the chaos screaming; striking out randomly at good and bad, everyone is equal before you.

My father-in-law never spoke about the period of the war and the partisans but one day he took me on a kind of pilgrimage to the place where the monument stood in memory of the Foibe massacres (when the forces of Tito murdered Italians living in the peninsula of Istria, the old province of Venezie-Giulia, today part of Slovenia and Croatia at the end of the Second World War). I had hardly heard about them. There was a crowd; the President of the Republic had come for the first time to honor the fallen.

He wanted to scream but couldn't even speak. He escaped from the crowd, shaking his head: brothers had fought against brothers only the forces of chaos had won; he had lived the results of that revolution everyone spoke about. He had seen his friends give blood to learn what they intended ... the Fascists and then the Communists and then the liberators ... for 'liberation'.

His closest friend with whom he had shared the everyday labors, had lost his life unnecessarily in that place on account of the Italians who were on the side of the Slavs; and then his loved ones had followed him on account of the Americans.

I remember a girl with an appealing figure, beautiful teeth, a face full of freckles, with an enticing smile, provocative, greedy for pleasures, always ready to burst out laughing in a vulgar way who was with a tall, skinny guy who always wore a 'decent' suit and tie and a crew cut (they wore their hair long then). With the serious expression of a bookworm and at the same time shy, top of the class. Silent and calm. They were complementary.

Evolution: the gene follows the usual laws of recessive heredity. Only in cases where both parents bear a viral code, is it possible to generate an affected child; also in this case the chance is only one in four, compared to a 50% probability of generating a carrier where the virus won't manifest itself and another 25% of offspring will not inherit the new code.

The pleasure of traveling; of realizing how much critical diversity is enclosed within a few kilometers of apparent sameness.

Always similar never the same!

Travel, to allow yourself to become permeated by sensations, lights colors forms; the landscape flows beside the car constantly changing and making one imagine, foresee, gradually, the appearance and even the character of the people living in that particular environment. And then to stop for a couple of hours, take a walk, go into a cafe, visit the market, so you can breathe the environment, check the sensations, seek the soul of the people to share it, understand. This renders each experience a pleasure trip magnificent, irreplaceable and unforgettable, no matter how long, no matter how far away.

I have sought to teach my children to respect themselves because
without that first, you cannot demand respect from others. I sought
to teach them to treat people well and with respect because they are
certainly worthy of that.
Respect yourself; you need it!
It isn't possible to feel respect for who they are, they do, others have
done and especially for ourselves without having the profound awareness of being and of representing something important. Something
that is worthy of esteem and respect. Respect at least of our selves
for the awareness that whatever we do, or we are doing, is always the
best possible in that particular moment; for us and for all those who
are more or less involved.

Many people at the fair and they were all there, noisy and full of life,
one space filled with happy people enjoying a vacation.
An acronym in Italian for the *truppe* – (troups), *relax e ospitalità* (relaxation and hospitality), *intrattenimento esercito* or (army entertainment),
TROIE or troops, relaxation and hospitality, military entertainment:
TROIE or WHORES, otherwise called PROSTITUTES (*prodi unità-tra-
stullo e trattamento amoroso per i nostri eroi* – warrior unit-playthings
and loving treatment for our heroes) from one army to another from
one war to another, times change, but the substance doesn't change.
Common sense offers an explanation to the world: saying that the
world appears roughly as it appears; saying that the normal conduct
of human motivation is reasonable.
In the world of common sense the commitment and efforts of a man
are irrational, like the blind and continuous killing of nocturnal insects
on the surface of a light bulb illuminating the dark.
Reality is a short life, full of trouble, a man born into suffering from a
woman goes to meet his troubles, exactly as the sparks from a fire fly
upwards into the hot air.

The world of common sense is totally absurd, coming from nowhere
and nothing to be directed at nothing with no objective. In the world
of common sense the world itself has no meaning.

Sequences!
The days are short and the years are counted; all is vanity in the moment, or is in contrast to the moment. But what is the alternative?
Everything seems to be senseless contradiction, so crazy as to be totally unbelievable for the lack of a precise objective.
It's hard to believe in something you've read or that you've been taught if we accept the mystical or magical solution or religious vision: in one way or another they state the world is just a dream, a moment of conscious perception among the eternal non-beings; the world of faith lacks substance and reality, but then where is reality? Madness? A crazy person motivates his being ...

Why wasn't this done? I don't know ... but if we had talked, discussed, the file has been open for a month ... it isn't possible, you've talked to someone else ... but the ... documents ... were open on the table you must have seen them ....
I wasn't there ... if I was there, I was sleeping ... maybe I wasn't sleeping but I was certainly distracted ... I didn't understand ...

How I hate this attitude that is used only to justify laziness and not the assuming of responsibility!
I am the center of the universe, the whole universe, or of the many universes in any known or unknown dimension; I'm the reason, the only reason why there is reality, because I exist and perceive with my biological, natural senses.
If I die, the reality of the senses disappears ceases to exist.

I don't think anything because, to begin with, there's nothing to think about. There are facts to be observed.
On reflection, though, it is so wonderful to feel yourself among people like you!
Indeed there is happiness in hearing the noises, sounds, words, music that comes from all living thing. It is nice to know that everything is alive and conscious taking part in your life as you in his or hers or

theirs or them. To exist is beautiful, it is beautiful to know the unity of many, appreciate individual diversity; reality cannot cease for me because each person is at the center of their universe and their reason and reality ... eight billion reasons why the universe exists ... and if I die ... reality won't cease to exist: it will change, it will remain, but without me, and therefore it will be even more unreasonable, unnecessary, senseless as it has always been for the rest and always will be, perhaps for eternity. What is the alternative? Paranoia.

But what is the meaning of life? What are the existing people doing? All life, of everyone, revolves around the need to work to get money needed to buy food that will provide the strength to go to work with the money you earn to buy food that gives you the strength to go to work; and to work harder to get more food that will serve to work harder. A continuous search for the strength to go to work, until you die ... all ... in the end.
We have a short time to live: partly we will sleep, and partly we will certainly be miserable.

In the only life we have, why not decide to be as free as possible? To realize something that can distract us from it? For example occupy the thoughts, confront, discuss aimlessly, like the rich people of ancient times called philosophers?
If the life of a man is just an unreal and baseless dream, a simple concentration of energy called thought, maybe life itself is a mechanism aimed at distracting us, to keep us from committing ourselves to evolving in the pure pleasure of thought?
I want to free myself; I want to be so caught up in my thoughts, with the study of details, that I won't have time to think about the true meaning of life. Quite a paradox!

I want to use logic: if you want a logical test it can be used to discover some truth, then you cannot start from the unproven assumptions since in this condition logic could prove anything.
We are the world, the only common meeting place at the center of the world.

Proven preconditions: the world is what it contains within itself, evidence of itself!

Each living being exists, exists because they have direct experience of the self; they exist and perceive themselves in the world thanks to their senses.

Each living creature faces the reality of its existence thanks to the lessons that arise from the senses, and not just the five, we were given. The senses and the perception of reality are unique and unitary, the only reliable teachers. I *see touch listen smell taste perceive elaborate* a context; and these are the actual facts that permit us to define and enjoy life every single moment. The world as we perceive it is beautiful. The feeling of the sun on the skin, of hot water under the shower, of a woman's hands is beautiful. The scent of flowers or seawater of food is pleasing; the succulent flavor of a steak: I like to listen to people's voices at the market or music. I like to look at a panorama of the mountains that extends and continues seemingly to infinity and back, from a distance, from the sea; the colors of the leaves and the sky are beautiful. Your eyes are beautiful, the sun that warms me and the cold that makes me shiver. I am, they are my perceptions that are as real as I am.

Self-consciousness therefore exists and is a rational and absolute phenomenon!

Every day life makes me feel that I am part of everything, in every possible way, at least in this arc of time while paltry, this fundamentally temporary period of my existence and of the universe itself, of the whole of reality that surrounds me, for sixty – eighty years.

There are more things in heaven and earth ... I don't remember for sure, but I believe it's a phrase from Horace that over time has taught me, as far as possible to keep an open mind, not to believe anything or reject anything until the evidence has been irrefutably proven; and even then, given past experience, to remind myself that with time other new proofs will intervene to return it to the discussion of what we think we have established, to deny it; it has always happened; new evidence has refuted what has been taken for granted, that has been blindly believed, for centuries.

There is no limit to the human power of rationalization that always tends to want to explain everything that is unknown, through what little is known; the result is the triumph of ignorance.

The result of ignorance is fanatical acceptance or fanatical rejection; to believe or not to believe; an unequivocal choice; from time to time absolute faith or its absolute negation and this only in function of what each knows, or believes they know is presented as known.

I've noticed that intelligent people and those coming from a normally good environment, who have received a normal, good education – in conclusion their culture is much greater, not their learning (two entirely different concepts) – are tolerant, open-minded, people who are normally thoughtful and willing, with the fewest prejudices.
The opposite is true for those with money and learning with little or no education and culture are equal to people, who though, possess and have lots of money but didn't earn it directly. These last are possibly, conventionally, even highly educated, result as substantially uncultivated; today they say they are 'specialists'.
Both types, united by ignorance, are at least closed and intolerant, with a tendency towards fanaticism and oppression.

Unproven premise: I was born, I was told, a certain number of years ago; when I began to doubt, various stories were proposed to me over time, which were all rather clumsy or fanciful, to explain where I was before I was born. I was told, taught, that I am mortal and destined to stay here in the world for only a few years, after that I will disappear and will no longer exist, but the whole universe will not end after me because there are others who will continue to live and I somehow obscurely will continue to be part of it all.
If life were like that, it would be only the manifestation of a species able to feed, to grow to survive, reproduce, identifiable and recognizable in a determined limited environment. The life of the individual would have no meaning.
Other explanations followed, tales, stories, logical, rational and irrational, mystical and atheist, to convince me of what will happen to me

after death at least in this form and in any other form of which no one, though, knows anything. I have some memory of all this, the memory is only an aspect relative to consciousness so it can be processed, altered, manipulated, modified, can vanish. The memories do not justify the facts.

About immortality, many religions have existed and have been proposed to me; all preach immortality to guarantee continuity as an alternative to the gram of real life, according to logic but all depart though from unproven assumptions form the beginning of life to reach after death.

If I were immortal, the life lived would be just a random phase of my overall experience. Why not! I might just be a three-dimensional manifestation of a curved arc, maybe a knot, in a seemingly closed curve but instead it is open, has neither beginning nor end: only an infinite path or a convolution.

Even the religion preached by the undefined and indefinable 'scientific community' does the same to prove or better to say exactly the opposite, the absolute randomness of an unrepeatable perhaps insignificant period, or maybe only unique, of physical presence in the world without purpose but of absolute, relevant, unquestionable priority.

Without man, in fact, there would be no 'scientific community' as there would be no religion.

The 'scientific community', rational, secular not gullible, uses logic that departs from conditions that cannot be demonstrated, from the definition of itself.

The world, the whole universe branches towards the external starting from my center, therefore exists. But if each of us is the center of the entire universe, then the universe is illogical.

Logic cannot then prove anything!

For the rest I knew this already, logic is the safest method for convincingly telling lies. Permits it.

Each one of us is nothing and no one if not defined by a set of relationships, terms that being such are mathematically constant. Everything is relative! Everything is related to the constants, the relation-

ships, the terms between two or more parameters, such as in an equation. I am AB, son of ... born at ... in the province of ... Italy, Europe ... I was born seven years (approximately) after the declaration of the end of World War II and thirty years (approximately) before landing on the moon ... took place 1969 years since the birth of Christ, according to the Gregorian calendar, the actual ... etc.
Like time: it is what one needs to get from point A to point B at a determined constant speed and the space between A and B is defined by the time that separates them. The definition of one defines the other.

All those who have taught me anything, basically preach in the same way, that is, try to explain and tell the truth by creating persuasive lies in a way that does not convince me at all.
The funny thing is, however, pay attention, I'm not talking about philosophical obscurity at all but simply one of the main principles of particle physics: the uncertainty principle, according to which exists though simultaneously, perhaps in another or endless other dimensions, all that is not determined but which becomes real and perceptible, characterized, only when it is better observed or better perceived; therefore it is only when I perceive reality that it becomes and is!
Exactly like this, if my senses did not determine reality itself it would be more or less a mere fantasy.
Yet, since there are eight billion people and several hundreds of billions of creatures, and they, perceive in a way that is slightly different from each of the realities around them, then there are at least as many real universes, focusing on their perceptions and determinations and all slightly different.

My universe begins and ends with me because I am, exactly myself in every way, to determine it and if I didn't exist, then it would no longer be able to exist, becoming newly indeterminate even though it would continue to exist in virtually infinite possible realities for every being that observes, perceives and determines, but no longer mine.

They have always told me that it's the parents' job to teach their chil-

dren to live their lives in the right way: I am aware a parent can't teach anything to their children! All that a parent can do is give them the chance to learn, something they do on their own. Maybe the only thing they can teach them is to be responsible and they can do it only through demonstration. They can make them take notice of situations and give them the chances which, according to you, would permit them to realize themselves but they decide if and how to take advantage of them. You can guide them to always face greater responsibility and they ask you why they can't live according to their own rhythms. You can try to be an example but realistically you cannot always be the example to follow, in anything to be avoided.
To grow up and become adults is a war fought on their own, by them, and that doesn't make them winners or losers.
Today I believe parents should first think of themselves: it is only in this way they can provide their children a possible example of happiness or at least of serenity. If you always make sacrifices for them, and still only demonstrate the need for sacrifice, then they'd think they owed you something in return, even in old age; something that won't be responsibility but thankless sacrifice.
Your children will never be as you would have created them but they will however always and only be themselves. A parent can just accept this and stay calm.

When you're born you're alone, the infant in the house, mother and father, the world is pink or blue but then the child begins to meet other children; no one discovers evil until they begin to spend time with other children. They are egoists, wicked, merciless and I, as a child, had to be like them and play with them? Was I also quite bad at that time? I don't remember very well, but now they are evil, selfish, ruthless, so they say. Maybe I have remained a child? I didn't grow up enough?
I fear that I don't remember how I felt when I was a little boy: there's nothing to be done about it, I just can't.
When you become a man you have to understand the adults' point of view.
Children are strange creatures that are protected by adults' many interests, or at least the adults, for the most part, do so; there are infinite codes and conventions. In the early years of life children are not

interested in adults because they are too big, they don't bother them
and then are always taken up with things that they're not interested
in.
Children grow up when they realize their presence affects adults: for
example, when they realize that when they are absent adults never
do the things they do when they are present.
When they discover adults suddenly stop talking when they enter a
room and the conversations change and they begin to talk about this
and that about the weather, of other nonsense, then children begin
to hide to watch and listen. And they take advantage! They say that as
you get older you become a child again ...

I thought of myself and of my life as a straight line: in fact not a
straight line but rather sinuous, which though has no beginning and
no end, it is made up of a sequence of close and connected points.
I can see me as a straight line and therefore also as a curve, and that
is still a line or a line segment, an open or closed line, it makes no difference.

The purpose of my life? It could be the search for truth, if however I
could believe that truth exists.
The truth? Perhaps the simplest was temporary of an opinion, imposed or strongly shared, until the point of view changed or the underly-
ing issue.

The unknown is not a mere hypothesis but an unknown reality that
exists beside our normality and in fact usually after looking closely at
something that seems strange at first sight, the strangeness vani-
shes until it gets to become something that is common or almost.

It often happens that you just brush upon reality, almost miraculously,
without even realizing it; it happens since we simply live in a narrow
range of ready-made ideas, customs, prejudices, and we tend to relate everything to ourselves and ignore the invisible because of simple
ignorance of its existence; proudly not admitting to our ignorance, ra-

tionality would always have the upper hand. Those who believe in the rational are right, or better, rationality will always have the upper hand over what is now defined today as the supernatural?

I like the concept of 'ignoring our own ignorance'. Stimulating and binding: up to where it could lead us to reason about it? Now I don't want to at all, too demanding and maybe a nauseatingly pointless exercise?

I took a trip on the highway. I stopped several times. Hundreds of kilometers. Yet at every place I stopped the road continued, forwards or backwards, always continuing. Strange!

There are people with skills equal to my own yet with their imagination they manage to see colors, shapes, sounds, noises, music; they manage to get to the other side of the world and beyond, to describe and convey emotions. I unfortunately am bound to the letter of things I see and know; I can only glimpse shades and glimmers of what is or could be: I'm limited!

A painter must know how to paint not only the things that can be perceived or known in the world but also those that are hidden that they intuit; in nature everything holds secrets to be discovered, investigated, answers to questions that often we don't even ask: the age of the trees is hidden, concealed and stored within the rings of the trunk.
The power of a watercourse is demonstrated in the power of its current. The sun hides its incandescence at night in the dark; the birds and the fish can unlock the secrets of flight and the laws of nature with their movement.
A painter can conceal and suggest the mystery and the secrets of nature itself. Things exist and are different; a tree in the painting can be a red maple tree, elm, hazelnut, a willow or a walnut.
Man, the painter takes nature itself, crushes, crumbles, reducing it to elementary components in a mortar to reproduce it at pleasure; ta-

kes a little malachite and black bitumen and gives form and substance to the thick shade of a leafy tree. Uses organic and inorganic, mixes green with the yellow of turmeric or gall if a lighter tone is required, white lead to veil the appearance.
The full light requires the pure yellow of gold, of cadmium. The colors are light and the light reveals nature in its multifaceted complexity. Carefully observing each leaf seems different from the other and so it is also in the painting! The capable artist needs only a few touches, only green, and the painting becomes unique, alive, full of profound meanings.
On an existing tree all the colors are already there.

Did you ever happen to notice Italians abroad? Where do you find them? They are certainly in an Italian restaurant ordering spaghetti or pizza. It is as if they find themselves in a different world than the one that is a little chaotic, a little approximate, we are used to it being even a little dirty and run down, involuntarily people try to find something familiar and reassuring, a kind of point of reference.
I like to travel, simply to go to a different city and I always see the same thing: if I go to a news stand in Rimini they are selling the Gazzetta di Parma, just like in Cortina or Rome: everywhere there is at least a parmigiano or parmense (someone from Parma) who asks, searches for, finds 'la gazzetta' and they won't read another newspaper. In Parma they would read 'La Repubblica' or 'il Corriere'.

I think maybe changing environment, reality, traveling as a tourist to discover situations in the world and ways of life that are entirely, the most completely different from our usual, certainly finding all the stimuli and the sensations sought for and expected, the real satisfaction, the real fun comprises the surprise in finding something known and familiar that, mostly, provides you with an unexpected, reassuring landmark in the place you find yourself, which will then be talked about, at home.
You know I was in Urundabugundi and you know what I found? A Neapolitan who sold fake watches! An Italian restaurant serving pasta with tomato sauce and it was full of people ... a Sorrento pizzeria where they made a delicious pizza.

Perhaps the Germans by chance find a place that is tidy and spotlessly clean and functional or a traditional brewery and a pub in France or in Italy or Greece and they fill it, in wine country, equally satisfied.

I'm admiring a splendid winter scene: the sun is shining, the sky is clear and completely, totally and solely a uniform blue. The air is dry, cold. The temperature below freezing for days; the light is dazzling and is refracted on the snow, still and crystal clear, blanketing the ground. Bare-branched trees; icy crystals. It is beautiful but still until a solitary bird, a moving black spot breaks the spell.
I like it better.

I have friends who are restorers, of furniture, paintings, books. Restoration, I am reminded of man's attempt to reconstruct his past world by recreating certainties.
I have learned each restoration is something different from all possible others.

There is no universal rule for restoration. For each object or painting, needs to be first studied, understood, and at least interpreted. It is a work of interpretation and thinking about it better this criterion is applicable to any area of life, both private and public.

The facts always depend first on the intention that has caused them to come into being and then on the interpretation everyone wants to give them.

The essence of what we know, we see, we understand, is always proposed by others who are not us and is interpreted by us: like in the game of 'pass the word', it's fun to see how the first phrase comes out at the other end of the chain of transmission.
I once attended a sabba! In fact a quick dance in the round to a rhythm called tarantula, a tarantella, a dance that is popular all over the world that in the particulars of the province of Puglia should help tho-

se who are bitten by a spider survive the effects of its bite. A dance like the ones danced by the medieval witches. A magical dance, definitely liberating, energetic, engaging, alienating.
For the ignorant, as I was, sabba comes from the medieval and simply means to kick, that is to dance nothing more.

The strategy of the first Christian church, to assert itself on the pagan substrate where the missionaries worked was the same adopted by the Romans for extending the empire: if there were temples and gods, with a little holy water they reconverted the temples and Christian saints, the existing holidays were adapted and maintained (like for example the festivals of May, of fertility, of waiting for the crops Mother Earth was re-consecrated to Our Lady, the Celtic feast of the fires Beltane in May, and again for the autumn long rest, the feast of All Saints' Day in October and the memory of the dead on Halloween or the Celtic Samhain with the same meaning). Christmas for the birth and return of the light, for the lengthening of the days, and the festivals of the solstices and equinoxes. Saint John at midsummer for prosperity and abundance for the next harvest or the resurrection at Easter and rebirth to new life at that time nature blooms and require sacrifices which, once again, were human lives or animals and so on to Mithras and the cult of the bull or Isis and the Black Madonna, and so for many, indeed all, of the oldest events or earlier.
Do not fight or destroy but integrate, maintain the habit by simply changing the name and context until spontaneously the awaited change will occur over time, people doing and continuing to do what they have always done.

Obtaining power doesn't require strength but the suggestion of change, for a new order. Unfortunately the power obtained then needs to be maintained and this yes, the maintenance of power requires strength and oppression. This is how it was and how it is for everyone today as always.

The newlyweds wait for the wedding night to finally consummate their love, maybe not rarely maybe only often. Today it is not that normal.

How many problems have been created by an expectation for a night
that most spouses will spend it mostly sleeping, exhausted by prepa-
rations, celebrations and travel, only realizing then that from that moment there would be many other nights when, in love and well rested, they could do so without having to prove anything to anyone but
themselves.

A friend has often accompanied the first expression of my questions,
a woman with a keen mind and sharp-tongue, Neapolitan, cultured,
educated in the liberal arts, Italian teacher and the wife of my dear
old friend. Two intelligent and deeply cultured people. After a couple
of glasses of wine, the discussions at their home have always been a
pleasure: animated, combative; respectful of the ideas expressed.
They were simple questions I posed: I asked them as if we were at
the end of the lesson when the students have the chance to express
their doubts and their misgivings.
There were times when I hated the pedantic teaching tone of my
friend and her husband, the one they used with me to explain, as to
any illiterate, things that, after having heard them, seemed obvious
and banal; but I didn't know why it irritated me so much; I would have
preferred a less professorial tone, however he has never managed to
do anything else. He represented and felt as though he represented,
the system and its supremacy. Many years, many dinners, many question, many discussions, the embryonic stage of the subsequent processing and, of a few ideas, the basis of mine and theirs' today. Ideas
about anything always discussed from one dinner to the next. I have
noticed strong and radical changes in their current thinking.

Confrontation always threatens the stability of convenient acceptance.

More than the questions however were a charged reflection of expectations and for some reason in proposing them I was always per-
vaded by an intense inner energy, of a vital exultation that filled me
with optimism; to try to wait for the answer provoked the same emotion I felt like a child when I came home from the newsstand with a

new album of my favorite superhero comics: it was the smell of freshly printed ink, the clean lines of the drawings; each time the incomparable excitement, of the beginning of an adventure.

The need for penitence almost always encloses and contains the necessity of death. Are we dealing with constant training?
In historical reality, given that no man or no normal woman could achieve eternal life on their own merits, some preachers advocated the worship of supreme suffering as a means to earn it, and many demonstrated their devotion by even accepting to die after a cruel ritual. Development of fanaticism and its use.
Suffering impedes happiness!
Suffering isolates you in a bubble, and no one can reach you to comfort you. In suffering one undergoes a feeling of affront, blind, hard to contain; one becomes hostile to the world.

There are people who come to desire their pain and defend it with tooth and nail, as if it were the most precious thing they possessed. Others, the world, become the ones who want to steal the privilege of being the one who suffers most, the right to win the prize of the crown of thorns.

From fanaticism to war, from war pain, from pain to the development of medicine from the herbalist ... we have to prepare a potion to help the patient sleep and rest so deeply and in this way free them from suffering. Narcosis by inhalation; a high concentration of chloroform and methyl chloride is a very powerful and highly toxic anesthetic, use by surgeons in the Middle Ages until 1800.
In small doses aconite or monkshood, aconitum varigatum or napellina, relieves pain causes sweating, reduces inflammation. In high doses it can cause terrible pain in the limbs, fainting, suffocation and eventually death. Applied to the skin it produces a feeling of warmth, tingling, and then dulling. The skin remains numb for several hours.
Splendid reading: I have read so much about medicinal plants I am familiar with the treaties and know the properties of many plants even if I don't recognize them in nature. This is my great limitation, some-

thing I was never able to remedy and that I'm ashamed of.
... take a little stinging nettle, a little belladonna, mallow root, mistletoe: crush them to a pulp in olive wood. Now warm it up until it is infused. Drink it with a little honey: you'll soon see the effects ... I'd be curious to see them!
An image of my sister who had the flu ... who knows ... She was there, curled up under the sheets, despite her small size, and shook as though shaken by tremors, she didn't speak ... strange.
I thought that silence or talking were two opposite ways of influencing destiny that intervenes: the skeptics keep silent, the diffident, or those who are convinced to have, at least once, something to hide.
At times we have the audacity to express our opinion about what has happened to others and we aren't even able to understand what is happening now, and has happened to us.
But why speak if you have nothing relevant to say?
It is better to listen to who is talking and rattling on and then decide if there is something to say.
The modern world is full of 'serial ramblers'!
Normally one seeks to cancel or reduce their faults attributing the blame to another, or to others, or to the world in general.
We don't listen to the signals common sense sends us: and we ignore them? Pretend that nothing happened. Close them up in the drawer of fantasies. A way to ward off danger, not giving it importance, like nonsense that is not worth considering. Maybe you strongly believe it is like this. Nobody wants to live obsessed with fear.
I've cut myself so many times with my box-cutters but one time my father told me to think I was holding a weapon and I understood that weapons are used only to make human blood or life flow from humans and living creatures. Since then, when I think of a weapon I also think of what it is exclusively used for.
When I received my military call-up I had an interview with the district lieutenant, a motivated man, who firmly believed in what he did in his goodness and importance. I told him: "I will come and do what I'm told to do; I'm Italian and I've been asked to surrender myself and be willing to defend the State with weapons and my life. Men against other men for what will be defined as a just cause. Don't ask me what I think and I won't ask you! You'll order me to do what I must. You'll give me a gun and teach me to use it but are you sure, when you ask me, that the barrel will be pointed where you want it, just because

you want that? The finger on the trigger will not be yours but mine and I'll decide, by myself, what to do."

He answered, "A man does not exist alone, he is limited, if he goes against the herd, its will, his freedom of speech and actions end in the same instant he stops adapting himself to what everyone will do and because it is requested by the group, the state, by the people, you will do what we tell you and you won't think at all."

Perhaps he was right, history makes him right. Or else I could imagine: who is the accused? Insubordination: does not accept orders!

Having taken part more or less actively in the 1968 riots I did all my military service in Sardinia with the best, even with the foulest and the worst. For thirty years the state has classified me as an object of concern, and yet I've never hit anyone, I've never broken other people's belongings. I've only discussed and openly expressed my dissent, freely expressed my views, which were not always expressed, in practice, the best possible. Today I know it but still do it.

No one can go back to being how they were, what they were, the same as before. Never though after something happens; especially if it's something that causes pain and is difficult to overcome.

No one has the right to judge others.

There are people who faced with a misfortune react, seek to move forward. There are others who don't make it, and decide to stay in the same place they find themselves. They drop out; they simply stop without choosing anymore or wanting to because they can't do anything else.

What you are unable to change must be endured.

It's been said, Napoleon I think, that if on one part of the dividing wall someone pushes and on the other side someone pulls, sooner or later the wall, while solid, will cede resulting in change.

All scientists sooner or later, depending on the historical period, were branded as heretics or something similar.

When the sun shines and the wind blows, at times at least, I feel free and strong, but I wonder if I hadn't read so many books, lived so many lives, felt so many emotions, would I feel this way? Thank God I can read and I love it, and in this way I come into contact with the minds and thoughts of others. Writing, as I'm doing now, instead I come into contact with mine, my mind.

Tonsil operation: I was five years old and I remember it like this ... The nurse Bianca, was overweight, had large hands like oars a white ponytail very high on the head; I screamed and kicked and she held me as she sat on the white metal chair where we were both tied with bands. A ghost slipped something into my mouth and the more I tried to close my mouth the more it yawned. A steel bowl in the shape of a bean collected the blood that filled it. For a few days I could no longer speak or perhaps I refused to do so.

That damn nurse came, looked at me interpreted my accusing look and for all the answers shrugged her shoulders, raised her eyebrows, as if to say, what can be done? I never forgave her. When I think of this and what happened to me, of tonsils removed without anesthesia, tied into the arms of a nurse sitting in a chair, of the extraction of teeth, of cold, of the light anesthetic finally applied to the 'skin growing on the nose', of dentures, the only remedy for my parents at that still young age, it comes to mind that the Middle Ages is not so far away in time.

In around 1750 … he lifted a miniscule ampule of silver smaller than a thimble: "Mandrake root powder in exactly this dose no more". Pour the contents into a container, "And now the poppy extract, in a larger dose, fill a saucepan with water up to two fingers from the edge of the container; bring to a boil. Stir well to heat then allow to cool, stirring constantly until you can hold it without burning for three breaths so as not to burn the patient's lips and tongue". Lift the patient and support him while coughing, panting for breath, when he has calmed down help him drink. In the space of a few minutes he'll fall asleep … At least they tried it, they had not excluded anesthesia because it was "potentially harmful" or "not sufficiently heroic".

I tried to paint: what a disaster!

It would be nice to get into the mind of painter from an ancient pre-industrial era. It would be like entering the palace of 1001 nights.

The painter would move in nature through his pigments, like a free spirit. He would gather, weigh, test bark, gather up the components and dilute the juices with water or oil or blood or egg white, like a baker mixing a cake.

Malachite, cinnabar, and vermilion, the red earth, yellow. The vegetable black of carbon, lapis lazuli blue from overseas and verdigris for the blue and the green, white lead, cadmium yellow and iodine: the seeds crushed or boiled that provide unimaginable colors to the aspect. The extract from flowers that changes color and acidity over time.

The painters know wine yeast and walnut oil are the best oils as the baker flour and yeast. The painter knows what to use for the boards: spread the surface with mastic smooth with gesso, make it shine with essence of turpentine, white; add one or two layers of alcohol or spirits in which, however, first a little arsenic has been dissolved to create a yellow opalescence, then apply hot linseed oil because the whole panel needs to be impregnated. At this point, once the canvas or the panel is dry you can go over it with white paint that is later rinsed with urine immediately after to fix the color. Fumes dust strong smells.

The painter as the dyer of fabrics is a craftsperson who knows the material but as he prepares his canvas and works his board, captures the movement and trajectory of light; he knows how this light will hit his canvas, knows how a woman would bend to pick up a handkerchief that had fallen or how she would wrap her red hair in a turban of wet towels after showering.

The surface of an old picture tells the story of the painting; in the same way tree rings tell its history or the rock layers speak of geological ages, speak of the eons.

A single micron (thousandth of a millimeter) of that surface correctly observed and analyzed, tells its history, at times, more than any monographic treatise; sometimes it throws light directly onto 'history'.

As children, we are all fascinated by mysteries.

At 13 to 14 one acquires a certain skill in producing invisible inks, with lemon and salt water, which reappear when heated with the heat from a candle and to create secret alphabets, cryptograms reserved for communicating between two friends; two tablespoons of salt, two of water a few drops of lemon juice, dissolve everything slowly and hey presto.

My sister used an iron and passed it over the white paper: magically my incomprehensible and invisible message reappeared because the water evaporated and the salt appeared in relief.

When I went to school and became a chemist I learned far more sophisticated methods: for example a mixture of gum arabic and cobalt chloride is used today in figurines that predict meteorological developments: pink for good weather and blue if it is going to rain. And to think that this wonder dates back to the fifteenth century at the time of the Medici in Florence, the principle time for intrigue and poisons. Magnificent entertainers, hucksters, who like to intrigue the audience, those who like to be at the center of attention; casting their observations like a handful of pills and then at some point they become quiet, end the story and stretch a smile; waiting for others to construct the discussion that should be theirs.

The storyteller never tells the same story twice.

...Women shave yourselves; three blades hundred lire!

...Cry children, cry so mummy will buy the little toy!

...Five thousand lire, who will give me five thousand lire for the sheet plus the surprise gift for a value of five hundred? Come on ladies do yourselves a favor, there's a gift for everyone!

...Wrinkled sheets of newspaper, folded sheets of newspaper, make them look at carpets from Foggia and different colors hanging behind his stall, he took a snake out of a basket and made the children stroke it, but what was he selling? The show started about an hour later, he had gathered a little curious crowd, at last we knew: he was selling and sold, dozens of large plastic pens with more tubes of colored inks, a hundred lire each.

The cat restricts itself to remaining motionless in the same position looking straight ahead; faced with the nervousness of that group of white mice that had escaped from the cage, running here and there in the room.

Its paw hit out every so often, like lightning, at one of those rodents writhing on the ground.

As in the Old Testament with the Almighty, who occasionally indulged in a few outbursts of anger. Faced with the mice, though the cat also surrenders. Maybe it does so when it is overwhelmed by the number or doesn't know where to turn: then she gives in but she does so without giving up, haughtily, dignified in defeat.

The mice seemed frightened but not impressed, intimidated.

Mice are like humans and the death of their fellows doesn't bother them. There is nothing that can stop them from continuing and waiting for the daily activities in the face of anything that may happen.

Mice are not timid, not in the group; as a group they are fearless.

There is nothing more terrible and dangerous than a man who knows no fear.

The rich and wealthy are realists; they are convinced that nothing is worth more than life. The rich want to keep everything.

The poor are good soldiers. They have nothing to lose!

The war. As in those ancient tragedies where at some point all shout,

cry, scream, writhe together, it is nothing more than the periodic representation of a path to collective atonement.
Man never ceases to live even when he dies.
He must always run, ahead or behind himself. This is why he is always
so tired and forced to complain. Eternity and boredom.
Our bodies don't have the vocation to endure. They are only provisional mixtures of flesh and desires; inhabited by our souls for a lifetime,
thus little more than a breath in eternity; coming from who knows
where, before leaving for who knows where.
In effect we're just piles of shit, the result of the work of billions of
microbes that live clinging to our bodies. For as we stretch our neck
and give ourselves airs or worry about everything, Saint Augustine
said that we are born between dung and urine, and there's no way,
there is no escape.
The breath of God? And if we were the wind? The wind that in eternity
continuously breathes in and out? The breath of the universe? The
breath of the world?
The wind never dies, like the soul, maybe!
Man comes from the unknown to go into the unknown. Only one
bubble bursting to then give birth to the same bubble?
However you'll never understand what happened!
Déjà vu that oppresses us at every turn. Maybe we were all someone
or something else in a former life?
Another bubble?
This would explain the waves of nostalgia that often beset us for no
apparent reason; nostalgia and melancholy that expropriate our bodies, our thoughts, confuse our time for no reason, a place, a because.
When man travels, he learns what desire gives birth to, which by definition is never satisfied – is nothing but pain.
Yet a man who travels in eternity cannot be oppressed by pain, it is
his destiny.
The monotheistic religions have a great defect: all their priests support mediocre reasons, in which the impact can only be terrifying: In a
round of two centuries or ten centuries it doesn't matter, thousands,
millions of men will massacre each other in the name of absolute truth that each of them believes they possess.
Man invents anything in order to justify his different choices regarding
the most popular religions: they are called heresies, and over the

centuries there have been so many more incredibly disparate absurd inventions, just as unwarranted and unproven as those of the main.

There were the Abacedariani, who affirmed that in order to be saved and have eternal life in paradise there was no need to know how to read or write, and especially not to know the first letters of the alphabet.

There were the Anthropomorphics: who declared that God could not but have a human body reading the basic story, Genesis, in the Bible.

There were the Bacolari, who built on the pretext that Jesus condemned the use of force and stated that it was a crime to carry weapons of any kind even a simple stick.

There were the Stercoranisti, who claimed that the host of the Eucharist is digested like a common food before being evacuated normally into the sewers, or better into black wells.

There were the Nestorians, who denied the existence of the Virgin Mary because they believed that no human creature could have given birth to the Creator. According to them, the Creator would have only entered into the body of his son later. Therefore she didn't need to be pure.

There were Calvinists, predestined for who nothing was worth absolutely more than nothing, therefore, hooray for fornication, let incontinence live.

There were the Waldensians, the poor of Lyon who didn't want to harm anyone. They simply copied the apostles, who lived renouncing superfluous goods and privileges, they believed in sharing. This was why they were so dangerous they were at the center of the most ruthless religious war ever conducted.

There were the Massaliani, the followers of Sabas, that to be more realistic than Christ himself were castrated, sold all their property and gave everything to the poor and, as Jesus told his disciples not to work for earthly nourishment but for eternal salvation they decided that it was a crime to work.

There were the Sodomites, who avoided fornicating with women because they judged pregnancy impure, dirty, and in fact fraught with ramifications. God himself destroyed Sodom, which conflicted with his plan for incarnation.

There were the Nicolaitians, who denied the existence of God the Father as the Creator.

There were the Agnostics, who denied the omniscience of God himself and his son because they declared they didn't recognize the Day of Judgment.

There were the Practicals who claimed that human flesh is a result of the work of Satan who deprived man of his spiritual universality.

There were the Giovaninianisti, who maintained a virgin was indistinguishable from a whore, referring to the two Marys.

There were the Allegri friars, with the cult of rice which was transverse to the Dominicans. The Dominicans, the authors of the Catholic Inquisition didn't appreciate irony, with the pretext of having a science directly infused by God. They always spoke with very loud voices to overpower the other voices.

There were the Circumcellions, who extolled martyrdom and suicide.

There were the Bogomils, who rejected baptism and the miracles of Christ and denied the power of water.

The Cathars: continuously purified themselves since just living dirtied and desecrated; ideals of poverty and self-hatred itself carries evil.

There was Manichaeism who blamed man and only extolled the virtues of piety and renunciation: destroyed by Christians and Mohammedans associated in the work.

Why should the divine be revealed to only a few?

The Cathars believed that every man should have a direct relationship with God so church structures were unnecessary.

Simple souls are often unable to understand cultured words but they also have a right to God. They couldn't be heretics and as a result should not be destroyed?

The Pelagians simply believed in free will! Every Christian must actively choose to serve God, by their free will. It meant that man was an absolute entity, different from all the others; absolutely free to choose his path and thus turn from God to the Devil, from goodness to oppression, without having to account to anyone. Choose 'alone' and 'voluntarily' as the way to follow to get to heaven. To admit it was permissible and possible to have rendered God equivalent to any pagan god selected at man's discretion.

Refusing the authority of the 'Church'.

What matters to a church, an institutional religion is in any case that

people believe and more specifically confidently trust its mentors!
Justification of the existence of the personal relationship with the superior they needed: God!
Heresy was and is therefore practically in every self-regulatory regime, an exercise of individual will, outside the Single Way inspired by the One GOD within his DESIGN. The inscrutable divine design but translated as a result of Divine Providence and indicated by the CHURCH in its grace. Essentially applies to all churches and priestly structures. Jewish or Mohammedan amused themselves in dogmatic precepts and delusions. Magic like religion, Witches and sorcerers; six legions of demons, 66 cohorts each, 666 of 6,666 companies of demons: a total of 1,758,064,176 demonic creatures. Fanaticism is a good game. Comprising, the service of the temporal institution of the Catholic church, the Inquisition.

In the dominant religions, the nature of man is bound by the precept: the gravest sins, idolatry, and then sodomy and incest. Going to the last two that have a biological justification but idolatry, which simply means finding another God, this is unacceptable.
Reincarnation: if that were so, even Mary could return to the Earth in the form of a worm or a carrot. This is unacceptable.
Ascent to heaven body and soul, removed from corruptible earthly nature to take it to the place dedicated to the deity: the deity is in the sky!
Christianity, Buddhism have the same moral, basically the same essence also according to the Franciscans. They carry the same message: the one who hopes for nothing from this world, those who hope for nothing from beyond, who are free from all hope, free from all ties, who deny any impulse from the will, who is a perfect idiot poor in spirit, who has killed the thirst of desire, who has detached from the pleasure of pain is a perfect man.
God is aloof, immutable, simple!
Like the Franciscans, even Buddhist monks go to obtain food: their own and for those they help. They go from door to door with a bowl in hand offering prayers, mercy and hope. They are lovers of joy. The image of the God they have chosen and who they tend to be like.

The mysteries of the initiation are always reserved for the elite, so here is the greatest injustice.

The ideal would be to believe in all the religions at the same time. As God is everywhere at the same time and is always the same; God is everything, regardless of how he is expressed and manifested in what we desire.
India, the magnificent land for religion; ground for loving missionaries from all religions; a country where the poor don't have the strength to protest or steal: they are hungry, extremely natural, they can only beg. Society is divided into unalterable castes where there is no lack of the rich who are few and run too fast for the poor, who can be preserved in their primordial ancestral swill for centuries. Everyone loves it. Isn't there the desire to see beggars groveling at our feet? The intimate enjoyment of seeing others, reduced to humility, losing their dignity? The sensation of omnipotence and real power?
The future: nothing else but the past that begins again. The history of the world spinning round. From peace is generated prosperity from that wealth, from that vanity, from that pride, from that contention. From strife to war, from war to poverty from poverty humility from humility peace. Going around and around, the world falls, the earth falls, all fall to the ground.

Chatter ... humanity lives on small talk. There are so many things people don't want to hear but others never think about, because it is so praiseworthy to be sincere.

I wish we could have started in the middle of the romance, that we had known each other for two weeks, that we knew everything about each other, we felt good together: then I would not be so nervous, you know I'm not usually like this, I'm really interesting when you get to know me better.
Every time you fall in love you notice the song that is playing and remember it forever even if you can't remember the other person's face or name.

She was one of the prettiest girls I'd ever seen: dark shining hair, immense hazel eyes, mouth slightly curved at the corners, upturned even when she wasn't smiling, a fascinating expression that spread happiness.

Blessed students, they all look the same, same down jackets, same jeans, same boots or sometimes scarves around their faces, and yet in those uniforms quivering with life they fall in and out of love, quarrel and make peace, improvise parties where they drink and smoke all they can immersed in music that speaks of their dreams of their plans for the future; dreams they share like everyone. They shout, "Save the whales". The world for them is completely open and just as completely closed; everything is possible for them, but it is never difficult: to find a job, even more success, fame, wealth. Given time they would be pleased with even the simplest security.
They study but they do so in a constant state of anxiety, to get good grades. All of them remember that after graduation you have to earn a living. The world is so unstable there is little to believe in but work at least they would have money.
Marriage in the time of my parents, grandparents, was something quite different from what it is in today's world: the grandmother, the mother, knew their love in a unique moment and from that moment he became the man of their life. They were not afraid to leave everything, family, friends, rather it made them feel like adults, mature. They would have lived with them, husband and also best friend.
The engaged would live happy and content; married they'd have children who would bring meaning and continuity to their relationship.
Little by little they would have bought furniture, books, records, rugs, quilts, a car. Every purchase made together was a brick in a wall, solid and resistant, which would keep them together forever, safe. Mother and grandmother were ambitious and did their utmost to make their home a happy harbor where grandpa and father would return in the evening after their hard work done for others.
They were happy with the prospect of living through the husband, sharing in his successes, his glories.
They had no doubt they would grow old together. Even betrayal would never have been reason enough to destroy everything.

How could they think that boredom would have taken over, delusion, that they would have accused each other of the blame, that the children wouldn't be a sufficient reason to justify their relationship, that one or the other or both, would want or have to rebuild a new life at some point?

Don't eat a McDonald's hamburger: don't you know that when the animal is butchered that it is so frightened that its body becomes saturated with hormones that prepare it to flee or to fight, these hormones then enter the body of the one who eats the meat?
I'm worried about the children, I realize they are afflicted with many problems we don't have, they are victims of depression, unshared secrets. Carelessly they take risks, because they believe they are immortal, always seeking the maximum, excitement.

They seek approval from others but not from everyone only from their companions. They move in herds where there are hierarchies ranging from leaders to the victim: if the leader is positive good, but if the leader is negative, the victim can't escape his fate; he can be pushed to sacrificing his life. Outside the group they are trying to hide their soul from the world and therefore end up victims of sects where the figure of the holy man is such as to be able to look into their soul. For this reason the holy man is feared and respected. Being part of a sect means being part of something larger and more elitist but also more dangerous.

The war has ended! The cry leaps from mouth to mouth. All activities were suspended to give vent to this unbridled happiness that followed the first moment of disbelief.
Unfortunately at the time no one thought of those who were absent who could no longer celebrate anything: the Italians had lost 650,000 soldiers. The French 1,300,000. The English and their Empire almost 1 million. Romania alone had lost more than 300,000 soldiers. There were more than three million soldiers who belonged to the Triple Alliance and its allies. More than seven million civilians were killed.
Yet at that time they had to and could have at least celebrated hope

for all that had happened it could have at least served to warn people, to warn the world, the next generation, that war is shameful that war is bad that war is misery that war is death, pain and desperation. Hope had to be celebrated so that all that had happened would not become an excuse, only an excuse to justify revenge and demands, which could be expected but not accounted for.

The Moon oscillates on a 19-year cycle during which the moon oscillates and is represented in different but constant positions for every point on the Earth at every solstice or equinox and is regularly in the same place at the end of its cycle. At Stonehenge (henge means circle) the arrangement of the sacred stones and access avenues, the Door of the Moon and of the Sun, allowed them to keep this cycle controlled and defined. This cycle was considered sacred to the goddess of the Moon, who protected hunters, because the Moon allowed them to see in the dark, in the hours the prey came out and they could be hunted. Halloween was a winter holiday, the end of the activities; the repose before new life. According to the solar calendar it fell 39 days after the autumnal equinox; it was Samhain, the ancient fertility festival and preparatory rest, the suspension of sowing activities. The tribes would gather in the sacred places for the Moon and in the heat of the fires banquets and orgies took place that served to mix the blood of the tribes and to create alliances and synergies.
The same solar calendar begins in the spring, more or less around the 21 st of March, but naturally not on that day, conventionally, but on the day of the equinox, which is different in each latitude.
Fifty-six is a number sacred to the mathematics of the sky, because between three calendar years and three years of 13 lunar months, there is a 56-day interval. Between five calendar years and five lunar years 12 moons, there is a 56-day interval. Isn't it strange that man gives such great importance to the magic of numbers.
All the current religious festivals have been superimposed on the ancient festivals that marked all cultures from the deepest antiquity, based on the example and the method used by the Romans when they conquered a new province, first they sought the similarities to their many gods because as conquered peoples, while maintaining the cult of the previous they integrated them into the current religion of the time, which at the time was that of the Empire.

The same thing happened when by Constantine's decree and political expediency the empire became 'Christian'.

The Roman Pantheon contained something for everyone and for all activities. It was an easygoing system, adapted to integrating and overlapping with existing systems on the periphery of the territory without creating clashes or confusion.

The goddesses of water, perfectly matched Minerva, the Gorgon's head with beard and halo, symbol of Apollo, was perfectly suited to the worship of the Sun god.

This was one of the strong points of the expansion of the Roman Empire.

The monotheistic religions were extended along the coasts of the Mediterranean, like that of the Jews, or those of the goddess Isis, the Moon, that of Mitra the Bull god, originally the cult of Freemasonry which included rites, discipline, sacrifice. Purification through the blood of the bull, icon of the fighter: the most perfect cult ever for armies.

The monotheistic religions, like all cults, foresaw purifications initiations and sacrifices, possibly blood, but unlike those polytheistic or animistic, they called for dedication, passionate, stubborn, fanatical up to martyrdom and always, loyalty to God before the leader or government or fatherland.

Christians claim there is only one Almighty God behind the universe and that man has an immortal soul: God's invisible, indefinable universe – imprecise soul! – where the sun's energy, the lunar cycles originated that influence the earth Gea and water, Minerva or Sulis, it's not important.

From the union or better the collaboration of these (which are defined and definable) life is derived, biology and from biology man and his living world Gaia.

The Emperor Constantine had a choice, and subject to the power of one omnipotent God, who contained all the others, by reducing these to divine agents, infinite attributes of the divine comprised the whole of creation. Mostly, the choice put him in the position no more of a god among others, but as a unique interlocutor with the same omnipotent and unique God. The same concept as the Pope. With one blow he gained personally, as emperor, the guarantor of direct loyalty of all the faithful of all possible and existing cults, without disavowing or countering anyone directly. Why do that indeed? Worshiping the gods is nothing else but adoration of the idea of divinity.

Sacrifices to the god or gods became a civic duty, a matter of observance not a mystical encounter.

The principle is triune, energy spirit and structure. The divine is in heaven! The figures of the gods, or the deified, necessarily lived in heaven. For the normal dead the soul returns, the spirit, but for the incarnations of divinity the entire body necessarily had to ascend leaving no material trace of impersonation: thus were the gods and so it is for Jesus, the son, or of Mary, the mother.

The gods now become messengers, intermediaries of human causes with the unknown, who cannot be accessed directly by man and who hold up the heavens.

Still today within a few codified religions, paganism matters, in fact, many followers more or less knowingly, are often far from being in contrast to or in antithesis to the primary religion.

The cemeteries placed on consecrated ground, are still shrines for ancestor worship as they have been since humans have existed.

Any madness happening under the stars, they continue to shine with impunity, with their pure and constant light for those who are looking, but even this is only appearance, justified only by the different reaction times in the respective life cycles.

In effect in this motionless splendor even the stars mutate, change, live and die, exactly like us and so also on the other end of the cycle so do plants, rocks, mountains; and also things that seem immobile to us.

For this reason the cemeteries, from the most ancient to those of Christian origin, were places designed to contain the motionlessness of bodies whose movement or change could no longer be perceived by humans. They were always oriented towards the stars, the sun, the moon and comprised private sanctuaries for the ancestors. In particular, all the graves faced in an east-west direction.

It was a time past by many thousands of years ... Looking into the distance from the top of a hill the teeming morass of a profusion of birds and other animals could be seen; all were hunting and devouring hunted countless fish; herds of herbivores grazed, hunted by mighty predators. The hills, the prairies and the entire river delta flaunted abundance: natural abundance of wealth displayed without

shame, untouched, governed only by the laws of nature. It was mother earth that was delighted, prolific, created and sustained life in all
its diversity. Could one ever imagine the Earth could lose its productive capacity for creating and sustaining life?

The domination of the earth cannot be imposed; the riches of the
earth cannot therefore be taken away without her consent and her
co-operation and in accordance with her needs.
The earth devastated by the predatory domination of man, deprived
of its resources, despoiled by unchecked pollution, corrupted by excessive greed, in effect, however, it can lose its ability to create and
sustain, at least for a short period. In the end it will certainly triumph.
Even stripped, robbed, insulted, the land has always had the power to
destroy what it has helped to create.
Men, its creatures, so presumptuous to think of being able to dominate her, would pay the highest price since if it were possible to remove the will to live from the earth, then only its creatures would be
unable to survive, while she resting for a while, a long time for humans but insignificant in the art of her life, she would soon begin to
live again, in a different way, in a way where man will probably no longer exist. The dinosaurs have already demonstrated this.

The appearance that the earth has today, so varied so strange, so unpredictable, results from unknown creatures that have lived in the
warm ancient seas. Over the eons, countless millennia, the seabed
was covered by their shells and their skeletons; other eons and the
calcium sediment hardened, was raised by opposing movements of
the earth: it became rock, limestone.
Under the large expanses of fertile land available to us there are caves formed in the limestone by the rains, of running water.
The seemingly hard and eternal rock can melt as a result of a small
variation in acidity provided by carbon dioxide produced by plants in
hot, humid climates.
In the atmosphere and then in the water, carbon dioxide turns into
carbonic acid and dissolves part of the rock and the acidulated water
flows along minute fissures in the vertical joints of the layers of limestone widening them deepening the fissures: it has sculpted out

uneven irregular floors usually intricate, then fleeing underground through narrow vertical shafts of springs or sinkholes.

The caves were gradually expanded, and their summits have drawn
closer to the surface thus, as a result of the weight, they became
thinner, they collapsed creating steep sinkholes, sometimes leaving
natural bridges, surface residues, or plunging water into deep wells
letting it flow deep down and leaving entire dry stretches of rivers
which then reappears downstream with amazing results.

The soil irrigated by the rich and green wooded rivers becomes bar-
ren and rocky because the water moves the thin layer of soil and
then suddenly again it becomes green and full of life with birds, flowers, animals.

Water is the life and blood of the earth and flows through its veins
carrying and taking away the main components that support all that
exists, where it is today and where maybe you'll find it again tomorrow.

Humanity has settled and then evolved in this environment.

Steppe or tundra, a treeless plain where the subsoil is frozen in the
summer, thawing, it becomes a sea of black sludge. A hostile environment, only low grasses with a life cycle of a few months tied to the
moon and the seasons that however can feed horses, musk oxen,
reindeer, and a number of other herbivores and their predators. Every
so often a patch of evergreen trees at a uniform height stain the expanses with green like oases in the desert: the taiga. The trees are all
the same height because the cold wind blows constantly bringing
sleet or dust, every sprig shearing the one that dares to stand higher
than the others. The sun plays hide and seek between the peaks and
valleys of the surrounding mountains: storm clouds gather and at
every change of temperature, cold winds blow; the moisture-laden
clouds condense into tiny drops and the temperature decides whether they should fall in the form of cold rain or snow.

Glaciers are formed in small basins, circles nested against the sides
of the steepest mountains, beneath the towering spires where the
snow sticks; cradles of new glaciers become larger but not because
of the perpetual frost but because the accumulation of snow from
year to year transforms them in time into ice sheets that can cover
whole continents; basins where the powdery snow with the pressure
and the weight of the mass of ice water turns the depths into sphe-
rules with the magic name: Firn. These small balls are magic because

as they accumulate they resist the weight of the overlying mass and a
fraction of this energy is freed, in the form of heat in the depths, on
the surfaces of each one.
As with all rebellions these are quickly incorporated into the system
that slowly freezes this small free surface and, indeed, uses it to
strengthen all the spheres at their points of contact. Yet this gigantic
effort to contain the freedom of the spheres prevents the ice from
remaining motionless and forces it to flow, dense and seemingly solid, crystalline, it is forced to move to the lower levels, like a common
liquid, separating itself around obstacles such as the tops of mountains, rejoining on the other side, carrying rocks and debris. An eternal struggle between the desire to freeze into immobility and the
need to constantly fight against the continued presence of the mel-
ting liquid from the small indomitable firm, which are always present.
During the Earths many eras its surface life has been shaped by the
continuous struggle between the elements.
The ice was formed, it grew, it extended across continents and once
it even dared to cover the entire surface of the earth, trying to dominate the volcanoes. The ice however has always had to recede dissolving. It retreats to return again, in a repeating cycle in which the animals and then human beings have had to enter and seek niches to
survive and evolve to become so conceited and certain they have the
power to overcome and dominate both.
Poor fools.
At lower latitudes, the angle of the sun begins to warm the earth just
after the winter solstice, but the ice reacts and reflects almost all its
dazzling energy. What little is left is enough to melt the first superficial
snow on the grasslands and the permafrost, the frozen ground, begins to warm giving the shoots a chance to sprout.
Seeds and plants need very little heat but the effect of light is powerful combined with the available moisture: the surfaces of the glaciers
begin to melt, a little water flows into the crevices flowing down to
the parched land. Mists evaporate from the ice masses form rain
clouds. Spring always comes and in the spring the glaciers also release water instead of absorbing it.

At the height of their civilization the ancient Romans and Greeks defined beauty in this way, true beauty, the harmony of movement, the

plasticity of a body tensed in athletic effort and for this reason they admired and thus carved and took pleasure in the male body, preferring this to relations with the females of humanity who surrounded them, whose bodies were soft, slack, drooping, useful. They painted or sculpted as existing, alternative, different and interesting, which they couldn't do without but whose voices surrounded them whining, complaining, requesting continuous attention to annoying everyday things, which forced the men to work without the abstract fascination of discussion or the inebriating pleasure of a fight between two men. Better yet amongst them all was the fascination of the domination between a minute man or also a girl, who had just come out of adolescence and so similar in appearance and vitality, in their postures in their fundamental desires in their approaches to life.

According to the ancients, philosophical discussions were unsuitable for women, as they required a state of 'decent idleness' that was incompatible with the condition of exploitation and effort reserved for women; they weren't even suitable for the ignorant, because a philosopher who conversed with them, would only obtain their excitement and therefore fanatical behavior, the basis of all people's revolutions. The prophets have always cried out and demanded justice for their people. The man of genius and culture had to preserve the virtues of balanced judgment, temperance, restraint, courage, patriotism and honor for the fight: the things that man truly needed and also their leaders and most of all, the emperor.

Struggle is the word that describes how nature exists, lives, evolves and changes. During spring all animal species take advantage of the wealth of vegetation to grow and reproduce but when the season changes, in the tundra or taiga as in the sunny pastures of the tropics, the competition for eating what remains becomes ferocious.

The animals move possibly migrating, without fighting each other. Species doing this have practically the same eating habits or the same genetic needs, closely linked to the environment in which they live.

In this case only one of the species, the dominant one survives, all the others either migrate or become extinct. Humans are no exception!

Winter on the Earth is hard for all living beings; in winter the only objective is to survive scarcity.

Animals adapt, they share a productive complex territory, where many different species are able to survive because their feeding habits fit into those of others, like the poppies that bloom a little before harvest time protected by the ripe ears of wheat.

Man does not adapt to the environment, the weather, the seasons: man is setting up and changing the environment based on his requirements, his needs. This characteristic feature renders him, no more significant than any other living species but certainly more dangerous, not least for his own species, that has been immersed in nature for a long time.

Cars passed on the road. Here and there some little children were playing. The neighbors were watering or mowing the grass. It was a normal day. What I saw from the window was neither more or less than normal.

The announcer's voice came from the television in the kitchen; here are the top stories: a landslide derailed a train, dead and wounded; a truck ran into a number of cars, the dead and wounded; a husband kills the lover, the lover kills the friend; there is an attack on the institutions, a bomb, dead and wounded! The report... and more this who has stolen, that one has cheated, political scandal, financial scandal, sex scandal; also this is the norm.

The next two hours I spent crouched in front of the television pressing the buttons on the remote control between one advertisement and another, bleary-eyed, my mind more confused than ever glancing occasionally at the window where there was always the same picture, if not for a detail of illumination. The sad image of reality, covered over with normality and disillusionment. Absurd!

I love the moment of tension, of waiting that precedes discovery, the only time when every eventuality is possible.

The desire to do, to obtain, to enjoy a coveted pleasure.

Things change. Things change all the time!

In nature, in the universe, everything is possible, if anything, to varying degrees of probability.

I am certainly not the most fervent of believers, I have created my path, my children will make theirs.

To discuss things also with yourself, about innovations and differences after they've been learned, is more important than passively believing. This is why I am writing this diary.

I like the concept of 'ignoring our ignorance'. Premises that are stimulating and binding: proudly not admitting to our ignorance, rationality

would unavoidably always have the upper hand. How far would it take us to reason about it? Reasoning about the unknown or inexplicable about what is now called fanciful or supernatural?
Now I don't want to do anything at all, too demanding and maybe one maudlin pointless exercise?
Man, understood as a species of animal, is never 100% male or female. He is always a hybrid, a mixture of both qualities always in different proportions. Normality is defined as the minimal variation possible from the mixture up to 50%. They are considered different extremes, the mixture approaching 100% or more deviates further from normality. Nevertheless, these also exist, and they are real, alive, moving beside us every day and fully interacting with us.
It is for this reason that it is absurd to talk about races or of differences, but rather with humanity it is better to speak of similar types and be aware, simply of their existence and their total and complete humanity.

People are used to believing in the printed word, in newspapers or in various global media or television communications. People realize there is a problem, not when a problem truly exists but when journalists begin to talk about it.

If the newspapers or television speak of a phenomenon, here one begins to wonder if something wrong or if we are even actually on the brink of a catastrophe.
The mere mention of a problem can have and arouse negative effects; only at times positive instead.

If you want to organize a television program on the problem of crime or homophobia, then you must realize that the problem will become the increase in crime, or the presence of those who are 'different' next to us, regardless of location.

Nothing gives power to man such as lying. This is the principal thing. Only if you don't know that you really do have the power to make others do what you want.

Men live by ideas and those that can be driven as you want. This power of being able to manipulate ideas is the only power that really counts. I myself am part of the power I've served power to have my share, also if in a different way than what you could do yourself and everyone else. Nevertheless I've never been an absolute servant of power, unrecognizable, without will. It has always been a continuous choice. When I was young I was told you can push on one side to break down a wall, but if there is someone on the other side pulling, the effort of breaking down the wall is very much reduced.

Perhaps it will serve to help to induce people to buy things they don't need perhaps, serve to make them love or hate things that they don't know, maybe it will make them believe things that will cause them to become obedient, or make them question things that could do them good or save them.

You may even have become an important person, involved in big business, unleashed wars, founded empires, or you may stay in the shadows and speculate about the actions of others looking around and passing unnoticed, pretending you don't exist, pretending to be quiet, making yourself as small as possible. Who knows!

The world is full of poor fools who think they are naturally very intelligent and sincerely believe they are useful for the sharing and dissemination of truth. Perhaps it will be useful to themselves.

You may be convinced, perfectly convinced, that you want one thing, perhaps for years you cultivate the desire, at least as long as you know that desire is unachievable. At the same time when suddenly, there before you is the possibility it will become a reality, then it becomes a unique ulterior and sole desire that is the one you never wanted to have.

A voice could be heard singing, a very nice voice, subtle like a child's voice, clear as the tolling of a bell whose tone however was not happy and inspiring but infinitely sad, light as a breath of wind that rose, fell, paused, moved away or approached like a sob, a whining sound without words and then suddenly close to the ear. It seemed as though the wind were speaking.

Who am I? I don't know what to say. Or the impression of having known a long time ago; who knows when.
But is it really important to know? In the end I am! And there will be time for useless curiosity. There will always be enough time. For now we think of eating and drinking to live, to enjoy.
What does the phrase really mean *do what you want*? Does it mean that you can do whatever we please? Interesting question.
No it means that you must follow your own true will. Nothing is more difficult!
You need to examine your own desires one at a time, good or bad, going from one to another, from time to time always different, adapting to the circumstances.

The last wish and only that will be your true desire.
All, at least as children and then as young adults, want to show their qualities as compared to other people; everyone wants to be admired, everyone wants to achieve glory. These are not the desires that express their true identity, their true will. They don't even need to meditate, deeply for a long time, analyze, engage in introspection.
There are things you simply cannot figure out, simply by thinking; because they are so profound we need to live them.
It is like going through a maze, you have to go through an infinite number of doors, find yourself in an infinite number of rooms, to find yourself in situations you know you've already seen, experienced. Every time you must make a decision and every decision you make leads to taking another, successive, which in turn leads to an additional decision.
Life is a Y-shaped road, a succession of Ys at every intersection where you need to choose between two alternatives. Only at the end of the trail will you know where you've arrived. You can always choose without having any criteria but every time you realize the choice could very well also have been another. Often you can't return to the point of choice and you have to follow the decision you've made, this time trying to use minimal criteria, to exercise a minimum of your true will. Relying on chance you risk wandering endlessly around the center of the maze without going in any real direction.

At a certain point in your life you often decide to combine your own path with that of another person, this fact leads to doubling the choices and possible pathways. Sometimes you decide to have a child: a child is like a revolution; you know you can give life but you don't know and can't control how this is going to end.

It is essential to learn to develop critical thinking; so instead of just blindly accepting what you are told, you will be able to identify what is realistic. Learning to think should be the basis of everyone's education.

"Holy Virgin Mary, pray for us all and that we shall also be among them all!" (*Madonnina santa pregate per tutti che tra tutti ci siamo anche noi*) my mother said this continuously, my grandmother Mia, said it in the Bardigiano dialect: *Madunénna holy preghei per tùtti che tra tùtti ghe summa anca n ö n* ! You immediately understand the natural and divine mystery looking at an image of the Madonna and child. It is a universal image. In ancient Egypt the goddess Isis, the Moon, holds her son Horus in her arms, and he is black. The male is an instrument, temporary and complementary to nature, which is absolutely and totally feminine. Maybe you need to insert a note about variability and unpredictability, being more easily and less controllably prey to instinct. If you have to give one sex to divinity it's natural to consider women because it is the female who gives life, and even the Son of God, or even before, the gods had to be born of a woman to be able to take human form.

God loves the poor, which is why he made so many!

We are eternity, we are what lasts and will last forever: life instead is only what does not last!

All gods are one God and all goddesses are one Goddess. There is a single unifying but mysterious principle, at least, for now. Does it make sense to focus on eternity so much as to lose sight of the truth of this green and wonderful world?

I don't fear the world or even scorn it! The world goes on, though following its own course and taking very little interest, indeed not at all, in humanity. But it suffers the influence and repays at the same level. Each human experiences the world in a different way; there can be no single way of understanding it!

Introspection is revealed as a deceitful approach also this because it is essentially based on memories and these are often the fruit of re-elaboration and therefore unreliable, at times not even real, but they leave traces of emotion, felt or attributed to them over time, compared to the moments they refer.
Some memories are more stable than others, and as we age we tend to recover the more distant. They are fixed more deeply and form the basis of our growth, bricks in the path of the mind on the way to reaching maturity.
I try to go as far back in my mind as possible to search out certain memories. I sought the first because I realized most of the intermediate have been consolidated or even established by seeing photographs, by comments, discussions; family conversations. Well certainly my first memory or at least the one I'm certain of, is a kind of photograph, a crisp image. I'm there, a small, blond boy and in front of me is a huge white rooster. For years this image convinced me that roosters could be huge, dangerous animals. In fact, I then realized, that roosters are simple and normal roosters but the disparity lies in the fact that it was as tall as I was and therefore I must have been very small. Since I have always heard I was a blond child who then became brown haired, and I have pictures from before I was two years old to prove it, I conclude that this memory goes back to that period.
Many other memories crowd into my mind as I plumb my memory but I realize the criteria of dates is unproductive, not even of places, because I am always able to perceive the path of reconstruction or revision of this memory. So I select the path of seeking the strongest emotions, memories of unrecognizable moments, recognized affirmed happiness, or painfulness. I realized that painful or traumatic ones have substantially been removed, replaced with a filler emotion that doesn't allow me to identify them more precisely: I know that mother and father died and I know how, but absolutely cannot recall when or how long ago. I don't even remember what they looked like but certainly recall their essence, a word or phrase or moment, an attitude, but nothing that can be more precisely defined: dashed off in

an essential sketch and anyway completely understandable and exhaustive, at least to me.

I remember I had a car accident, perhaps, the first time the family car had been entrusted to me for a trip alone: I was on the way to Carrara to take my final exams. I had an accident, I have an image of a heap of stones that opened onto a cliff under the car when I tried to get out, I know I climbed through the forest, that I was able to get a ride and then waited for my parents to arrive as I stretched out on a wall near Pontremoli. I certainly phoned them, maybe I drank a coffee or a glass of water, but I don't remember. Mother had white hair soon after, as they hadn't seen any trace of the car along the road, they'd been tormented by worry.

Even this, though, I don't remember, I know it but I don't remember, as I don't remember their arrival, how we left, because then I went to Carrara to take the exams. Everything has vanished and also the place where I had the accident and I was so sure about the place at the time. I've never again been able to precisely identify the location; I know more or less where it happened.

And it is like this for many other memories. So even pain and unhappiness is not a reliable pathway to the identification of a memory.

Then I tried to find a memory, the most beautiful, linked to more intense emotion and as happy as possible. I tried to remember my wife, when I met her, there is, I remember some of the circumstances, I remember the moonlight on the beach where we stopped after the dinner where we met but it is a simple memory. I think about my marriage and here, while usually recalling everything, in effect I realize I remember absolutely nothing, if not for some moment, some image, some small snapshot that all together makes up the complex memory that I'm able to retell, even to myself.

There are full and pleasant memories of trips taken with my wife and my children but when these were already big because sharing has allowed us to better focus on the facts and emotions later.

I finally found the one true memory, embossed, cemented, indelible; however its connections were made in retrospection: the birth of my daughter! In fact I attribute the memory, I locate it exactly, at the moment she was conceived: my wife, barely an hour after the act, stated this with certainty, a certainty that came from her being a woman and certainly nothing else, of being pregnant! This was confirmed at the time and in the usual ways, but my memory focused on the smile on her face, on her expression, on her absolutely simple certainty, on this full knowledge, even if I cannot define any of these things. An emotion, a happy moment, then recaptured and recognized, consolidated only after Enrica's birth.

I was there when she was born, I saw and felt a very strong emotion, first because of the previous difficulty of giving birth and then at the sight of the little girl who reminded me of the Martian in the famous film ET.

Today it is not that these two or three sharp images take me to the delivery room while her birth takes me with absolute, immediate, total certainty, to the emotion of her conception, of that unregistered time, difficult to describe or narrate that instead makes up the firm point of my recollection. The thrill of discovering I'd always 'wanted' a little girl. The desire, now modified into the curiosity, of seeing how this little girl would, of course, fill life with her search for a personality and, I was certain, it would be a continuous search on her path. I now know I wasn't mistaken and I know this child will continue that search throughout her life, until the last moment and never abandon it because she is so full of character, personality and potential that she can never be satisfied with the result reached on her path, however great. And the memory unfolds, and yet I believe forever from that moment, unique and focused, the strange certainty and acceptance of its existence to become, certain albeit still only possible.

Naturally, just as expected, satisfaction, pleasure, emotion, are connected to the birth of my son, Roberto, but it is totally different, more hazy, more indefinite, indistinct, perhaps simply because it was not the first time while he is connected to different memories: the discovery of his talent and his passion for music. I don't know how to define when and how, but at some point, perhaps the first time I heard him play, still uncertain and hesitant in a little concert with a group of friends, I learned he had talent and I was inclined to curiously wait to see where this awareness would go. I thought of how proud my grandmother would have been if she could have seen her grandson carrying on the innate talent that emerged here and there in the family. Yet the memory is structured in time without definition, while it is certainly linked to an instant, bright as a star in the sky, a moment before, well before the passion and ability was manifested in every way. It was carnival, and he had to have been about ten years old, he presented himself in the living room dressed like a punk with a guitar improvising around the diffused notes of Zuccerho's rock *Funki Gallo*. This is the established image, a snapshot from which it unfolds and evolves and where the memory arises.

The mechanism that defines and consolidates memories I think is not so much the fact nor the emotion, defined, accompanying the time or the fact itself, but rather, the beginning of a new curiosity, a new search for a new expectation that it brings. I believe you fix the time of birth, recognized, by the new curious desire and expectations derived from it.

Memories are like the stars in the infinite sky: they exist, are real, small lights, scattered across the sky and they fill up as they fill our lives with memories, amplifying them to make them appear or perhaps are almost infinite; a multitude of sharp images, shining brightly and accompanying our darkest moments, clarifying them and creating companions that make us aware of our own existence but with which we struggle to recognize the distinctive characteristics of each one.

I remember how the stars, sometimes while we watch they group together, and tell us different stories from how we've classified them: the greater or lesser bear, the eagle, the lion, the hunter, are only dream images of something that doesn't really exist and can be changed at will, making them become, without changing reality or the relative position, the airplane or the turtle, a cannon, a flower and anything you want them to be, the memories, represent and depart from their singular reality or position in time and space.

Just because we feel the obligation and the need to create images, therefore to describe what in fact can't be described, then divide them into gods or goddesses then assign them names and stories, making them compete for the favor of the worshipers like candidates in elections but they can provide us with examples and motivation. It's hard to love something that has neither a face nor a name. No one is wrong, neither those who claim that a true unique God exists nor those who worship many but in a different way.

A single multi-faceted crystal like a diamond, the whole is glimpsed in transparency through a single face; to each face a form, a name, a face, a face at a time that reflects the need of the moment, of anxiety, desire: Apollo, Mars, Isis, Hera, and all their clones or duplicates in the various cultures, are invoked to protect those who ask, and only that one; no one can escape the jealousy and envy that are part of humanity, and that is how Yahweh or Allah, or the same God of the Christians protects, despite being universal, one people, one group or just making a single cause, a single war amongst them all.

He proudly walked around with his beautiful wife and his two children, a boy and a girl. He knew he was immortal because he had these two children: if you leave this life without having generated a child, then you die! Otherwise you only fall asleep.

Speaking of women, sometimes it has been said: it is no wonder that the man who was made from a soft material like clay is the more pleasing, while the woman who comes from a bone is much harder than he is. (The Greek philosophers ...).

"But how were you able to find her?" And he responded with sarcasm: "Because she is a woman created like all women, who demonstrates the intelligence of God who created her from a man's bone, like this he rendered her jealous by nature; she was not made from the ear of the man, which would have made her a gossip; she was not even made from a man's mouth, which would have made her a chatter box; God created her from the rib of a man; I searched everywhere for what I was missing until I found her ... But do you really believe you are able to choose a woman? No man does anything to a woman during the first moment of infatuation, no man is able to; it is always she who takes the initiative and the result is that you are left with nothing else to do, no choice is possible, if you don't put a good face on your slavery, but don't be alarmed and from that moment you can count the days of your freedom ... all women are fully aware of the importance of the time factor and that it plays against them. Women use their initial advantage to put down roots in certain habits, certain relationships of particular intimacy with the man, until the force of desire is overwhelming. They know that men tend to be creatures of habit; therefore, they lay the foundations of their survival long before their charm begins to fade. At a certain point unavoidably it happens that it will be you who reacts, no longer her and incredibly you'll seem to be

much younger than she is. It is the reward for having endured so
many years of obedience in an attempt to satisfy one or other of our
women's caprices. Besides, at that point if you delay too late, or if
she's been very good to you it will seem that life is unbearable and
empty without her. And you will know that you are now too old and
you will be content to be able to do so. Besides women God gave us
wine, like women, the devil had a hand in this and he showed us how
we can improve both. In effect at the time of the first man who managed to make wine Satan said, "If you sacrifice four animals your wine
will be decidedly better."
"What animal should I sacrifice?" asked the man, because in fact his
wine was a little bitter and not always pleasant.
"A lamb, a lion, a pig, a monkey."
"And where will I ever find them?" replied the man.
"You'll have to give the best of yourself, engage in research, just so
you can get results and then be satisfied." The man spent his entire
life looking for the necessary animals and eventually sacrificed them
in the vineyard. From that day, the wine, at the first sip, makes man
meek as a lamb; if you drink a little more, the man becomes a lion
ready to face the entire world without fear; a little more and the man
becomes a pig prey to his own instincts, without brakes, he rolls in
the mud, in the mire of his own vomit, and can no longer recognize
good from evil, beauty from ugliness, the good from the bad. In the
end, if he doesn't stop, when he gets sopping drunk he returns to his
deep roots, and behaves exactly like a monkey, laughing rudely he
yells, jumps from branch to branch leaps around without knowing
what he's doing, because he forgets the world and everything including his own ...

We had gone to Mass, as on every Sunday morning and as on every
Sunday morning as I took a seat near the back of the nave on the left
close to the door, ready to run, but as always, found a place near the
usual friends, like me forced to take part in the Sunday ritual with no
great enthusiasm. And listening to the Mass, between getting to our
feet and kneeling down to pray and singing, it became a pleasant time
of conversation for us so that we were strictly on our feet leaning up
against the wall. We chatted of this and that stopping occasionally
when the looks of praying worshipers struck us like thunderbolts.

One time I remember the celebrant continued his chant with no apparent interruption, Mass was strictly in Latin and the celebrant turned his back to the people, therefore without interrupting his chant, he turned around and looked at us. As if on a given signal almost all heads turned disapprovingly towards us. It was a strange feeling, incredible: no criticism, no action; only this particularly outsized attention that made us feel like the smallest of children. We stopped our chatter immediately and then making ourselves as small as possible we backed out of the door being careful not to let the door slam shut.

Asshole, you're nothing but a fart among the impetuous living and your death would mean nothing more than a vague momentary stench of putrefaction ... Of course you could always become a martyr, then, yes, people might say that at least 50% of the time you were partly right ... If you want I will help you to become one, immediately! Which God made you so sublimely stupid? You're nothing but an unfortunate idiot with a brain wrapped in the mire of presumption ...

When others criticize, you smile! When others spit judgments, you declare you agree! When others are blathering nonsense, you don't interrupt rather you praise their wisdom!
Learn to observe more than others if you want to become a leader: declare yourself happy with the wise suggestions of others, when you realize that some would disagree about one non vital point in a discussion about many points; to the most tempestuous entrust tasks that do nothing but appear important. Declare your agreement and follow your wisdom. Leaders are not a fortuitous coincidence; they follow inspiration whatever it is, don't heed the unasked for opinion of those around you. Act and get approval. True leaders have no qualms about achieving their objectives they consider only one thing really important. Leaders have no conscience, what you call conscience is nothing but foolish pride. People don't appreciate the truth in leaders. They don't want it, especially if it isn't exciting, motivating, rewarding or a source of pride.

But am I really a learned man as you say? Is it true that I know logic, am familiar with philosophy, know a little about science but come to think of it couldn't milk a cow, I wouldn't know how to steer a boat, I don't know how to even build anything lasting or really useful. Then am I a useless man or simply an ignorant man? So what is culture and how is it different from learning?
The best way to know a man is to stop and take a drink with him or do business with him or even observe him when he's angry!

I look at the city, seeing another place and another time. Images overlap in my mind, images of fire and wind, hot kisses and two hearts beating together. We will be companions in a new world. We will be together forever.
I was in love not with the girl as much as the revolutionary idea; it cannot be anything but like this, everything we do unavoidably affects everything else. She cared. It mattered to both of us.
I was in love with the possibility of change, I was in love with the wo-man that she could become as well as ideas of a world that could be. She went away closing her eyes against the moment of separation. It's been a long time since then. And today I don't even have the chance to dream. Yet we must move forward, never looking back, I knew, I've learned but sometimes I couldn't do without.
I found her much later and looking at her, in a moment of infinite sur-prise, I barely recognized her in her role as mother with two small children clinging to her skirt, a very ordinary missus, apparently very well off, on her arm: her husband! Actually many things had changed, even in the world, but certainly not as I dreamed, I believed, I thought.

The tide was at its highest. From the dock the surface of the water, where it was stagnating was foaming iridescent, oily, it was coming closer. The images reflected as though in a distorting mirror while the powerful, monotonous voice called. It was not a beautiful moment. Luckily the environment was ugly, it was cold, the wind was icy and I hate the cold. I walked away. Life had lost an excellent opportunity to convince me to abandon it, to stop fighting and to move forward.
I went back home, I felt stronger than ever, more peaceful, serene,

relaxed: life was beautiful and worth living.
I lit a cigar, poured myself a shot of gin and decided to go to sleep:
tomorrow, tomorrow is another day.

The so-called environmentalists, those in the bars and fanatics, exag-
gerate statistics based on poor scientific interpretation drawing conclusions that are produced and disseminated more from desire or at
least with the objective of scaring to push for change rather than to
truly inform.
It is also true that the edges of the Amazon forest are being increasingly seriously destroyed, but it is to make room for pastures, sugar
cane fields, the only things that allow the local farmers to survive.
Overall in the world though the green surface, and therefore useful, is
steadily on the increase especially in Europe and in North America,
where people are rich enough to afford to use alternative resources
for firewood and have enough agricultural fields and resources to cultivate and feed themselves.
Farmers burn tracts of forest to create fields and pastures to survive
while in the northern United States, for example, regularly controlled
fires are started to stimulate the regeneration of vegetation and to
encourage the growth of repressed species, shrubs, smaller plants
including those that are medicinal. The real difference is that here it
is applied to control; there need dominates.
Rainforests are certainly fundamental for providing oxygen to the atmosphere, and of the rest also carbon dioxide, whereas in fact oxygen and the system of atmospheric gas is a closed system where
plants take part, but only minimally. In fact in the rainforests only the
top leaves take part in the production of oxygen while underneath it
is simply consumed and thrives precisely because of the scarce percentage in respect to carbon dioxide. On balance, the net production
of oxygen is therefore minimal. In the north of the planet, where instead there is a net increase in young forests, the plants produce
plenty of oxygen.
In fact controlled deforestation, I repeat controlled, may be a blessing
and could represent a real benefit to the atmosphere of the planet.
Certainly it is that in every ecological equilibrium, the forest, the people and the animals that inhabit it, the availability of water and light
are closely related. If the forest disappears the equilibrium is altered

in one way or another in respect to the current state: biodiversity, our unexplored stronghold of interactive possibilities tends to shrink, therefore, men and animals that are involved and interdependent are destined to risk numerical reduction, to disappear or change their state of existence until they become extinct.

For example, how is it that mammals, unlike reptiles and amphibians are unable or at least not easily able to regenerate their parts their organs? This is because over millions of years of evolution this has allowed them to defend themselves against the rages of cancer in its various forms. Inhibiting regenerative capacity has also inhibited the development of cancerous cells.

Everything that represents a limitation in an ecological system also represents a protection, to the same degree. It evolves and survives numerically in the majority, the ability to produce the best and most effective beneficial effects as long as these exist.

Indeed the essential qualities necessary for a researcher are basically three: they need to know what to look for, must know where to look, they should be able to see beyond the theories that would represent a major limitation to their objectivity.

What are the spotters? I found this to be an invented system designed to rip off the casinos. They are people who wander about around the tables where you play cards and they don't play. They limit themselves to checking how the cards are dealt: one spotter can track two, three, even four players. They must limit themselves to keeping track of all the cards played at a table: giving a negative sign to low cards and a positive sign to high cards, the 10 and aces. It works if they manage to keep a single number in mind, the total at the time when the relationship between the low cards, negative, and the high, positive, rises above a certain value among the cards in play, then the probability is transferred from the dealer to the player. If they are able to identify this moment, especially in the game of blackjack, where there is a clear influence of high cards remaining to the dealer's disadvantage, then they alert the player. The player knows that his chances have increased and begins to bet higher. The spotters continue to count and indicate when the favorable relationship

returns to equilibrium with the unfavorable: at that point the player
stops playing or reduces his bets. What marvelous abilities man has!
But who could have imagined that?
The only precaution against these card counters is to increase the
number of decks in play and shuffle the cards every time a new player
sits down, or when a player begins to heavily raise the bets.
Naturally this system only covers professional players who don't stop
playing, but limit themselves to merely changing the way they bet
when things are going badly, because they know that sooner or later
their moment will come.
As always for every armor manufacturer, there is a cannon manufacturer and the fight between the two continues into infinity.

I have deepened the definition of a Public Officer: a person who takes
a role of responsibility ... for others!

There are many ways to enhance concentration and meditation, but
what impressed me most is the method of disentangling a knot: it's
about focusing on a complicated knot and to attempt to loosen it by
making it slide towards the inside of the protruding end of the thread;
but it isn't done physically, you have to do it mentally; the knot must
unfold in a smooth motion like that of a snake winding or unwinding
its coils. The effort of concentration required is immense and the resulting trance can be very deep. It is very, very difficult!
The great Lamas, experts of oriental meditation are able to integrate
their physical and mental systems, universally mysticism is typically
oriental, all the fundamental processes of the universe, those that we
express with concepts of mathematical relationships, neurological situation that are typically western. If it is like this, it demonstrates the
existence of the deep interaction between living things on earth and
the cosmic whole.
Perhaps, at a deep level, very deep, fundamental, our brain reflects
the basic geometry of the universe, of which it is completely part: in
this way it acts; maybe it is controllable.

Science and knowledge are like a luminous ball in the darkness; the larger the diameter of the sphere, the greater the darkness that surrounds it... (a quote that struck me and I recorded it on the second page of a book from the eleventh grade but I can't remember who it was).

It is impressive to realize that knowledge of the basic mechanisms, the perception of nature and its inherent co-natural interaction with what lies beyond the visible, the measurable, have always coexisted with humanity in the form of what is normally identified, but not explained, as *spontaneous religiosity.*

Some basic knowledge has commonly been part of humanity since the beginning of conscious existence and has historically been used with opportune manipulation by those who from time-to-time, over time, had the need to manage power; that is it has occurred for millennia applying the same script: enclosure of knowledge within initiatory circles pyramidal structures and increasingly sector-specific, specialized and partial information with the effect of total disinformation in relation to the mass of the population leaving their ignorant perceptions in place, their natural religiosity, faith and hope, at all times and in all places, making believe that everything was very difficult to understand and manage.

We're in the third millennium and knowledge profits from the infinite, technological ways to spread itself but remains being the mechanics of the correct, useful and concerned, misinformation in every branch of knowledge and its obvious social and sociological applications. For this reason I consider it necessary to offer some reflections on the definition of Life, Ecology, Interactions in an ancient, new approach that leads into the distance.

The scientific method, naturalistic classification, before the approach of physical engineering to natural phenomena: measure, mechanisms, insights, technicalities, I believe they are not as important to the understanding of nature as the observation of the interaction between all the parameters of a defined ecological system, always and in any case in relation to space, time, number and the objective characteristics of the principle interactive parameters.

Using the words of C.F. Gauss, the German mathematician who contributed to number and matrix theory (1777 to 1855): *lacking the math mindset so that those who cannot quickly recognize the obvious as much as those who linger over the calculations with an accuracy greater than required!*

We need to understand what the most interactive parameters are,

how they interact and how they affect the evaluated system, what are
they, what are they doing or don't do, and especially what can they
do, interacting among themselves or with others, in different conditions defined each time.

Classification: Under what conditions, what equilibriums, while dynamic, are based on varying the conditions observed or imposed.

It is certainly important to know how they do it but it is especially important to understand if they do and what the results are, considering these as a possible evolution of the systems studied. Why do
they do it certainly, but only if they can do it.

I recently published: *Dalla teoria dell'evoluzione alla teoria dell'instabilità
costante . Dalla teoria classica alla teoria del disequilibrio* . (From the
theory of evolution to the theory of the instability constant. From
classical theory to the theory of non-equilibrium).

The common sequence of natural evolution is that of continuous variation of the basic equilibrium between temperature and pressure,
slowing, cooling, acquisition of mass and mutual interaction; thus
amassing and therefore structuring and finally organization. *Fiat lux*.
Gradually passing from level to level one comes to increasingly cir-
cumscribed phenomena, engaging parameters and environments that
are increasingly smaller and slower, cold, structured, organized with
an ever increasing number of effective interactions and greater possibility of modifying to change in the situations-systems that involve
them. From chaos to melody.

One could speak of universal ecology, galactic ecology, planetary biological ecology, gradually to more structured and organized levels for
the creation and continuous formation of new parameters, to variations in the overall conditions of the equilibrium of energy, or though
we can talk of, varying the scale of definition of the environment-sy-
stem studied, of the actual interaction and new possibility of interaction.

Nature evolves and renews through infinite repetitions of simple mechanisms and of little cost energetically: for every new possibility of
interaction, a variation.

All mass and universal energy were concentrated at an initial point
and have been unfolding until now.

It may be said, of the universe, that being the total compendium of all
that is NATURE, is self-referential. The universe is always present to
itself, in all its ecological manifestations, as small and peripheral as it

is, in the economy of scale evaluated. The universe is so large that it exists without the possibility of undergoing great variations in the overall dynamic equilibriums that form and evolve at its interior.
The universe-entity is essentially eternal, also considering the tendency to reach the last energy level of least interaction, of least possible energy exchanged, that of the most frigid motionless that would also prevent the smallest and insignificant variation in the equilibrium between even the smallest active parameters, of the smallest ecosystem possible. This situation if reached would be equivalent to the definitive death of the universe-entity, if reached, or perhaps to a further change. The universe would exist as an inert, ulterior parameter, modified active and evolved into an even larger-scale encompassing multiple or infinite universes coexisting in equilibrium, then once again dynamic, between them. In the end the universe-entity would be carried to its resurrection, because of the impossibility of existing without interacting (living), in some way, with any of the other existing parameters.
We can now define the biological whole as a system, relatively cold, slow, amassed, structured and organized.
If for living we only consider it as a biological structure, it is certainly not the simplest interactive structure possible.
It isn't possible to think that the interactive equilibrium between individual cellular beings can substantially alter the structure of the universal system, and yet it comprises one of the infinite dynamic equilibriums between active and interactive parameters in the entire universe and in fact, contributes to its change. Each parameter, their combination in the whole, are identified and exist (they live) with this ability to modify and be changed. Single inanimate components realize the most complex organized structure of a single living being. Also the smallest cellular organism is alive precisely because it comprises an interactive parameter and interacts according to the conditions, variables, of the system-environment in which it is inserted.
Only structures exist that continually and dynamically interact with others, in every system of two or more parameters, in the search and achievement of a more lasting and stable equilibrium. An equilibrium of minimal exchanges and expenditure of energy. The existing structures are thus in continuous evolution of the ecological behaviors that involve them.
The smallest biological parameter in play is in turn determined by the

interactions, not biological, of its elementary components, which thus
are also living.
These elements also have life, determined in duration, defined in space, in time and in the number of parameters that, are dynamically in
equilibrium between them, continually changing their mutual forms of
interaction. It follows then that ecology, far from being the science
that studies the relationships between living things and the environment is rather the science that studies all possible interactions between all possible parameters; it does so by from time-to-time selecting the most suitable scale of observation, useful, effective, of the
prediction of evolutionary phenomena of the equilibrium in place.
In essence, studying life, without distinguishing whether it is organic
or not, whether it is large or small, whether it is conscious or not but
simply, far more simply, if and when it acts and interacts to the energy stimuli, caused by other parameters present: where, whether,
when and as they are.
Life, thus defined as the simple capacity for action in respect to other
factors and interactions in place.
Life is thus as simple brief, instantaneous or economic, lasting eons,
moments of energetic equilibrium, unstable and in constant evolution, in the interactive complex, at least of the universe.
Life as a similar part, always and in any case fundamental, functional
mirror of the broadest natural whole... of image and likeness...

The ancients considered blood a sacred substance, powerful, the sap
of life, food for the gods and yet we consider this simple biological
fluid, a suspension of plasma cells. An average human body of 70 kilo-
grams contains five to six liters of blood, no more. About 45% is made
up of cells, that is they are living organisms, unique, synergistic, active,
the rest is plasma: almost all water. Water with a few mineral salts,
made up of electrolytes, a few proteins, sugars, nutrients. Blood is
red because of hemoglobin a substance, an iron-based protein but
can be blue if the base metal is for example copper as in some reptiles.

If you are anemic, the conjunctive of the eyelid turns pale pink; your
heart works harder, faster, because the blood is more diluted. For

this reason when climbing the stairs you should stop every so often to rest the heart and slow the pulse so as to catch your breath. You cannot live well.
Blood gives life, it is the magic fluid that allows us to live completely, totally. For this reason the ancients offered it to the gods, in large or small sacrifices perforating here and there and letting the blood drip on the ground or a few drops on the rocks.
It was important to consider each other blood brothers, after exchanging blood.
Today this would be considered grotesque. Today, at the mere sight of blood a man passes out yet if they happen to witness violent and bloody incidents, no one can help but be attracted and forced to watch, even to search for them on television programs in sports events everywhere.

To educate for freedom of thought is like thinking of historical analysis as an exact science. An impossible consideration being the conditioned basis of departure and thus contaminated by the results, obtained or desired, by today's society; the same applies to medicine that is affected by the fact that each individual is absolutely and totally unique and cannot biologically be standardized or at least not completely.
In this historical period, we are forced to suffer, the migration of people seeking a chance for a better life in respect to their own countries.
Many of them are Muslims, the majority; this means a relative increase in the Muslim population in Europe, the population has grown enormously in the last thirty years.
When I was small, there were no black men in Italy, the first one I saw was in England, I was taken to see him on purpose, like to the zoo. To travel to Paris today or in many French cities is equivalent to traveling in mostly Arab cities. The largest mosque in Europe is in Rome, less than 2 km from San Pietro. Getting lost in the local markets is like traveling to the east or south of the Mediterranean. The world capital of the Catholic Church is 10% Muslim.
The large presence of Muslims in Europe today makes them aware of the power they represent. They no longer live in the shadows. They freely proclaim and strongly demand to be recognized even more

than known. They are no longer willing to tolerate contempt, indeed; they counteract it. They are always asking for greater concessions to their culture to their way of life, they ask for as much or equal consideration of their places of worship as those of Christians, but they always require more than those of other religions.

Unfortunately you cannot fail to realize that all over the Muslim world to be a Christian is something forbidden or, at least, very limited and conditioned. The missionaries are often outlaws and risk barbaric punishments firsthand such as flogging, prison, if all goes well expulsion, at the worst death and for their converted, the accusation of betrayal of the true faith and the sentence of stoning. At least marginalization. Fear, resentment, ill will towards Muslims is widespread among Europeans who no longer feel at home in their countries. Nobody is happy. But is that true? Or are there mediating phenomena that stimulate this sick perception?

In Westernized Arab countries the resumption of Muslim restoration is accelerating increasingly. We are witnessing a new Islamic expansion, secular but that is necessarily followed by religious expansion, often fanatical, fundamentalist. Europe has already gone through this; it took 1,000 years to get rid of it at the cost of so much violence and abuse, war and carnage blessed by equal fundamentalism.

We live in dangerous times, daunting. Yet unlike then Christianity today is far from being European, indeed it is cosmopolitan, African, Oriental, belongs to Latin America.

Nothing should justify the opposition in place.

What do you want to activate to counter history? Maybe kick out all immigrants, fortify the country; introduce police states and oppression: do we want to return to the Middle Ages? Stir up a crusade? The query exists and it is more dangerous than the question: the time is right, there is room now for the birth or rather, the rebirth of the opposing fundamentalisms, of fascism, of racism, of Nazism, of strong dictatorships, nationalism, localism, of nations, of just and holy wars. What is the simplest solution to a war between Europe in an economic crises and the Muslim world in demographic expansion?

The Catholic Church is not lacking in historical memories, not exactly exhilarating, its struggle for other religious expressions or otherwise of thought: heresy, the Templars, the Inquisition, Giordano Bruno, the Borgia family, the ruthless repression of any contrasting ideas, also the constant affirmation of temporal power. Today it seems, to rather

ride the wave of tolerance, patience, work and prayer, perhaps simply because one feels weaker, less involved in time and less able to deal with the Islamic invasion. Maybe because we have only changed, we have evolved socially. The young are oblivious to the infamous and shameful war, aspire to a revolution to a change.
Stop men of the West, of the North and South; stop we are approaching the hour of our destiny, we are experiencing the beginning of a nightmare, the same common nightmare for many. What will we do? There needs to be an adversary and that is not Western oligarchic capitalism, which indoctrinates them every day, which turned them from men into consumers.
About half of all the oil that exists or if you prefer remains on the earth, is located in Arabia and in the surrounding areas where reigns, absolutely, a unique religious and economic power, just as oligarchical; a geographic area where they are born, they grow and where groups expand such as 'Al Qaeda and ISIS' terrorists, supporters of the revolution against capitalism and the colonialism of others, fundamentalists and fanatics.

The Taliban in Afghanistan, the Muslim Brotherhood in Egypt. In Europe the Muslims, even those who have been integrated, are giving up the idea of being considered European in favor of being considered members of the Islamic community.
A strange thought comes to me of not understanding how in a Europe of more or less 500,000,000 inhabitants there can truly exist a problem of reception and of management of one or even two million poor people who attempt to immigrate, escaping from situations of risk or poverty, or simply looking for better luck in the land of utopia. How many millions of Italians have done the same and still do so today?
We must ask the dead! They can teach us many things, they can explain many things, but maybe you just need to remember them and, remembering them, remind ourselves of what has been to understand what could be again, and yet again, and yet again.
Power is based on fomenting hatred, bitterness, anger, hope; the promise as always, of rewards in the hereafter. A silent ensign, severe. Who supports it appears to be lost in the memory of remote and distant things, armies spread out on the hills, under a burning red

sun. Shouts and screams full of anger or hope, of companies of ruthless warriors that clash crushed at sword point against the adversaries, blood, honor, glory!
The question is who will be the first to find it worthwhile to wage a
new war between Christianity and Islam? And what will the Hindus,
Buddhists do and the others who would unavoidably be involved?

I like to look back and think that even when I had apparently made
mistakes, or made choices that proved to be losers, in effect I had
done everything I could on that occasion; none of those actions could
be considered a step back on my path but instead a continuous progression, even though sometimes determined by reasons whose motives were so deep as to be unconscious.
We need to get rid of old habits, old opinions, old ideas, and also almost all our old friends. Although often its very difficult to break free,
to let go, detaching from what has become a part of you. That's how
we grow, at forty years old we cannot continue to believe and think
what we believed and thought at seven. Freeing yourself of old stuff
and only in this way, can you make room for new things.
Why does everyone ask me about things, opinions, for answers? What
makes people think I always know everything, that I've got the answers?
There's an almost constant rule that predicts a turning point in the
path to a man's maturity, a change that occurs approximately every
seven years. At seven years, we leave childhood, start school and
start to learn, at about 14 middle school ends, at about twenty we
enter early maturity, a diploma, a driver's license, university starts and
the problem of choices; a little autonomy comes quite quickly, hype-
ractivity and the awareness of our limitations; then college ends
and/or the path of the prime of life begins, usually various work activities. Then we begin to move towards the normal routines of life.
Usually at 27-28 years we fall in love and plan to live together, a family; around 35 years one or more children determine subsequent decisions and increase responsibility. Also at work activities begin that will
become the career. A progression continues until around 50 years
then aging begins, you lose enamel, you risk less, if there are children,
they are grown and require more attention. The time of stability begins: we prepare concretely and physically for the age of rest, or of in-

direct guidance, in the family, in politics, in business in general.
Around sixty years, we are also beginning to feel, the infirmities of age some more or some, and now, presumably, we are preparing to face old age with all that it entails: slow rhythms, little hope, few desires, poor health and so on. And to think that not many years ago a 35 year-old man was middle-aged and often the end of life was placed at just over 60.
Think about how long an hour is for a seven year old and how short a day becomes for an elderly person. And all this is precisely what has been left behind.

One night by the sea, there is another memory. It had been a good party down on the beach, with the black sea roaring, the wind or rather a gentle breeze that carried cooled air from the tops of the nearby mountains. The black sky full of stars as a result of the few lights excluding our fire that seemed to contribute to its fullness and maybe it really did, shooting cascades of sparks that rose in spirals and then disappeared from sight: who knows if anybody in the world will become a star, as my grandmother said! Several of us were together in a circle around the now languishing fire, the night was far advanced, and even conversations, jokes, games, had reduced to a mere buzz of low voices or contemplative silences.
A fantastic moment of serenity and calm where some slept some thought, someone whispered; someone simply looked at the others.
I remember watching the guy sitting opposite me in the circle, one that until recently had shared much of the evening and also a lot of my life until that moment. Now I think back to what I saw in that person who was partially illuminated by the light of the embers and the flames: he is no longer a physical person; it is his spirit. All physical features you don't like, suddenly, you realize they aren't part of him but instead are part of you: it is your appreciation, the pleasant and unpleasant feelings are aroused only in you! Taking away your very personal decisions about the being in front of you, all that remains is to observe the spirituality that emanates: you also realize seeing this aspect, observing, evaluating, analyzing, is nothing more than your thoughts because you decide what he is for you. It follows that the only possibility of existing concrete change is the change in our own point of view, of our personality, because we present ourselves to

others with this; how we behave what we do, we will be perceived by others exactly according to their different personalities.

And with these thoughts and perspectives, for now, I relinquish continuing to think and allow myself, have decided, to enjoy the dark and the sea, the wind and the stars, the sounds and echoes, the silent company of this moment and I allow myself to wrap myself up and go to sleep. I will think about it again, who knows, another day.

Life is a series of trials that follow one after the other: each must eventually be overcome and the only way to do this is to face them.

In life personifications of different roles follow on from each other, social roles, roles where you accept the responsibility to do something, sometimes obeying, sometimes even commanding, and finally, unfortunately sometimes it is also necessary to judge.

There is no easy way to explain or understand each of these roles that sooner or later everyone has to play. No one can know what the role of commanding will be until they take responsibility for this, and it involves them deeply and completely because their choices will affect the lives of others. Yet you cannot avoid it, sooner or later we will all have to command or judge.

They said: don't judge unless you want to be judged; as always a threatening message and segregating: be afraid, live in fear. I realize the message was not exactly like that, I think the correct one is: Don't judge until you are forced to! Until then avoid it. It is the right thing, since when you must unavoidably judge; then you must overcome all doubts, all feelings, all personal issues.

In any other role or moment, the valuation would have involved you most of all, your sentiments, your hopes, your expectations and your choices, the results falling around you. In this case however the same things will have effects, large or small, on the lives of others, probably of many.

When one of us describes something natural, in effect, tends to reduce everything into the four principal elements – *water air earth fire* – all that exists is in these combinations. If you think of describing the dimensions or directions in which all that exists, automatically you think of the four cardinal points extending to the north extending west stretching south, folding to the east. Very rarely, and only with great effort do you realize there are at least two other fundamental dimensions: *inwards and outwards*. And so space doesn't only have three dimensions and obviously not even four counting time.

Men constantly aspire to acquiring new skills, ever new knowledge; an endless search for the expression of what is in the end a few simple things: the awareness of the physicality of the senses, pleasure, pain, everything that describes the being and mind, whether conscious or unconscious.
Every artist – poet painter musician sculptor – seeks a way to express this knowledge; any thinker tries to attain wisdom. But how is wisdom expressed, also through all our arts?
One question that haunts me these days: is the most important thing we do and why we do it? Isn't rage perhaps a demonstration of cha-racter?
The emotions and actions were not always connected to each other but isn't man free to decide whether to be angry or not, whether to be greedy or lustful? Aren't these feelings worth as much as all those that permit a man to feel rage?

Is anyone wise enough to learn from himself? Lying is at the service of power to achieve or maintain power. References to now, yesterday, today, tomorrow, aren't they simple creative theories (it was, it was not, it is not, will be, could be or not) for the aspiration of controlling himself and his emotions, to manage the intensity to obtain a use, whatever that may be?

War and peace, harmony and discord, sharing vision, satisfaction with oneself, closure in respect to all the others, performance anxiety: al-ways and in any case, yesterday was, now it's happening, it's what I do now, I'll try now, will create tomorrow...
How will my tomorrow be?
If you were really wise tomorrow would be exactly as it should be, no more, no less!
I would be perfectly integrated into the whole and indivisible and the-

refore tomorrow wouldn't exist, as it wouldn't exist now, and not even yesterday.

Time exists only because it has led to the extreme subdivision of the moments of our comprehension.

If I were wise my behavior would not necessarily be aggressive, and thus directed towards defense and survival: basic instincts that create emotions that create actions that create futures.

If I were wise, I would recognize the few key behaviors that would allow me to integrate myself into all that is natural and I would adopt these, always and in any case. But doing so I would tend to resemble an animal, full of fears and instantaneous reactions: can an animal be wise?

If I were wise, would I give up on possessing the things that improve my state of being? Or vice versa I wouldn't renounce them because it would be absurd not to improve. I should discriminate but, if I start to discriminate then I make myself choose the time and to do that I have to follow the emotions. I should, therefore, reach the state of anxiety arising from the indecision about the best choice.

Beautiful or ugly, dull or polished, black or white, skinny fat, shy or brilliant, colorful fantasies or monotony?

Perhaps man is not made to be wise, to be integrated into all that is natural, we can only hope sooner or later to stop having to live, in this way renouncing the need to choose. Whatever happens after death, this man doesn't have to (maybe) play another role again, will not command, will not choose, will not judge, therefore, he will be limited to obeying and to submitting?

One of these days I'll have to re-read these things, I seem to have sunk a little excessively into the depths of profundity, who knows! To live and continue to do so making mistakes all over is probably much simpler.

In front of me I have an image of a butler, created after seeing films: I've never known one. Very typically English, I imagine him in a delicate twilight approaching the door of the house to open it to an unexpected guest. I imagine the impression I'd have at that welcome from the perfect butler: the impenetrable face forced into a perfect mask of impassivity, not a servile attitude. A professional who is perfectly conscious of the service, perfect, which in fact he is selling to his master.

Elegantly dressed but without that ease that signals the difference between him and his boss. It is impossible to make a mistake. According to me all in all it must be quite dull! I don't want a butler.

It was warm, standing on the narrow riverbank; I was flushed, nervous, anxious. The view of the river where calm water flowed couldn't give me the peace I sought. The river snubbed me, unlike at other times I was a stranger, an enemy; insects, ants, gnats and mosquitoes, bothered me. The wind was light but raised dust. The bushes tangled at my feet. Nature showed me indifference. Cursed nature, if I could I would burn you.

I'd learned to observe others who had no suspicion they were being watched, listened to. And I liked it! But sometimes I felt I was being observed. I caught snippets of conversation around me where I seemed to hear comments about me. I was being judged and I didn't like it; really.

There are contradictory people; intelligent but for this reason they are victims of their fantasies; they allow an idea to enter their heads and all of a sudden they start playing with it in bursts of enthusiasm, a contagious enthusiasm, until all of a sudden they find they've been swept away.

A landscape, a moment. A painter painting a park: almost perfect pure lines separated into squares and rectangles of different colors. Here and there black spots illuminated by the yellow-orange sun: the birds. On one side of the dazzling river the sun was reflected, with dark spots, black in the bend. The blue sky, a cloud of dust where a man – a farmer a gardener? was working. A sketch but enough to channel the subconscious onto metaphorical paths full of who knows what meaning; of who knows what expectations, of who knows what emotions. I asked the painter, "What are you painting, what do you see, what do you want to convey?" He replied, "I'm working! When I've finish I'll let you know!" There is no turning back and no way to move forward: maybe we will die like this as well? What is reality? A crazy externalization of mental confusion.

I remember love, like everything afterwards. Mine and I think like that of all young men and young women... in that moment I decided. To have faced all and everyone, she/he included, hoping to win but conscious of losing everything. Decision explodes in the mind like a flower blooming suddenly violently exploding; shockwaves shake the heart. The sun dazzles the eyes. Lightning crosses the sky! A chain reaction has begun that makes you feel alive at last. It seems always that it is after a long time.

The evenings I remember as having spent with the most pleasure were those in small groups of friends, so to speak, usually acquaintances who had a few friend in common or for some reason, hung out in more or less the same environment: generally perfect strangers with sometimes diametrically opposed tastes and experiences.

They were evenings when we talked a lot, animatedly, over a few glasses of wine and a plate of pasta, at the home of one or other or at the wine bar. The themes were totally interesting and engaging, as they only can be if they are very personal or very general.
Passion and animation were never lacking or the rest of the discussion that went on pleasantly, between interruptions and overlapping, not in an attempt to convince but simply in the need to reveal and compare ideas.
Religion, determinism and free will were discussed, more often than philosophy of religion or pseudo religions, love, happiness, of inner suffering. Mind you we were in the full development of thought during the revolution of sixty-eight.
I remember the slightly sadistic pleasure of insinuating grounds for disbelief when some staunch believer was present or the pleasure of fiercely teasing, to the point of making the love of the moment angry.
Love was often spoken about in seeking to understand it since none of us understood, despite everyone living it constantly. Love is simultaneously suffering, expectation, doubt, uncertainty, seasoned with

glimpses of happiness but not quiet: angry, intransigent, obsessive; like a drug, causing severe withdrawal symptoms when lacking and it was most of the time. More time was spent talking about it than spending time with it.

Rarely we talked about politics, because the politics of the time was just a real mess, there were no indications, only the aspiration for peace and change whatever it was; and often discussing politics was not limited to being animated but could lead to real, unpleasant, fighting. The catchphrase of the moment was China is near!

Forty years later I can say that someone was right, now China is here! We smoked and drank; every so often someone got up and left indignant and irritated but the discussion continued among those remaining and often, those who had left, returned after a while with a new load of beer, wine or spirits, and resumed their place as if nothing had happened. And in fact it hadn't really been anything, even though for anyone listening outside the windows, it would have seemed like the end of the world. There was no limit to what you could hear: concepts about absolute rationalism clashed with positions drenched with rhetoric, also it depended on the cultural background of those taking part in the evening and being young, all were certain of what they'd studied, because they'd studied it, maybe to the maximum possible, and absolutely ascertained and indisputable. There was a tendency to assume, *I know because I've studied it.*

Often at the end of the evening I walked away, as it certainly was for the others, believing we'd wasted yet another umpteenth evening that could have been better spent in some other way, perhaps studying, something that I needed to be doing or simply listening to music and reading something pleasurable.

Girls were rarely present at these meetings, simple and brutish, for the concrete and simple reason they considered us exactly too simple and too brutish to converse with us. The opportunities for having discussions with them, which were also often but were calmer and more elegant and therefore, they were always right, which did not limit them to saying what and how they thought but they wanted to, unavoidably, convince and convert us to their point of view.

We felt overwhelmed by women. And we then tended to fall in love with them losing all rationality and distancing ourselves from our friends, to be made fun of at the first convivial event. The woman and I believe also the man with youthful dreams, is always unreachable!

It was certainly beautiful but sincerely I wouldn't return to reliving those experiences. A continuous destruction only to rebuild, often again,
nothing.

Curiosity has led to death or amputation at least of the proverbial cat
(as much as the cat often goes to the lard ...), therefore if the pro-
verbs bring us popular wisdom, then curiosity is harmful. The resulting
moral would appear to be hostile. Is there a kind of frivolous curiosity? Maybe lacking motivation, possibly unnecessary, perhaps needing
to know things that are superfluous? To poke your nose into things
that are not your business?
It's simple a way of saying, I believe; curiosity is a serious matter, perhaps the most serious existing and I believe it should never be killed
nothing but ignorance! It is out of curiosity, the innate gift of man and
many animals, that the most rational applications of scientific inquiry
are derived.
Could we enjoy a glass of beer if someone had not asked what fer-
mented cereals would taste like? Or would we smoke if we hadn't
wanted to know the taste and effect of tobacco?

Those lacking a strong will, the weak, are simply eliminated: it is the
brutal truth of the natural order, the world of Darwin, evolution and its
hierarchies.

The mountains are beautiful, to look at from below, they are motionless and allow you look at them. They are not like the sea that will never be still. It extends it ripples, it creates all colors, is never constant,
reliable. Also the sky is beautiful at night, and even the flowers on
fruit trees are beautiful in their promise. The scent of hot bread is
beautiful, flowing water, the distant sound of bells and those hung
around an animal's neck at pasture; water flowing in a stream is beautiful.

Research is pleasurable! A basic pleasure that can last a long time:
also a lifetime: the search for pleasure, from simple common pleasu-

res, within everyone's grasp, but for this reason they escape from sight. They are for everyone, thus also ours and therefore we don't seek them, because we own them.
He who seeks, finds, and vice versa those who don't seek don't find. Especially if you don't want to find, you don't try! It is common practice in my profession.

All cities die. They are creatures endowed with energy in continuous movement and this energy constantly changes places, directed towards the development of some directions and abandoning others to the fate of degradation and extinction. All cities die because they are born, they have an economic, cultural and social life; they grow, expand; live for a while and exactly because of this, like everyone, they are destined to die. Shadows and dark against the light. Offices and shops glittering buildings, glass and steel, asphalt, colored lights, crowds of people on the move and beside them, falling offices, small fast food kiosks, tiny restaurants with colorful posters of kitchens around the world, traffic, prostitutes. All and everything comes together in complex patterns of human migration, cultural exchanges and the expansion of global civilizations.
Civilizations are born, they have evolved, have been fought for and then disappeared, leaving behind calendars, measuring systems, buildings and tombs, ghosts of their existence.

When war breaks out everyone knows why it explodes, or at least they think they do. The beauty is that when the war is over no one remembers why it broke out.
When man lived in caves he had to fight, of course, to survive and needed to act like a wild beast. In his development, children were used in the labor force, easily replaced and therefore of little value but today they are pampered, protected, washed and polished; they have no hair but this would be eliminated anyway and the children will be trained to live technologically, without running, learning to communicate and move around without using their legs and their voices and most of all will no longer be eaten ... at least that is what I believe!

Reason was man's evolutionary achievement. Reason has controlled
his instincts and from reason man expects an infinite number of
things including many answers, many answers that at times lose sight
of the questions. The instincts always work in man and are the reason they cannot always control them. And what are these instincts?
Reason and instinct, what are they? Who's in charge? What does it
really mean?
If man acts according to reason, then there are no clashes or wars at
his home; these will happen at other people's houses; the ferocity
and freedom for all instincts are permitted in other people's houses.
They call it the civilization of reason, the organization of billions of
beings thinking they've gone from primitive savagery in the epoch of
the caves to that of technology and mass destruction.

At times, there are days and moments when I feel helpless: small, defenseless, impotent and incapable of reacting to overcome present
situations or those that lie ahead in the day, in the coming days, in
the coming period.
I've learned that then passes and that action, any action leads to one
or more reactions that change the context and also my mood.

What are hierarchies and how are they established? They don't need
rules, you don't need to fix positions early on: in every situation
groups are arranged, hierarchically adjusted for those habits rooted in
tradition, in culture; habits once taken up become stronger than any
that are imposed. The boss will spontaneously act like the boss and
as such will always and in any case be recognized in any critical situation, like for the negative leader there will be the designated victim.
Woe to the communities where both natural and negative leaders are
found to be present at the same time: the community will always
tend to be split, divided with a part, tending to protect the weakest,
who the mass relates to but also with most following the recognized
leader.
The boss has opinions, subjects don't have any, don't want to have
any, and only want instructions, precise directives.
Outside the window I am fascinated to see, out front on the church
roof: a flock of pigeons totally intent, busy, dodging and crossing,

going up and down along the edge, cooing who knows excuses or th-
reats. A community that is totally indifferent to the carved angels and
devils and otherwise busy. Parallel lives.
The main differences between being human rather than angels or devils: man is more or less free to choose how to act, angels and demons cannot behave differently than the way they do; they are very
powerful but as such are slaves to their being; angels cannot be happy, because they are happy by definition and therefore they are unaware of being so and are not forced to seek happiness: they can't
imagine or dream about it, they don't recognize it. The same applies
to the misery of the devils.

Father always told me that money, real money, heavy, not the kind
you use to pay the baker or the florist, is nothing but numbers placed
on different columns of the financial statement, which must always
be balanced.
We spoke of data and models, predictive models, summary tables, a
whole world of data that should be used to understand what is happening, what has happened; to imagine what might happen.
The problem in the use of the data is that if we want to estimate the
production of a donut factory, if we want to demonstrate to sharehol-
ders that a situation, deficient for lack of production is instead positive, we don't list it or catalogue it by number, but by weight. At this
point it is enough to make each donut slightly heavier to make ends
meet. Magnificent solution.
It can be verified in the use of mathematical models, very powerful
and useful tools for the prediction of behavior. The choice of unit of
measure but mostly of the motives, the objectives make up their limits: you must try to seek to find but mostly you must know what you
want to find to define what to look for.

If my employees have to produce, as they have always done, simple
practices and I maintain their productivity is lower than the number of
hours of labor employed, for them it is sufficient to demonstrate that
the actual practices are less simple, require more hours of work to
be completed. At the same time they demonstrate that not only has
their productivity not been reduced but has even increased.

For every minute, every hour, every day that passes, each young person is a little less young, every old man is a little older. This is time, unstoppable, indescribable, cannot be transported, its flow is unchangeable: not even time can reverse its path.
At each time of life corresponds to a person who is different than the one before who without doubt feels completely different to the one who will follow. The more different he is the longer his life will be.
Is the world changing? Has the world changed? Certainly the world has changed and it can't be anything but this way because people, every time I look at them, are in a different state: a person cannot relate to the world twice in the same condition.
Nature does not permit its creations to be masterpieces or failures, to last: they are works of art, like those that man sculpts in sand or ice.

A couple with a child in a pushchair holding two by the hand: a motionless smile of a representative stamped on the face, he says to her, "But anyway, I work all the sainted day, spend time with the children as long as I can, play with them whenever I can..." and she in return always smiling for the public onlookers and passers by, "Certainly, you play a lot of games with your children, I just... do all the rest, I feed them, wash them, dress them, I take care of them when they are sick, take them to school, I take them to parties... Certainly, exactly like you I only do it in my spare time between washing, ironing, setting the table, cooking, making the beds, drying clothes, doing the shopping, going to the post office to pay the bills... It's true that occasionally while taking your clothes to the laundry I stay a couple of hours at the hairdresser and I chat a little at the pharmacy. I cannot ask you to do more for our children..."
I believe that housework should be valued and paid for like any other job: the state is the employer. Those who want a career, then, could decide which one to take up.

I met a friend who'd just gone on a trip to India I asked him for his impressions and he said: noisy, crowded, dusty and colorful. Simple and effective.

I have the impression, listening to people talk, in bars, meeting places that every day the life of each one of us is compared to the movies, soap operas that fill our homes at any time of day. Once they called it evasion and the films represented fictions that allowed us to escape the monotony of normal life with the only difference being in respect to books was the images were imposed and the figures of people, the actors real, of course constraining the free and spontaneous identification of the characters and environments. It seems that life today has become, on the contrary, evasion compared to the standard imposed by cinematic reality: ... It happened to me like in the movies ... He's nice as an actor... it's happening exactly like it happened in that film ... It's funny that today we have to go to a film to explain and tell our life and much more that we should attempt to adapt to it.
I understand that it's not been here long in America, celebrating Mandela, there was a giant poster displayed to the crowd with a photograph paying homage to the famous actor who'd played him. You are no longer who you really are, but become those represented.

My garden is beautiful, there are blackbirds that keep me company; they own the place. Right now I'm looking at a big blackbird perched on a branch and looking around, apparently curious, tilting his head from side to side with his black and shiny eyes like obsidian and his yellow beak. I pass by near him, I even greet him with my hand; he simply restricts himself to hopping a little further away, perching on the ground and quietly devotes himself to pulling a worm from the ground.
There are endless ways to be happy, for example appreciating the absence of pain; every minute every hour that passes in its way. Happiness is the search itself but the search, an end in itself, cannot bring about the awareness of happiness. To be certainly happy you must declare it, admit it, shout it when by chance you come across a moment, in an instant of grace. Who does this will never forget they were happy at least once, at least for a moment, completely and utterly happy, well aware that happiness does not last.

And then the search along a path of certain points of recognized happiness becomes the pursuit of serenity; less exciting but much more concrete, real, lasting and satisfactory.
With advancing age unfortunately, perhaps fortunately, one stops exulting. Rarely are you surprised, more and more often we become irritated, not because of unexpected or unpredictable events but the sudden that disturb the long sought for serenity and overcome with so much difficult.

I'm thinking about the woodpecker, which nature had to provide a double layer, one inside and the other outside, to contain the brain, between the two layers there's a shock-absorber system; like palettes, able to absorb shocks and everything to allow it to bang its head hundreds and hundreds, thousands of times a day against a wooden trunk to puncture it and make a nest, its only ambition, its only motivation.

I'm thinking about how God could have been so 'out of his head' as to invent such a being made in such a way, simply to allow it to exist and reproduce.

I don't like Venice, don't like its smell, you know constantly rotten, moldy; I don't like its dazzling white colors under a scorching sun bordered with rotting green and brown or when there is no sun the base is grayish without life. Normally gray, boring, dirty and smelly, or incandescent and dazzling, full of people lined up as in any market any place, all intent on looking into the air or buying necklaces, bracelets, postcards and souvenirs, jostling and shoving to see things that everyone should be able to say they've seen, on going home, in order to share a common experience. Or semi-deserted in the inner alleyways, neglected and decaying, ignored by most; almost uninhabited because they are too expensive to live comfortably, in respect to the more modern dormitory city of Mestre, just outside.
Enveloped in an unhealthy climate, where moisture has the upper hand, winding paths, narrow, lined with bland walls all formed with perfectly matching bricks, color and size, exacerbated by scraped pla-

ster, of paint, of paintings embellished with saltpeter, interrupted by identical rows of small windows with detached shutters; some rope stretched between the two sides of the road where underwear and socks hang. The cornerstones impregnated with the urine of dogs or cats, yellowish or stained by sulfur used as a disinfectant; small deserted balconies with a few geraniums. The stratified stench of rotting seaweed that rises from the canals and permeates everything and the air we breathe is like the breath from mouths infested with bad teeth and decay.

Today we speak of aberrations, perpetrated by the pharmaceutical companies that seem to routinely disseminate the products of their research containing pathogenic strains and later vaccines to counteract them. With great carelessness disinformation in the media speculates about theories of a global conspiracy.
All are surprised, scandalized, no one remembers, apparently, that biological medical science has recently developed a pace, starting with the concentration camps and Nazi research centers, Japanese, Russian and American. Amphetamines were once the salt and pepper of war, the strength and ferocity displayed by men.
All seem to have forgotten that post-war America hosted and funded all these 'scientists' and that only a few were tried and convicted in Nuremberg.
All the others have quietly bartered their freedom in exchange for the results of their substantial research in experiments where 'animal test subjects' were injected – and the word animal must be understood in the wider and broader sense – all the more fanciful garbage, chemicals, viruses, bacteria, poisons, the most outlandish substances, to study the effects and all the guinea pigs that survived were later killed and dissected, if not vivisected, to find out why this happened.
Perhaps most of these criminals are now dead but certainly their methods are not dead, their schools, their teachings. In civil society use of the test subject 'beasts' in experimentation has at least been declared as restricted, where it is or may become visible and noticeable.
Perceptible and imperceptible, as it appears today the universe or all the universes seem to cause oscillations of dark energy acting on dark matter, causing perceptible, measurable gravitational effects.

Science and faith under the eyes of man when you are approaching
the mystery: both must be used if you want to see not necessarily
everything but at least something.
The deeper you penetrate the structure of matter, the closer you get
to its source, the energy, all that can be measured represents comprehensive reality.
Man is made up of body and soul: something that can be measured
and something else that however cannot be measured but that appears inseparable from its naturalness and that depends largely on
the motivation of what man is, the risk man assumes.

How do you feel satisfaction about being honest if you haven't even
experience the feeling of being dishonest? Words that explain other
words to attempt to classify, in the end, what is not classifiable, to explain what cannot be classified, to explain what cannot be explained
but certainly exists, because its existence is common experience:
the sixth sense, instinct, the instincts, philosophically insolent.

When the consensus of the scientific and social community is called
upon to make any statement as demonstrated and reliable, we forget
that progress has always arisen and only from dissension, from contradiction and opposition precisely to scientific and moral consensus.
The stagnation of creative thinking lies in consensus.
You speak of philosophical thought when you can afford to say, out
loud, all you think without having to think about the consequences of
the words expressed, freed from the constraints of what is or should
be, what must appear.
Philosophical thought belongs to everyone when they can afford to finally be themselves and this happens almost exclusively when each
one finds they are protected in their own home. Only in their own
home can a person allow themselves to be rude otherwise, allowing
the instincts freedom, you unavoidably arrive at conflict and by extension war, a liberating moment where finally you can stop loving your
neighbor and can kill, smash, destroy, rape, amply justified by the fact
that we're fighting a war, just and holy, in order to consolidate a future
state of peace and definitive harmony.
Philosophical thought, unfortunately, has been codified over time until
losing its essence, its meaning of liberty and liberation. The Sophists

came into being who put everything into doubt; there are the Plato-
nists who only believe in archetypes; the Pythagoreans believed in
the mystical and finally worst of all, the Aristotelians developed logic,
the greatest form of mystification and control of common thought
that could have been invented.
However for those who have learned to develop critical thinking, every philosophy is a guide to better understanding and interpretation of
the world and its mechanisms. Everyone has the right to have their
own opinions and the fact that a man, whatever his status or his rank,
speaking in the name of God doesn't mean he's telling the truth: it
just means that he's providing his interpretation of the truth.
The excess of prophets, oracles or preachers was the driving force
that increased the development of interpretive codes unified within
which the variables, acceptable, are few: in this way the current major
religions were born.

The mother figure is the representation of the greatest power existing, that of creating life and of giving form to the species but it also
represents the greatest tragedy that man must face: the mother has
seen her children grow, the children she has cared for and protected
against everything and everyone only for them to become protagonists and victims in their own lives. Even the mother of Jesus suffered
this tragedy, and had to see him abandoned, suffering, alone and
then crucified.
Every mother cannot but represent a goddess. Every man with a mother, divine, who could never abandon him or leave him alone. The
queen is the queen, no matter what a woman is, the icon is what
matters, what she represents.
They are always mothers who have to first start and then complete
their men's works to transform them into something that solidifies
their memory after they have foolishly and courageously fulfilled their
own destiny.
They are the mothers those to whom men turn to be buoyed up or
consoled or motivated cuddled and looked after: they are the only
force he turns to when feeling small and powerless, frightened.

The goddess who is in heaven, and can only be there, because the

deity resides in heaven and for this reason there are no gods on earth but their sons or daughters who have completed the tasks for which they'd been incarnated, they have to ascend to heaven to bring together the spirit, which is already found there, with the body they had
once borrowed. In this way they return to the whole of everything and
leaving individual thought, which is human, vanish to be replaced by
the common 'finality'.

I watched a few episodes of the (old) show The Invisible Man. The
story presupposes that a substance was discovered and experimented on that made the subject invisible. Invisible therefore transparent
to light. From there, a thousand adventures and situations.
I thought about what permits us to see things? Color: a few grams of
colored matter, pigments, which reflect the light into our eyes.
Now compared to the television program where things were added to
the man, if we could instead take a few grams of pigment from the
human body and if it is true that a man is composed mostly of water
and that water is transparent because it's contents are not fixed,
then the man could under normal conditions become invisible or at
least very transparent. His mass certainly wouldn't disappear and as a
result his weight. The concept of "what exists but is not seen."
In effect, an easy experiment that allows you to visualize this concept:
if we look at a sheet of glass in different lighting conditions or from
different angles, we can go from seeing it, to seeing through it to not
seeing it at all. If this same plate was to break until it crumbled and
became dust, it would definitely remain visible but it would no longer
be perceived as a plate: it becomes an opaque, white pile. If light enters this pile it will reflect the colored light rays of the spectrum. Yet
they are the same thing, seen in different moments, viewpoints or
conditions.
Looking at a group of crystals in our reality each reflects and refracts
light, you can hardly imagine or connect them to a sheet of glass that
has only two reflecting surfaces and a minimal degree of refraction;
and that is, notwithstanding that in this form, the sheet, is considerably more bulky and occupies a much larger volume in space. Even the
possible uses of the two forms are different and differently effective
under the same conditions. You can change the conditions to examine the same situation in another world. To change the world you can

simply change the context!

The dust or the glass pane could be immersed in water and you can see what happens in this fluid world. Perceptions would be different. The refractive index of water is similar to that of glass, therefore, in this new world, absolutely real and natural, both the pane or the powder will be virtually invisible to the eye but their mass will certainly not disappear.

The search for knowledge pursued by man as a necessity continues and this simply because knowledge, always results as being incomplete and a certain source of new ignorance, can never be satisfying. Scientists, then, often become arrogantly presumptuous, refusing to admit the discovery of their own ignorance and so come to deny that a formula itself, mathematical expression, an artistic representation, musical or geometric, might suggest revelations to other scientists, scholars from various and different branches, which are for them inconceivable and elusive.

There are millions, billions of choices we make every day, but only a few in fact, very few, involve free will.

I am a soldier, armed, with orders to shoot and kill. Somehow, choice after choice, I have come to this point but now, only now, with the enemy in front of me under the same conditions I really have to choose freely. Who knows if he will make the same choice as I do? My life is at stake, I can shoot, (to kill intentionally or not, it doesn't matter: to frighten, to injure, etc.: are only palliative justifications because, shooting, I may not intentionally kill).

Is it an arbitrary choice? Subjected to the pressure exerted by the survival instinct, the strongest animal instinct, justified by the order to do it for 'just cause', the choice of yes, I will, is definitely easier, probably more useful than the alternative, of refusal, which requires a process of thought and an extremely strong and costly personal conviction.

Exactly because of this, No is the only, true, possible choice! It applies to all choices but not all have the same value, the same price to pay. To be cruel or not: is it a real choice? If this were like, masochism and sadism it would not be part of human and animal nature: they don't require thought, just action. Yes, I will, thus becomes only the easiest choice.

But then does free will exist? It exists or doesn't?

I believe and want to believe that it exists; I believe it is part of almost endless possibilities offered by nature, from its biodiversity, governed by a chaotic yet precise and functional system of interrelation and equilibrium. The set of choices, instinctive or rational, generates 'the case' that affects and governs the whole.

Free will – if understood as a possibility – is perhaps, exclusive to thinking man, possibility is perhaps only more complex for him than for animals. The lion decides whether to attack and eats you in the end on the basis of the relationship between hunger, need, fear, its survival instinct. Man however attacks the lion for completely different reasons, and sometimes, just sometimes, out of fear. Free will becomes therefore one of the many unpredictable variables that allows nature to maintain the system's dynamic equilibrium. The system's equilibrium is crucial and allows you to conserve the greater part of the energy and reduce it with the universe to frozen immobility at the end of time (Entropy/Enthalpy) awaiting a new beginning, a new vibration that will shake the motionless universe.

Free will exists and I believe it is a concrete possibility that doesn't necessarily involve however the totality of choices; only a few, fundamental, challenging, requiring a huge effort of will and mind to justify the alternative possibility of rejection and the energy required to carry it actuate it generating the results, whatever they may be; choosing to go against the tide.

We are certain that the consequences of refusal, will certainly be less predictable than those of consensus and they will trigger a flow of new choices that will influence the entire system overall. The entire universe will be shaken and all there is, starting with the implementation of a single variable with the least probability of being, among all the others.

The enemy soldier in front of me, will he make the same choice as I do?

I dedicate myself to some volunteer activity; when they ask me why I do it I reply, *because I see that it is right to do so*. I give a few coins, a wretched contribution for my means, to the homeless and to all those who ask me: why? *Because I see it is right to do so*. They are neither good nor jerks. I am not the judge of deeds or of intentions: why? *Because I see it is right to do so*.

Looking deeper I believe that after all being a man could mean being an individual, an organism at the service of the natural living community, men included. The definition of service, should be feeling the need to do something for 'them', without thinking of personal gain or gains, of gratitude or reward. To serve doesn't mean being a servant. To serve means to be available to others for what others expect of you or because they feel they have the right or because they've been paid. This is certainly not the same concept.
To serve means believing you have some capacity for making yourself available and to have the responsibility for doing so.
Most people think of 'service' as a servile condition, a servant, a low social status, and then reject it. Most people are ignorant!

I'm listening to a television service with scientists, or declared as such, they are driveling on about the catastrophic developments that would take place with the displacement of the Earth's magnetic poles: catastrophists paid to fuel fears and phobias and justify economic policies. What I'm listening to is putting the rising levels of carbon dioxide in the Earth's atmosphere in relation to climate change that apparently tends towards global warming and totally ascribes guilt to the current Western productive economy.
No mention of the possibility that a temperature rise in the seas corresponds to an increase in carbon dioxide in the atmosphere and this is independent of the productive economy.
No possibility for error in connecting the productive economy to the increase in global temperature and its devastating effects. (Devastating for what? Where? For whom? For how much?)
For me it is obvious that we are dealing with the economy of survival of the human species 'consumer' in its current ecological context and foreseeable future. Will I be mistaken? They don't tell me.
Not even the hypothesized possibility of being in a moment of a cyclical path between maximum lowering of the global temperature and maximum rise in the global temperature, a recurring geological cycle, therefore, of much longer duration than that of a civilization or economy.
It is equally obvious that they don't theorize even that the same trend (appears established and actually non debatable) to heating in

our latitudes and in each case to the change in the other, both, at
the same time, a cooling trend over a longer period.

A simple mechanism: the seas are heated by absorbing the sun's
energy, they release carbon dioxide but also much more serious,
from the viewpoint of the greenhouse effect, water vapor and methane, far more powerful agents; increasing evaporation and clouds, they
relatively change the high and low pressure centers; change the path
of the winds and ocean currents, the times the places and the quantities of water released in the form of rain. Many more clouds the
greater the greenhouse effect and mostly the planet's heat is not dispersed into space; for the same reason, though, also the sun's energy is no longer able to reach the sea.

It will decrease, thus, the amount of heating available, thus the seas
will absorb the carbon dioxide and hold the water vapor; reducing the
clouds and precipitation, the temperature will continue to fall until large surfaces will freeze; the larger they are the more sunlight will be
reflected. And so it will proceed up to the new point of extreme equilibrium where the heat of the planet, held by the surface must and
will be freed, with the release again of vapor and gas and new clouds
the reflection will be reduced and because of the greenhouse effect
will allow the temperature to rise again.

The seas would need to rise considerably in order to drown coastal
cities, according to them, in the last thirty years: it seems it has not
happened but is that important?

The information doesn't give any details about how everything is va-
riously changeable and unstoppable but exalts the role of industry in
the acceleration of these processes, for better or worse. Moreover
research is paid for by industry. Certainly these processes change,
gradually, the ecosystem and exactly for this reason for man, to be
understood as humanity and its economies, it is essential to plan
production based on this trend by focusing on a valuation of limited
spaces, over the duration of around a century.

It would be opportune that these people also remember change affects the entire ecosystem and affects biodiversity in an area. Man's
action, in addition, can accelerate natural action causing chains of extinctions and sudden loss of biodiversity: all at his expense in the
long run.

Man convinced of using nature for his purposes in effect would lose, in this case, resources and alternatives, possibilities offered precisely by nature that until now has brought him up to this point and that he can no longer use.

Also the inversion of the poles is a cyclical phenomenon and also very precise, the poles are regularly exchanged north towards the south and south towards the north and vice versa. Geologists use this criterion to date volcanic activity on the seabed, a bit like reading tree rings: the Earth's crust melts and being composed of plenty of iron, its particles submit to the magnetic field of the time and line up accordingly: when the crust cools the rocks maintain this alignment, and you can date them well beyond documented history.

The use of scientific information, the attribution of banality and obviousness to the scientific community that guarantees the shared consensus of pseudo certainties; the rediscovery by the information media and pseudo information, normally known for years and abandoned which is then recovered and partially re-proposed years later, represents a real paradox, justified only by the absence of truth, a fundamental characteristic of our 'civilized' systems that scientifically maintain the state of general ignorance, the inability to develop critical and free thinking, through incomplete and partial education that is more like a form of indoctrination spread as widely as possible.

It seems to me that commonly everyone tends to attribute their most venal ambitions to others believing, perhaps in good faith, that the others want the same things and with the same ardor.

I have never heard a simple affirmation like "Nature is not simply loved or respected, but feared, because nature is never man's friend". Fear is the founding principle of all religion: all gods are to be feared because they are unpredictable and normally man is disinterested but needs to ingratiate himself by loving and respecting them so as not to helplessly submit to ire.

Our planet is teeming with life forms and everything is always in any case extremely busy with killing each other!

If it is not ire it is desire. If it is not indignation it is pride.

My convictions are neither solid or wise, nor saintly.
I am a man who is constantly burned by passion.
My animal symbol, the one I most identify myself with is the eagle: lar-

ge and strong capable of soaring free, independent, often alone, but doesn't disdain being social, in an area of the sky where it fears no one, where it lives, living in and visiting environments that are accessible to only a few; with sharp eyes and a capacity for discernment that allows it to choose the time to act, without haste, without constraint, directing its actions, its efforts, its sacrifices, to achieve its objectives and, in particular, especially, to raise and protect its family and with it its eternity.

There is one thing that everyone does when they resign themselves to waiting for death: they force themselves to remember things, strive to remember the details of their lives, all the events that until recently seemed important, impossible to forget like things tasted, those smelled, words listened to, thoughts, the great illuminations that once seemed to be revelations.
I liked a definition, I don't remember whose it was; I read somewhere, I don't remember when or where; it went something like this: *man is the missing link that connects monkeys to civilized beings*. And another: *if God had concentrated his creative thinking only on the earth and man, then he would have proved to be a very wasteful and inefficient author, having filled the entire universe solely with his waste.*
Every atom of matter composed was born inside a star billions of years ago, it was expelled, with energy, it became cosmic dust and a packet of energy that has come this far together with others to become, now, what we are and then what we will become.
We are part of the universe, a minute part. Among the terrestrial creatures only man possesses, in the brain, a structure or perhaps another creature, autonomous and symbiotic, evolving, capable of imposing its will on organic mechanisms in his body, occasionally successfully, even at the expense of the same. To restore a lost equilibrium takes time, conditions and toeholds.

Also it would be useful for the rich to remember what it means to be poor. It would be useful to learn not to buy the superfluous before having purchased what is necessary.

A conversation is all the more interesting when the participants are cultured and have tastes, opinions and experiences that are very different if not opposed, speaking of engaging and interesting themes and that are either very personal or very generic. The philosophy of religion and the reasons for disbelief are certainly among these. Remaining silent causes others to suspect that you're thinking about something. Prolonging the silence indicates that you agree with them.

Living? Or not is simply vital?
We must decide on the priorities before making choices.
The air at sea is humid!
How many platitudes and common places infest our knowledge, we aren't used to it, as we are, to the critical analysis of the available information.
The cell? Is round, small and alive. Absurd! An egg is a cell, from a chicken, or duck or even better still from an ostrich, which is certainly not small. Alive? Not at all: they are structured and organized in order to live, but they are not alive, if anything they are full of life. If they are not fertilized the eggs rot without living.
Life is a simple mechanism, sequential, where an appropriate and organized structure, in a compatible context, manages to become larger, to grow and therefore to survive a little longer than others.

Born to live. To eat, selectively, grow and survive; survive to reproduce, in any way possible, and then to die and return to everything, unique and interdependent which is the universe and to take part, in some way, in the evolution of everything.

Being an anarchist means to be a free thinker, a critical reader, an active listener, to be fully conscious of having to understand to be able to choose, each time, based on known science and sentiment and also – why not? – based on urgent need.
Anarchy is a philosophy of life jealously individualistic, but also generously inclusive. It cannot be that an individual, who is unique, and also and inevitably the product and social subject of the era but mostly of the context he lives. The 'state' is me and I entertain equal and

peaceful relations with as many singularities!
The state is a service institution, it doesn't represent me but supports me and sometimes opposes me, indicating the social rules of majoritarian current conformity, and this can hinder a peaceful relationship.
At the base of the anarchist principle is the concept of the individual with some narcissistic components that can and could, in some cases, lead to anachronistically and paradoxically violent behaviors. The communities founded on anarchist principles, have historically proved to be an easy and preferred target for social retaliation.
No state or society or group can force any obligation or duty on me to take charge that I, the unique and indisputable creator of my life, unless I am willing to accept or share.
My judgment is irrevocable but not static; my ideas are rooted and justified but they can be modified and are continually being changed, by relationship and by comparison, egalitarian and equal, with others and their ideas.
Only the ignorant, not necessarily uncultured, or the stupid don't modify their ideas because these identify and integrate them into the social organization to which they belong, individuals in the herd awaiting instructions.
The only speaker I accept being equal compared to, is myself, when I assume the form and substance as my own interlocutor; an alternative individual that I could or would consider ideas, positions or decisions different to those that, in any singular moment, I consider just and applicable to my behavior.
If man ceases to make deductions, generally wrong, based on that portion, categorically limited, of facts that can be observed or perceived to then make suggestions and limits himself to taking note of the facts themselves, waiting for others to be added, then he would be a great scientist but would not be human. Not being human, he couldn't feel the emotions that define his essence; his behavior wouldn't be, however like this, influenced by his own mistakes.

Who knows why man uses the term 'whore' to insult and offend a woman when it is the only thing he really wants her to be!

I took some notes at a conference on risk and danger. They confirm
my impression that absolutely, for everybody, the greatest danger and
consequently health risk, with effects that are definitely lethal over
time, are simply 'the act of living!' Everything else are costly side effects.

If Adam had not had Eve everything would have been different. He
would have been, essentially, a simple biological anomaly, an acciden-
tal variation. Adam wouldn't have felt alone because he wouldn't have
known the concept of loneliness. Adam wouldn't have known good
and evil because he would have been isolated and in this condition
he couldn't have been able to ignore it: morality stems from our attitude, a form of purely animal empathy, towards others. They are the
gifts of the Holy Spirit: wisdom, understanding, and self-control! Adam
would not have known emotions if not the desire to increase his own
knowledge and awareness, always provided that this can be considered an emotion.
Would he have been a victim in any case or sooner or later eaten the
apple? I believe yes, but he would have had to wait a long time without the acceleration imposed by Eve. Eve's presence creating a society, and following competition, has irreversibly altered this simple
reality.

*Use... Drink... Go to... Eat... Buy...Travel with... Enter from... With... you'll get
better, you'll get the best, you'll be safer...* advertising, sound and visual
continually fills the eyes and ears forcing you to live in the world as it
is, or how you want it to be. People believe what they think they see,
think and understand. They know politicians well, those who aspire to
be elected, who live without ostentation, regardless of the money
they have, they enjoy it discreetly. They use the luxury to indulge their
passion in less obvious ways, and you discover they don't live in grandiose buildings. This is why they are considered honest and eligible.
Others, if they have an economic condition that cannot be hidden,
flaunt it out of proportion, to show they are capable entrepreneurs
and won't need to steal from people. This is why they are considered
honest and eligible.
Ordinary people, Christian rather than Muslim or Jew, go to church

more or less on Sunday or when expected, to listen to the word of
the 'shepherd' and accept everything he says; taking for granted that
he knows what he's talking about, whether interpreting the Bible or
the Koran.
Most of these people would be shocked if they were told that the
'pastor' is equally if not more ignorant than they are about most
things and only slightly less ignorant than they are about the things
he talks about.

The Americans win all the wars and this cannot be otherwise because
every long war can only be won by the richest, and they are rich.
In America, at the time of colonization, most Puritans taking refuge
had to flee there as they found they were in conflict with the ways
power was exercised and of being, of the powerful and of the Catholic Church. The Americans said that all are born free and equal, in
stark contrast to the history and constitution of every existing civilized country at the time.
The strange thing is that at the same time, the rights of man was affirmed, in the Declaration of Independence, for all men, to pursue
happiness. Maybe they were no longer committed Puritans.
The Puritans lived anchored in the teachings of the Bible and the Bible certainly doesn't speak of happiness, as in the rest of the sacred
texts of the Christian religion. The Calvinists in particular and they are
the majority in America, consider the fact of being unhappy and un-
lucky a virtue and it is a sin to indulge in anything that can give you
immediate pleasure, either music, or the theater, or wearing long hair
or taking drugs... Evil is all around us, the world is dirty... not to mention the various Baptists, Anabaptists, Brownists, the Quakers, who all
agree about the idea that any individual or group, each congregation,
if not every single individual, receives its own singular divine inspiration. All of them in fact wouldn't do anything that was not written,
exactly, in the Bible and without the necessary guidance of a central
authority; Presbyterians consider predestination a dogma.
There have been and still are conditions of thought at the limits of
anarchy, definitely religious anarchy, and without doubt, in contrast to
the absolute certainty of divine inspiration, and of the reality documented in the Bible, as is true for the Jews, to the point of being
creationists, to deny Darwin and evolution, to reduce geological and

human time to the flood and force six, eight thousand years, of Biblical time into which the unique and immutable design of God is expressed. Predestination, inspired leadership, reality revealed, the ambition of belonging to the small number of just foreseen, removing, simply eliminating exterminating, all competition!

Their culture beyond being evolved is based on the only available text for reading or set out, taught and commented on by the preachers who frequented medieval European towns, as opposed to the readings and truth imposed by the Catholic Church and its representatives. A church that they felt had oppressed and exploited them; surely rightly at least between the fifteenth and sixteenth centuries, a period in which the temporal power of the Church was rivaled only by that of kings and emperors, demanded and expected absolute obedience, submission and taxes. A life of extreme poverty in the service of the powerful and their henchmen, the only interpreters, invested directly by God, with the power to represent the will of God, in the name of the common good, between pomp and speculation.

The Protestants have simply denied the fundamental principle of Catholicism: transubstantiation, the act through which the power is invested in the priest, magically transforms the host, the bread and wine into the body and blood of Christ. The church, which has always opposed magic and burned witches for centuries, enacts, uniquely, this magical rite par excellence. It is not foreseen that the rite, will be performed in the memory of the passion and the sacrifice of Christ, something that could be shared by all Christians, but it is designed to really achieve transformation. The denial of this effect, and of the power entrusted in the priest for its realization, was the main cause of Protestantism in all its forms.

Only the Franciscans, in that period however disliked the temporal Church but it was needed to control the population, preached principles similar to those of the Protestants who incited the moral rectitude of renunciation, to the life of poverty of the early Gospels.

From the people, because probably they were closer to the true Christian message, even though within the much desired and despised hierarchical system, were universally recognized as positive; according to these principles they lived very closely to humble people, sharing their needs and poverty, with only one precise difference to the Protestants, of challenging not the authority and power of the Church but only the manner of exercising that temporal if not its ostentation.

Substantially, like all Protestants, there were also the Franciscans, fundamentalists and almost fanatical; all their sermons caused the powerful to think that Christianity of this kind, especially Catholicism, was a cult suitable only for slaves, as indeed it originally had been. The Church and the powerful, attempted to keep it that way. Humility, patience, sacrifice, submission to the enlightened guidance of the one who knows, of those who know, in the name of the prize after death, is a trait shared by all religions and if we remove this, also most philosophies. Plato teaches: the philosophers who know are the elect, unique, worthy and capable of governing the oxen population who otherwise wouldn't be able to.

The strength, innovation, of revolutionary and modern America, was its ability to unite and bring together all these strains bringing to the fore the population and the individual: democracy replaces or better integrates the values imposed by God with one difference, which is valid for all those who don't share the biblical message: consumerism, immediate reward and grounds for... humility, patience, sacrifice, submission to the enlightened guidance of the one who knows, of those who know and therefore, of those who own the greatest amount thanks to these abilities!

Homeothermy: is the capacity of being able to keep the temperature of the body almost constant in respect to the environment. It corresponds to the state of wellbeing, which is more or less valid for mammals, warm-blooded animals such as humans. Put this way it sounds simple but the mechanisms for achieving it are different depending on the metabolism. If the temperature is adjusted from inside the mechanism is called endothermic; if the mechanism is activated based on the outside temperature it is called exothermic. All other variables in between are related to the metabolism under conditions of activity or rest: mammals at rest that go into hibernation lower their metabolism to reduce their metabolism the most are *bradymetabolics*. The same applies to creatures that hibernate when it's cold outside but these are cold-blooded animals whose body temperature depends on the external values. If an animal warm or cold blooded exothermic or endothermic, increases its temperature during activity, it is defined as *tachymetabolic*. It is correct therefore to identify animals so distinctly into warm or cold-blooded animals when these pass from one category to the other?

A scientist, a good one, tends to avoid hasty conclusions; he is not impatient, not ready to jump to conclusions, doesn't judge the elegance of an idea rather than its contents. Visionaries, fanatical plodding investigators, obsessed with an idea, tend to let the imagination fly as long as it is related to a single logical thread that allows them to create a theory: perhaps they are not good scientists as defined but certainly form the substrate, the mechanism, the spring that allows science to move forward and not stagnate in certainties, only because it has already been proven in the past or because it has been peacefully accepted.
In itself, invention is so rare it practically doesn't exist. There are observations, discovery and research. At least it is to be able to invent something: as a rule something that exists is discovered or rediscovered and is applied or used in a different way.
The scientific community, abstract entity that wouldn't in fact exist if it were not continually invoked to justify the inquisition of the original ideas, is however a community made up also, and fortunately, by extremely competent, prepared scientists. Every so often even those who belong by right continually come up with silly ideas that they try to demonstrate, hypothesizing and speculating, jumping freely from one to the other possibility as well, simply for the sake of affirming "the impossibility of the impossible" but mostly their presence and to justify funding!
Science, by definition the official, doesn't work like this: first you collect the data, then analyze them then, and only then, propose an hypothesis and a project to test it. You cannot prove an hypothesis. The hypothesis can be tested to see if you can discard it: it is called falsification. At the bar, rubbish. If with time a hypothesis resists any attempt to prove it unreliable, then being very solid, it is called the theory.
One theory is not the truth but the best possible interpretation or the one that is available at that time, of what we know about the subject. One theory is good if it offers not only the best interpretation actually possible but most of all the simplest explanations possible. Nature is studied using natural methods: nature is simple, its evolution, its infinite diversity and complexity is based on simple, mechani-

sms, economic, endlessly repeated gradually discarding the least effective, least simple, least cost effective.

Evolution is not immediate, a mathematical vector, an arrow pointing straight towards an objective, rather it is a kind of radiation in all possible directions, wherever there is space and time. If there is a vacuum, the space and time required to consolidate the possible modifications, then fills an evolutionary niche. Starting with this niche, characterized by a natural species that is identifiable in that particular environment, this same species branches out seeking other possible niches and conditions: if found it evolves, adapting and modifying accordingly.
Species gradually evolve to adapt to environments and conditions that are always more specialized. Those that are more evolved are the ones that most exploit their potential, they are the most adapted to an environment and to a limited context. The most evolved species are those nearest extinction.
Pandas are bears, they took thousands of years to become herbivores and they eat bamboo. Koalas are adapted to the environment of eucalyptus trees and eat only those leaves. The essence renders their flesh if not poisonous, unpleasant and unpalatable to predators. Both species are restricted to the existence of bamboo and eucalyptus. Man can destroy these environments in a few hundred years. Will it be enough for the pandas to remember they are after all omnivorous bears? If they don't have enough time, they will simply become extinct.
And man will miss the bamboo he so obviously needs. Man is adaptable, survives in any environment, therefore he is anything but evolved. This is the animal and natural strength of his species. Is he made in the image and likeness of God? Then God cannot be fixed but is a real kaleidoscope of potential possibilities.
To study and analyze evolution, observing existing species simply out of context, does not lead anywhere except to a mere exercise in mechanical bureaucracy.
At the zoo you can see many animals but not their environment; you can describe and observe, but one can only imagine the ecosystem; you cannot verify their living conditions in the natural environment under conditions of freedom.

We observe birds but they, at least some, are nothing more than dinosaurs, evolved in contexts that have been changing up until today.
The equilibrium between the environment and the species that fill it
is called ecology. The destruction of a habitat causes, always and in
any case, a number of extinctions.
Although uncontrolled predation by humans has decreased in the last
century, nevertheless the number of endangered species is increasing, because adaptation is always very slow, and the species that are
most adapted to specific niches have nowhere else to go.

Could we enjoy a beer today if someone hadn't asked what flavor the
fermentation would have? Curiosity is innate and is the basic motor
for going deeper and research; questions requiring answers, the answers discussion and action.
The actions are more satisfying they have as an objective satisfying
their curiosity.
Curiosity is never frivolous or inopportune; it allows us to be aware
and liberates us from ignorance.
Discussion is a phase of confronting, a technical contest, and in this it
is different from a conversation.
Emphasis and silence characterize a discussion. The use of silence is
fundamental: to stay silent induces the assumption that you are me-
ditating on what you have said, extending it to induce the other to suspect that his reasons have been placed in doubt and invite him to
continue with emphasis, always explaining more to the possible critic.
A conversation is however an exchange between equals but able to
modify the ideas of the conversationalists and appears far more interesting if those taking part are cultured and have tastes, opinions and
experiences, very much different if not opposed, it is carried out by
speaking of engaging themes which are either very personal or totally
generic.
Philosophy, social and religious and the motivation of disbelief or of
love, are certainly among these.

I threw a small stone and watched the ripples travel across the surface of a small pond. My son near me threw another. The ripples superimposed, conflicted; generated others then on meeting a leaf were

further modified and so on. Some time passed before the surface returned to being almost calm even if in the meantime a slight breeze had risen. I understood the laws that govern the interference (Fresnel, the French engineer and physicist 1788 to 1827 who contribute much to the theory of wave optics), the importance of chaos and dynamic equilibrium; the stability of chaos and that of political democracy!

Technological evolution produces changes in sociological stability and this is called progress.

I heard a town councilor for the environment state, "We are in a time of crisis and 'unfortunately' there is green. We must intervene for its maintenance with all that it will cost..."

How does the soil of a meadow sustain all the animals that graze there? Because sometimes some groups migrate, they leave. They mostly graze on the shoots and grass but not all, they eat and fertilize, digging with their hooves burying the seeds; as soon there is less forage they move on, following the seasons on a more or less circular path at more or less fixed intervals. In the same valley, prairie, forest, there is not only one species of animal, but many. Some species alternate sequentially eating what others don't eat; for example the giraffe, doesn't eat grass but they eat the shoots of bushes and small trees. Everything eats, fertilizes and prepares the earth for the growth of the grass that feeds zebra, gazelles, bison and as a result all carnivores following eat the older animals, the sick, the most tired, the least efficient, and for this reason they will certainly be isolated from the protective mass of the pack. Needs are in equilibrium, a balancing of appetites, in time and limited space.

No animal is able to degrade and render its environment inhospitable because the ecology of the environment is in dynamic equilibrium that won't allow it: to alter it means extinction.

Why has grass taken the place of forests and mammals that of the dinosaurs? Because grass takes less time than plants to complete a life cycle, it is born germinates grows and reproduces in a few months, helped by the presence of herbivores that eat and spread it in the ideal environments and the carnivores limit their growth numbers. It is simpler, more energetic economical, more changeable according to the conditions, more adaptable.

Even the marine environment follows the same patterns: for millions, hundreds of millions of years calcareous algae, microscopic spherical plant cells, hard shelled, lived and grew and died, letting their shells fall, like a continuous snowfall onto the seabed. Kilometers of layers of mud; from time to time based on the species and the depth, the environmental conditions (calcareous, silicic, carbonaceous, chalky) have provided the structure and conditions for life. Life has evolved over and around them in time, based on its continuously variable conditions and its, from time to time, specific characteristics of economy and efficiency.

Everything is connected, biology and botany, vertebrates, invertebrates, chemistry and physics, behavior and ecology, geology and mechanics. An ocean that brings together all the sciences, as in fact it really is.

Today, the Dolomites or the White Cliffs of Dover are the visible result. Normal lives, billions of billions, monotonous, simple, insignificant to our eyes, perhaps less ambitious but they are preserved and propagated over entire ages. Are they worth perhaps less than seven to eight billion human beings?

We are few, fortunately, for the sole reason that we are at the peak of the food pyramid and predators must, necessarily, be far fewer than the prey! We will remain as long as the dynamic ecological equilibrium permits us then we will become extinct, or at least our numbers will be reduced, in one way or another.

Who knows, maybe rats will rule the world, as they are highly efficient and adaptable and live near us and with us, as the grass does with the forests. Or beetles spiders, scorpions. Or unicellular algae will return to dominate the expression of life at least for a new, extremely long period.

I asked myself about the features that really define the difference between the human species and all the others: I definitely believe scientific investigation is derived from curiosity, continual research is pre-eminent but second, is certainly bureaucracy, in the best sense of the term, the challenge of organizing and consolidating data, intended for the first.

If living were only to feed, grow and reproduce, essentially to survive enough to do so, the universe would be a cold and hostile place. It serves the purpose of being able to be distracted from the thought of being nothing more than a small spark of light in the universe. Knowledge is superior to ignorance!

But this established certainty is not enough for students: motivation

is not enough, you need bureaucracy: the familiar rhythms of lessons and discussions, verification and assurance that learning is being accomplished. To observe, record, discuss, analyze, sooner or later we will definitely learn something.
Each of our universes is extremely uncertain!

It is nonsense that makes the world go round! At times the best policy consists of deception! Sometimes in order to obtain something good you have to lie to people. It is very easy to do, just alter the facts!
Evolutionary theory has withstood 200 years of rigorous investigation, discovery and highlighting the facts that support it without finding concrete facts to refute it.
The creationist theory is the simple expression of a will even though in its principle dealings, at least in a serious and thorough discussion, at least about the point of origin, to the question about why from the start, not even it necessarily contradicts evolution.
The introduction of the concept of randomness into evolutionary theory substantially contrasts only with the concept of predestination, or universal design or divine will that sustains the fanaticism of creationists.
Fundamentalists believe in violence; they kill people!

The universe and nature, are interactions between extremes: temperatures that are so high that not even matter can exist and absolute freezing nears the most complete blocking of movement, concentrations of matter, density and immense mass, alternating with the broadest most extreme vacuum. Everything exists in the middle!

A paradox is a proposition that contradicts a real or perceived logical mechanism! Can life be, simply and solely, a random sequence of events? Often reality contradicts the paradox: the tortoise and Achilles, the arrow and the apple; Achilles always reaches and overtakes the tortoise as the arrow will in any case reach the apple and in finite time, although mathematically this would not result as possible. If there was a universal design, and I could travel in time, then all you would see would happen in fact as if it had already happened. I'd be taking a route already mapped out from start to finish. If the design exists, then it must cover all possibilities permitted because of free will.

How many dimensions or universes are possible, all these could exist simultaneously and all possibilities would evolve in them. In all the individual conditions, would necessarily be infinite, an alternative could not exist and therefore, in any case, free will could not exist. This is not so in the present and current reality of my personal and unique, tangible universe.

A society of very controlled individuals, especially if they know they are, is or becomes ever more submissive, pliable, malleable, able to be manipulated. People say stupid things, which spread. Spoken words have their own life. They contradict, deny the truth, detract their strength in one place, in one context and those same idiocies leap out, maybe later, in another place.

Human culture is based on four pillars: relationships and sexual dependence; supremacy and territorial law; the unconscious desire to belong and be accepted in a group; individual and intellectual domination. Absolute certainty and confidence become entangled on these pillars, for anything else is absolutely groundless, of human superiority over all other forms of life that is or is not intelligent and thus there is the tendency towards self illusion and consequently self-exaltation. *Introspection*: is the endless search among thousands of uncertain facts, erroneous conclusions, without any sharing. Do you want to share your thoughts? Is life an anomaly of nature? Isn't it's place in existence only an uncertain instant placed on a surface, of dynamic and variable equilibrium, originating in momentary interactions between natural extremes?

In Roman times no man was enslaved because of their ethnicity, skin color or class of origins and class at birth: slaves existed but were a condition generated by events involving failure, military defeats or economic losses, punishments for criminal offenses and not arising from a natural condition. Today it is anything but.

At the time of the Romans the senate represented all the peoples in the empire, they were all Roman citizens having equal rights, nobles and officials of all degrees freely comparing each other, a bit like now only happens in the Catholic church, the most globalized.

All ideas and faiths were present and equal, equally tolerated until the Christians had the upper hand, fanatics who abolished tolerance considering themselves the proprietors of the only truth, closely followed by the Muslims; since then the conflict of intolerance, has lasted down to this day, parochialism fundamentalism and religious peculiarities.

In a world of the tolerant, the aggressive intolerants and fanaticism risk getting the upper hand like a cancer in a healthy body.

The renunciation of the Catholic Church and Christian and Western intolerance in the name of peace and universal good, doesn't prevent the others from attempting to climb to total domination, in fact, as then, the contamination threatens to become viral.

Religion (all without exception) is an instrument of power for a few, the opium of the poor, the corpus of the Middle Ages showed asceticism and renunciation of earthly pleasures as an acceptable alternative to the lack of goods and technology and the market.

Capitalism and the god money and their divine representatives, immaterial, financial markets: are a new substitute religion; they derive from the evolution of science, which in turn originated from war that generated needs and industry and comprised the end of the Middle Ages, since those who had more material and technological resources, after the Middle Ages, won the war. In contrast to the asceticism and renunciation of material goods Capitalism proposed their research, construction and consumerism.

It is well known that children only like to see and listen to the stories they already know. Nobody particularly likes surprises and sudden changes.

The successful film and especially television series share three things: they represent memories situations and emotions, always these and a few, in which everyone can recognize themselves; otherwise the same situations alternate in all the sequences and versions possible to transform and maintain the environment of possible shared memories and emotions. Love and various issues, bereavement and failure, hope and fortune, success and victory sweated and merited. Alternating the sequences, all may know, or imagine, from the first to the last, what will happen to the protagonists and if it will be better than happened to them or worse, or even the same. In any case there will be an identification otherwise other people's memories would be as boring as home movies. Fall and rise and rise and fall, in the end they always take them there: they all lived happily and contented or retain melancholy memories in their heart. Rarely is the end tragic and leaving room for future consolation.

But it makes me smile to think that there should be weeping in any case to express as much joy as sorrow.
I ask myself: am I also a hypocrite? If the results of my actions are important to me what matters cannot be the only objective. A little hypocrisy, however, is at the base of civil life, it makes coexistence possible alleviating some trauma, it acts as a lubricant, like religion, like liqueurs, good food. A little hypocrisy cannot really be all that bad: the difficulty is in determining how much.

With age, I have realized my highest ambition is the appreciation of serenity. Serenity is the summation of all the small, recognized or remembered moments of happiness. To appreciate serenity leads to the conservation and the depletion of change. Happiness is unquestionably linked to the passions. With age I learned to contain my feelings: I just have one doubt, today am I a stronger man because I have contained my passions, or are my feelings much weaker and I'm always the same? How can a child grow only in happiness? In life there is always a counterweight for every weight and the price to pay: you must learn to accept it.
Children's stories are never happy, carefree but dramatic and complex about suffering, disappointment, unworthiness, horrors and fears, abandonment, choices and sacrifices; only at the end do they have everything in common as in life, despite all that may have happened in childhood, the result will be positive for the protagonist, notwithstanding and independent of the end that all the other characters have in the story.

These days I have witnessed a series of investigations involving the world of the occult, seers, sorcerers, healers: many people even in our rational technological age turn to them with trust and hope, although it is virtually certainly trickery and a scam.
I learned a few tricks from these charlatans: they are simple tricks that allow them to make reassuring prophecies that earn them a lot of money. If things don't work as expected it is the fault of the skeptics that have offended the spirits with their presence.
For years the skeptics, scientists, technicians, infidels have discovered and brought to light this trickery and cheating but people continue, and will continue to pay any amount only to be deceived; it will never pay because it's explained you can't escape reality.
The same as the rest, even the most serious academics who tend to push aside, belittle the facts and events because they find them uncomfortable, to the point of convincing you that all human knowledge, all that exists and is possible to know is contained, but solely and exclusively, in what is written and documented in books.

I came across the most absurd concept in the world: a hypercube! A square with four dimensions. The results are, or rather should be, if I understood correctly eight cubes that are seen in three dimensions only there wouldn't be more than two: it is what you would have if each side of the two cubes were a cube!
I never liked math, I don't doubt its accuracy and the capacity for making scientific predictions but too much imagination is needed and I don't have enough. For the mathematical equations, which I don't understand, because as far as they are real and concrete, abstractions and intuitions are purely mental, I prefer transposition in the form of a musical score that is always mathematical, a very long and complex equation, but permits us to understand the complexity of nature, simply by listening to the performance, the symphony. The beauty is that in this form everyone easily understands this enormous complexity.

Once, when I was a child they gave me a present the 'Little chemist': it was the start of a passion that not even school, university, work could dampen. I am basically a chemist and also a good industrial

chemist, I've demonstrated this several times but I've never stood
the mathematical contamination required to complete my university
education. Mathematics is not for me, for the simple reason that, I discovered, it requires too much imagination. When I asked why two
plus two equals four they answered that it was so and that's that.
Now I know there's a reason but I'm focused on things, on matter
that can tell me verifiable stories, credibly acceptable. I ended up
transferring my scientific curiosity to geology but, being a chemist,
and given to a practical approach, I dedicated myself to petrography
and thus to chemistry of the rocks and from there to water, and finally the environment and, thus, I discovered ecology, the complexity
but also the complete and total correlation between all that exists of
matter and having a mass, including what led to the limits of the least
possible mass becomes pure energy for at least a few moments, to
then again it becomes transformed.
My evolution actually went backwards from chemistry to alchemy, the
rediscovery of the philosophy of science, when I realized more or less
exact sciences do not exist but one science that can be faced only in
its parts. The important thing is not to lose sight of it, and many do,
too many, that each individual observation, each approach be it theo-
retical, instrumental, pragmatic, or intuitive knowledge, is only a partial
view of an immense whole that is called 'nature' and that expresses
itself in as many ways as you can possibly think. The beauty is that I finally understand or think I understand that nature; so extremely
complex and difficult to read and interpret, in the end is trivially simple.
Simple elementary processes, the simplicity repeated endlessly, billions and billions of times, delicate balances in countless repetitions
of the cycle are modified by creating new, changeable and complex,
forever more changeable and complex as they reproduce. Strong
equilibriums and weak equilibriums; the strong beat the weak but not
always and not everywhere, and most of all, not forever.

Following I have summarized some principles, for me they are conclusions but it is the same, that I've collected, appreciated, thought
about, summarized, that my 'alchemical' research up until now, has
permitted me to recognize, simply accepting the fact that many seek,
and many find. To share the little or a lot is the true source of human

knowledge. Against this simple, mundane, natural mechanism nothing can, not even the so-called 'scientific community' validate or invalidate the conclusions; closed as they are in the capsule of personalities, of immediate and financial interests, can only deny or more easily discredit what is at the time inconvenient, which is not financed, at least until it is forced to modify some position. To make it even come to discrediting itself, proposing absurd and costly research with outlandish conclusions that fill the main channels of existing scientific communication: women's magazines, bought by women and read by men *... From the results of research conducted by the prestigious university of ... it has been confirmed ... that chocolate is good for you but too much is bad! Eating too much can be bad for you! Passing time can make you old! Fruit can be good for you, too much gives you stomach ache! The color red stimulates the production of antioxidants! Sex is not engaged in, nor understood in the same way by everyone! Prevention* (and spending to buy unnecessary products to ward off death and disease) *is better than a cure* ... and so on.
And here then are my very personal notes on alchemy.

Notes on the Principles of alchemy
From fire (1) energy meets water, (1+1) and it is chaos; from the encounter, matter is reborn through chaos (2+1), the earth renewed, in the material order, solid, liquid and vapor is derived from air.
With water earth fire and vapors (Chaos + energy) generates novel compounds (structures) and new natural possibilities (organization). Here therefore is the importance of the magic of numbers!
Zero: collects everything but is filled with energy: it is unstable.
One: first, unique, unnatural (without nature), it is not balanced, it is found at minimum energy, ice cream, inert or immobile.
The universal principle (the universe) is sacrificed dividing (Big Bang) it also generate life.
Expanding and cooling, it slows and produces light (300,000 km/sec) the matter (20,000 km/sec), biology (cm/sec) and therefore life in complex forms. Goes from absolute heat and from the chaos of energy to the melody of organization, from fire to melody ...
Music: mathematically organized, capable of expressing and rendering nature comprehensible because it is perceptible and interpretable through the senses like the rest of the natural world.

Two: derives from the sacrifice of the One, which is subdivided into male principle (father) carrier of energy and the feminine principle (mother), which carries structure: energy (of the sun) meets the structure (the earth) and generates life (organization – biology); for the earth is Gaia the living planet. The couple represents material reality, the interaction between time and space, the stability of energy, the generating couple.

Three: is the perfect number for man: it represents nature, in all its aspects and the possibility to change and the evolution of forms, arranged in different and alternative equilibriums. It represents the third way possible, the alternative that stabilizes the material couple; it represents choice and free will.

Energy, structure, organization: the fundamental trinity at the foundation of the natural universe. Father, the Sun, masculine principle. Mother, the Earth, the female principle. Structures, materials. Son, generation biology, life!

From the initial chaos of absolute heat to energy; energy brings order to chaos; chaos returns (destruction, extinction) when the generating energy reduces and an alternative is possible.

Water dissolves everything bringing organized matter to chaos; the return to chaos (flood) allows you to start over again. Fire and water, the principle destroyers and regenerators (chaos) the earth (and the air) natural principles of the generators of life.

33: Christ's age, generator of the renewal through repetition of the divine sacrifice; it is the highest degree of Masonic initiation; it is the doubling of the symbol or the word that represents, is used like this also in the symbolism of risk. Geometrically represents the two faces of the infinite, the continuity of space-time between past and future through the present moment. In physical terms it represents, the consequentiality between the physical space-time cone, illuminated by the formation of the light of the past, a past known to the memory of the human observers and/or not passing through the precise filter and apparently certain of the present, which is determined by the human observer and/or not, who lives it, opens the space-time cone of future possibilities, the one that can potentially be illuminated, in its development generating the future, the infinity of possible events creators of different possible futures, each determined by the observer, in any possible moment, always like an evolution of the past. Placed horizontally, each of the two elements mirror the other, produces the symbol ∞ (infinity). The union of the two opposing faces (white and black, good and evil are equivalent). Used geometrically, it is represented again in development the triangle (the square of the Masonic builder already present in Egyptian culture and even before, from which you obtain figures that describe nature according to the golden ratio: 1,1618 of the sections (golden sections).

The three-dimensional shape can be obtained through the triangular generators: again two opposite and symmetrical cones, known past and possible future converging in this present point.

The observer is the determinant: is he who determines the events by choosing the alternatives! To study a system it is necessary that the observer is outside or he will influence or determine it. The mystic observer was the Pharaoh or the emperor: it is man who concretely becomes God even leaping the ascent.

The observer is the one who recognizes himself and his symbiosis with the universe and nature (among others this principle is currently the social basis of the esoteric community of Damanhur, Italian and almost unknown, not organized secretly except for degrees of initiation, like all elite religions).

Nature evolves through simple mechanisms, using *Opposite and Complementary* elements.

The elements were developed using combinations of pairs: 1 = H; (+1) = He and then – C – O – etc.; that is it took place during the progressive cooling of the universe and the consequent slowdown: heat = chaos then at 300,000 km/sec = light and energy then at 20,000 km/sec electrons and mass therefore cm/sec = biology.

The stable combinations of pairs – 2- 4- etc. Helium, carbon etc. – formed the material structure, matter, diversified, stabilized by the third possibility of bonding for each element that generated the complex structure. And now philosophy, knowledge, and its celebration, the religions: the universal tree that rises and at the same time descends; the gifts of the Holy Spirit descend to existence, intelligence, the possibility of determining the space-time cone of possibility, or better, of at least conditioning their own future through free will. The Tree of Life, the Menorah, is ascendant, spirituality, the divine is, remains, in the heavens and will however return to the heavens, after some brief illuminating passage on the earth; man descends from the universal and as a result of the descent, at the same time, with his actions in the end, ascends again to the universal.

The golden ratio: 1.1618; as always in nature a simple repeated mechanism permits one to obtain the symmetry of the sections. Complex natural shapes you can simply reconstruct through the use of a square, applying this section to the relationship called the golden section!

A commonly known symbolic and magical figure is the pentagon. Inscribed in a circle it represents the cyclical, immutable nature of the universe; if you put a man in the circle, representing him as a pentagon of the golden section, the five-pointed star, you will have the Vitruvian Man of Galilei. The man is at the center of the universe and naturally of nature. Again with the square and triangles, using a rhombus it is possible either to describe or to cover an entire surface of any shape.

The three-dimensional development, the rhombohedron is the pyramid; for this geometric capacity represents the universal principle of nature. The rhombohedral contains and reunites all features and universal principles in its figure and thus the capacity to generate or better regenerate nature is attributed to it.

That's it. Now, that's enough.

Life is simple and therefore beautiful, but every day appears to be so complicated that I often have my doubts.

I believe that cultures that have the least number of suicides have and vice versa the greatest number of murderers or hunters.

We have been protecting children for about fifty years, practically since there have been fewer of them and therefore they no longer make up the substitute workforce but have become the preferred recipient and the primary source of the consumer market. For this reason we would like and pretend children can be and live only happily, but how can a child grow with only happiness? Children are important only for motives of the market and welfare conditions; in any other situation they are the first to be sacrificed. This proves the assumption: an all animal species mechanism.

Can anyone deny that in life and nature there is always a counter-weight for any and everything?

Life is not a good friend, always ready to hit you and hurt you, when you least expect it and acting on the weakest point: yourself or your loved ones. It is always very difficult to endure the test; how can you not wonder what sense there is, had, or what sense there is in continuing! Often the response to an intolerable mental torment becomes an escape from the mind. Mental masturbation!

You shouldn't fear the use of medications for treatment. Drug abuse is virtually impossible when they are used to cure a state of disease; it becomes probable and possible, practically certain, when they are used for prevention, that is when they are not needed to cure something that is there but something that doesn't exist and may never exist. The choice in this case is long if not infinite.

The worst client that a professional can have is one that doesn't respect your professionalism and your ability to operate in his interests but believes, forgetting why he had consulted you, that you must do or not do what he believes must be done or not done. It is a clear demonstration of arrogance and lack of respect for the abilities of others. A client of this type should be refused and abandoned to himself but a professional learns they cannot always choose and if they have problems it is because they have not known or were unwilling to avoid them, and then, sometimes, one needs to act in spite of the desire to safeguard their interests first and then their expectations.

When you have a problem you recognize and feel is serious, talk about it but cautiously, because of the fear of being forced to discover the meaning behind your words and in the responses.
I have a friend who is a true snob! What is a snob? It's someone who hasn't earned all he possesses and not only money; people who come from a good environment with a real education behind them, are tolerant, caring, open-minded. Snobs are intolerant and believe they have the right!

I see and understand the pain in others if they suffer or if they smash a finger with a hammer; I know what others say and perhaps it's true but it certainly isn't everything because it is too complex; I can imagine feelings, those that are superficial: a flash of irritation, boredom, pleasure, enthusiasm, interest in those close to me; in fact, though, as much as I know them I don't know them at all.

I must admit I don't even know myself well, some memories escape me; I know there are memories in me that I don't even know I have any longer, shapeless thoughts, feelings I can't grasp to identify them individually, stray sensations, passions and emotions that are sometimes repressed and hidden deeply within that have been apparently removed or forgotten. All this makes the me that acts.

Man and the religion he practices defines him. Every religious person who attempts to explain his or her beliefs, in fact tries to explain himself.

I'm sitting in my garden, at my house, and I don't consider my home as a place, a location, a static container, a box with upholstery. My house is a living thing and dynamic, which changes with the mood of those who live there; my home represents a vital process for me. I'd like that it didn't resemble a bunker, a shelter anti-intrusion but rather than a hotel where the usual people come and go, but mostly, they return voluntarily because they feel good; naturally a hotel where the guests live, not simply existing, for a period.

They say I drive recklessly but I disagree: driving is an exercise of power and control, I find it relaxing.

People have a habit of repeating and continually affirming things that are absolutely obvious, "What a beautiful day!" Just because the sun is shining; "How tall you are," only because they are shorter. When they look at someone who has a bad fall and lies bruised on the ground, first they laugh and then they ask, "Did you fall off the ladder (or from a bicycle, or in a deep hole, or from a tree), did you hurt yourself?" It seems almost as though people continually profess and emit banalities from the mouth so as not to have to make their brain get to work. This statement has earned me the definition of cynic!

A child asked God, "But why do you so firmly refuse to demonstrate your existence?" God answered, "I refuse to demonstrate my existence because the demonstration would be a denial of the necessity of faith, and without faith I could not exist!"
I think of the supporters of creationism and of universal design: if man and nature were unable to evolve by chance as evolutionists claim, then God would have demonstrated his existence and in demonstrating it, would have denied himself! Long live logic!

The witches were the result of alimentation based on, among other things, ergot in the bread; the fungus that infests rye causes, ergotism or 'Saint Anthony's Fire'; the alkaloids contained are the basis for the synthesis of LSD, perhaps, I believe, the most powerful hallucinogen known. If we add extreme poverty, the need to revolt against this state of affairs; if we think that women were considered to be inferior beings capable of making men slaves and their deep, traditional knowledge passed down from mother to daughter, the herbal medicine and physiotherapy, dressed up with superstition and rituals, we arrive at the easiest targets possible in the Christian era. A religion that denied the pursuit of pleasure or ecstasy outside the church, whatever it was, in the various more or less heretical expressions, Protestant or institutional, including official medicine.
The dream, caused by intoxication and drugs that didn't come from God could only come from hell! And if noon is the time for God, midnight and darkness, which man fears, can only be the time of demons and therefore witches.
As we also know dancing has always been like the consumption of alcohol or drugs, the favorite target of the Puritan faithful. The sabba, the ritual dance attributed to witches, is still present in the American Puritan tradition as a kind of round dance kicking and amusement, which perhaps dates back to that time. Our example is the tarantella, the dance of San Vito for scorpion stings.

I'm still wondering what time is and have been trying to define it for images because I am unable to do so, at least with my skills, in another way: if you saw a series of 50 drops falling from a tap but could see them fall and run through a slit one every minute, I would infer that watching the 25th drop, that and only that one, represents time, at least what I can perceive because the former are no longer visible having passed and the following are not yet visible as they have not yet reached the fissure (the cone). The fact remains that if you could accelerate the fall I might get to see them all pass through almost instantly at the same time. I think it has to do with Einstein's theory of relativity.

How can you trivialize in the simplicity of human experience the immense complexity of nature composed of sequences and a series of simple processes, endlessly repeated, in continuing variations of the conditions of equilibrium that they, as they are taking place, impose? Arrogance and resizing within man's reach.

Since humanity has existed there have always been women who governed the world, directly or indirectly! How could it be any different today? In developed countries, women give birth, raise, educate their children until the end of the study program and make them fall in love and get engaged if not marry. Then they become mothers and grandmothers. At work they are absolutely equal and their activity pulls the economy along. In under developed countries, where women are not emancipated, considered inferior, limited, victims of overuse and exploitation, the economy stagnates and doesn't take off and she is the base, the foundation of the social world.
Man always needs a woman beside him in one or other capacity; not always, necessarily, vice versa.
A man wants an intelligent woman for himself who understands him, him and his world; a companion to help him understand and solve his problems; paradoxically also a woman who at the same time is however inferior, needs advice, support, strength and his logical thinking.
Men are willing to marry this woman, so special, in order to possess and show off something that few others can boast: a woman who is 'almost' equal to them in every field.
For these same intrinsic qualities, millions of women resort to tricks to ensnare millions of men, forever hesitant and frightened in the face of women's issues and that is for the obvious lack of one iota of

inferiority required to satisfy the ego and the woman is forced to acknowledge, intuit, demonstrate herself usually, as at least equal, if not
generally superior, only because of her abilities.
The purpose of the repeated conversation between two people previously strangers, smeared in recurring meetings, is substantially this
to get to know each other: I learn to get to know her and she learns
to get to know me. This knowledge is the first stage on the path to
intimacy.
Each marriage begins with a high degree of intimacy, with the desire
to be close to one another always; over the years this need diminishes but resurfaces from time to time. Physical contact, which is at
the base of falling in love allows for the highest degree of empathy;
the feeling that not only moods, emotions, but even thoughts can be
exchanged between the two lovers.
Not much unlike the relationship that develops between a mother
and her children. I often hear talk of telepathy, because two people
who know each other well, think of each other at about the same
time of day: it's not telepathy, it's the foundation of a close relationship and the deep knowledge established between two people and
that's what allows an old, long and frayed marital relationship to remain immutable but completely changed. They are, however, reluctant to totally exclude the possibility of telepathy, which perhaps was
a complementary means for the development of humanity before the
full development of language. If that were the case there should still
be the potential for consciously developing it. Or maybe simply the
first man's ability to hear could be stretched to infrasound, as still
happens today for many animals with the resulting possibility of communicating at a distance. Or even more simply, was it a silent world?

When a fanatic is contradicted he reacts violently because he believes his very existence has been threatened. I hate fanatics and I realize, in this, I'm even being fanatical myself.
Many of the most guarded secrets remain so because of the simple
ignorance or lack of interest of those who want to share or at least
know them. What could happen if 22.7 'pounds' of pure uranium 235
were brought together in a single room? It is extremely difficult to
come by, but physically not very cumbersome to build an atomic
bomb. I read of a terrorist act in a newspaper: a fuel tank was detona-

ted under a car chemically triggering it. No information here but in another newspaper it was written that the primer used was a condom filled with concentrated sulfuric acid, which corroded the latex causing the gasoline to burn on contact need more?
The aerial photos of that time made me laugh, where airports, barracks, accumulation of fuel, sensitive places in case of conflict, were masked with a white brushstroke. If the enemy army had wanted to trace these places it would have been enough to locate the white squares.

Death is just! No one escapes, young, old, rich and poor. There is life on the planet and it is abundant: nature is a big waste of lives; life can even feed itself. Whatever exists lives by feeding on the death of something else. Death on the planet is as equally abundant with life. The fact that every life is unique, and this is especially true for the conception man has, meaning only that he must compete in the same way as all the others against the entire hostile universe that requires death, for the only purpose of generating new life. The thing that is common to everyone is that nobody, ever, feels joy when facing death.

We carry around a burden of unspoken words; we go around saying the wrong things to the wrong people. We don't trust people who are close, who cover our backs, who look us in the face and simply tell us their opinion, sometimes advice, unsolicited, sometimes thoughts; sometimes simple suggestions, input. *Don't tell me what to do*! Our most common words are insults, verbal attacks against the first poor soul we find in front of us, designated victim of our desire to unload the anger is why our relationships go downhill. Words like *thank you, I'm sorry, I love you*, are extremely difficult for us to say.
Substantially not even I know for sure. More than anything I interpret, according to the most superficial layers of my rational and emotional mind; nor can I think of really getting to know others. There are many levels in every human mind that make the concept of being human abstract. Love and hate cannot be or really last very long.
I love you, I hate you, what do you really want to say? Nothing! Perhaps the easiest *I detest you or I like you*, are more realistic. What or who do

I really love? Who or what, whom, do I really hate? It's impossible to know.

The church teaches evil is in knowledge, happiness and good are in ignorance, where instead evil resides for the studious.

What does the word *evil* mean? Everyone is free to interpret the concept in his or her own way. The struggle between good and evil is thus reduced to the prevalence of one line of thought over another and thus nothing abstract or mystical but simple human conflict and for the most basic reason: power.

Leave every God out of this, is a threat that comes from man and only man. The pursuit of power is the desire to improve everyone, their condition as much as possible; this is only possible at the expense of the other's conditions.

In every time the slaves and the oppressed have rebelled to substitute their masters, because every servant can imagine him or herself in the master's place.

In every time, the liberations and the revolutions imposed from outside proved to be failures, because no one who is oppressed can empathize with their liberator: or the master himself becomes or remains only the servant of another master!

Recent history, which I remember or was close to me, always repeats the same theme. The Nazi despots were eliminated, fascists and imperialists used faith to unite the masses, united in the rebellion by libertarian pragmatism or denial of religious belief, men are then again divided between the two main thoughts that put the interests or the state society or of the individual in society at the center. And men have continued to fight with each other, in the name of good against evil.

I remember the USSR and Stalin, Lenin, Trotsky, Cuba and Fidel Castro, the god state: men live to work, that is the objective and the objective can only be directed by the state. The objective of work, man's objective is for the benefit of all, and thus the state. All men are servants of the state! The greater good of all humankind requires the renunciation of personal freedom. I can never accept that!

They were countered by the European and American capitalists: men are free individuals, each with their own ambitions and desires separate and different generating antagonism in search of personal advantages, generating secondary needs and consumerism, allowing the god of the market to prosper. All that has again created prerequisites for the rebirth of the proposed fideistic, this time Muslim: all united against the exploiting infidels and oppressors, for the glory of God, who is supernatural and superior to men, who are all his servants, and of course, his hierarchical representatives, deputies who command them, they can, in contrast to those who must obey and kneel, some may develop their own independent thinking, a source of strong gratification.

Fear: children are full of fears, when they grow up they learn to recognize their fears. The worst fears are those related to fear itself: the fear of being afraid. It is a difficult limitation to overcome without communication. Even with your own body, with your senses. Drink: when you know, it is communicated, that you are thirsty. Rest: when you are tired. Everything we oppose generates fear, opposing anger generates fury, opposing pain generates anxiety.

There is only one way to overcome our fears: to admit them and to surrender to their presence: getting angry, accepting being sad, accepting fear, don't be ashamed of these feelings, communicate them freely: there is no blame in departing from a mood, we must expose them and overcome them.

An experience in primary school came to mind: the teacher invited us to take part in a competition where the one who yelled loudest and cried the most won. Then, maybe, I don't remember, it would have been fun, now it seems to me it was certainly instructive.

I listen to the news and read today's newspaper, any day of the first twenty years of 2000, in Italy, at the bar in my town!

Cursed immigrants and also clandestine, what do they want? What are you doing here? They come begging to be fed and cared for at our expense in the state we belong, to which they don't belong, which they don't recognize and rebel against. They don't obey and respect the laws we obey, they don't have our same goals or our motivations, our faith; their race is different as is their language. They say they've come seeking protection from disasters in their countries ... but to get here they've broken laws and overcome others like them ... but they are and remain strangers ... but their blood and their culture is not ours ... but they are dangerous ... but they are a threat ... but there are many ... but there are too many ... they must be pushed back, sent away!

In the words of Vico, (the Italian political philosopher and jurist, 1668 to 1744, twists and turns of history but, I think, always only and in any case in function of a temporary simple definition of what is good or bad. You have to fight is everyone's watchword, always.

They are about to start the World Cup, the Olympics are over, some biking tours, swimming races, motorcycle, car, gymnastic competitions and dozens of sports. The only objective of the participants is to win! It is a truism: who doesn't win, loses! Winning is a commitment! Winning is not something you should do, it is not even real effort: winning is a challenge with a well-defined objective! Winning is the result of a simple recipe: don't give up, persevere, insist and try again at another time; never abandon the venture started!
Service is a commitment. Athletes compete; the world around them must serve them! It's a beautiful thing, something one needs to have either the ability to do or the responsibility of providing. To do something for the benefit of others! Providing great service is a victory in your competitive sector! Without proper service there is no chance of other victories, and therefore there is no chance of taking part in the team's victory.
Unfortunately, ordinary people, associate the word *service* with the word *servant*, thus lower class. This is also why cults exist and proliferate: people are part of a community, of a tribe; I'm a taxi driver, I'm an Italian, I'm a Roma fan, I'm an employee, I'm a writer, a tobacconist, a grandfather, a police officer, a traffic cop, a communist, a firefighter and so on...
It's a way of knowing who you are. It's a way to recuperate a higher condition of service: not only a servant, I don't take orders! I take part in the common good of my tribe, sect, community and so on!
Declare oneself Mormon or Jew or fascist or AC Milan: taking part in these communities means people are no longer individuals but become mere strangers. It is a dangerous, useless performance.
If you harm a firefighter, don't be surprised if some day your house is burning and help arrives very slowly: it is a shared but unspoken threat and feared.
Others belong to a sect, us never; because we are aware that a person is not the context in which he or she operates; we are different that is, us, we are people. A combination of typical human chauvinism and inhuman indifference.

The education, that we receive and we impart, is nothing more than a

programming or reprogramming of our brain that allows us to belong
to the context in which we exist.

Right now there are thousands of migrants from many different countries, with various cultures, in miserable conditions. We have two possibilities, or we take care of them or we chase them away.

If we decide to host them, however, we should remind you that
whoever provides them a place to live has to take care of the place
where the guests live, clean the refuse where ever it is found without
worrying about who has left it; entering a room the owner cleans it,
simply because his education renders it unbearable to see dirt
around him.

Those who host them have the responsibility of taking care of other
people housed because he or she is the owner, cleaning and taking
care of their own home. Whoever is the host should worry about human relationships because they cannot stand seeing people who are
sick maimed, suffering in their house if they can find a solution.

Whoever is the host should expect the guest is awaiting their consideration, they will dirty without worrying about who is going to clean
up; whoever is the guest doesn't pay.

No one however likes to clean up what others have made dirty thus,
if a guest dirties to the point that cleaning becomes insupportably tiring, the guest will become an enemy, it's inevitable!

I try to think about my city, my home, my country, the woods, the
mountains, the seas and the rivers: seeing how I treat it and the consideration I give to the environment I live in, am I the host or the guest?

I like the agreeable formula *no personal resentment toward you but it is
believed that as a matter of political expediency* ... fake and very effective, often used, depersonalizes the conflict by laying the responsibility
on ... no one!

All men have one thing in common: everyone, without distinction,
they are attempting to get the best out of their lives and then they
die.

I try not to argue anymore and never about other people's opinions
of me: it's useless.

Man, is the end product … maximum … of evolution … no absolutely no, indeed! But of what evolution are we talking about and since when? Since the stars exploded and a few planets exploded and the compositions present on the asteroids and in the comets have become hydrocarbons on earth and these in a spiral DNA chain, until arriving at a maximum difference of 0.5% to differentiate between man of today and the chimpanzee of yesterday? Or we narrow the field and we only care about the last 6,000 years after the universal flood? We can do this only by forgetting the last 600,000 years since man existed (at the time man was present in Italy, specifically in Abruzzo!) as a handful of species in their own right; and of course we also forget the last 30,000 years, since there were cultural and commercial exchanges between the tribes, also if they are few and scattered, at least on the ground they were exclusively European!

It is incredible to think there are about a hundred billion individual cells in our body, single cooperative individuals and each of them contains the entire, and unique, individual genetic make up. It causes reproduction of the uterine environment in vitro, that is, adding the twenty essential amino acids nutrients and enzymes that control the biological chemical reactions and successively the necessary hormones, which can induce any of these to replicate themselves, replicating even the twenty-three pairs of chromosomes that make us who we are.

Being able to do so (and today you can) naturally it is possible to skip meiosis where two half-cells, one male and one female, merge their chromosomes to form a new pair of twenty-three and substitute the entire nucleus in an already complete cell with another, already complete, of the chosen donor, with their complete genetic heritage, then inducing mitosis (division into equal parts and replication). In this case you can obtain a full clone of the donor, and a perfect copy and twins.

Say it is, everything considered, easy like it is easy to forget that more than 95% and up to 99% of this DNA is identical to that of other animal species, of the chimpanzee of the fly and that within each helix there are three billion bases coupled differently and the theory of errors.

The philological criticism: the art of explaining to someone why someone who is universally considered great, or vice versa, is and to do this
retrospectively. The art of explaining to someone who is right, after it
has been proven that he was right or wrong, when it is clear that he
was.

I read somewhere that the expansion of the American frontier was
not left to chance, but was planned scientifically, in the use of land
assigned to various farming communities that would settle gradually
on granted land: two rows of apple trees, 6 m of wheat, 6 m corn, 6 m
of cucumbers in the first year and then so on. A mandatory and accu-
rate long-term plan, I believe 18 years, before the farmers were left
free to grow what they wanted. It's something that normally goes unnoticed or is apparently considered minimalist but to me, having learned, it is absolutely brilliant.

I was listening to a television program about medicine where a woman in whose family death from 'heart attack' was quite common,
was strongly advised not to make any effort and to lead a life in slow
motion, possibly losing weight; she claimed to be much better than
considered, that every six months she went for a regular check up,
she had never smoked a cigarette, she walked and had walked
around for twenty hours a day all her life. She never drank liquor or
wine. She felt fit and didn't want to make any more sacrifices: the
doctor quietly replied that she was only listing the reasons why she
was not dead yet!
You should have seen her furious and bewildered face.
A hoot.

The Italian legal system: I am aware of thinking about the trials I've witnessed, fortunately only as an expert, which frightens me. The system, the way in which we deal with this sort of thing, seems wrong
to me.
I saw a judge summarizing the testimony for the stenographer, very
detailed texts. After years only his summary will remain in the memo-

ry for the next levels of the proceedings. Fortunately now there is also recording, more or less complete.

I have listened to public prosecutors referring, always and in any case, to the newspapers before each hearing ... that the prosecution will produce strong and incontrovertible evidence ... and so on and so forth. These trials often, too often, have revealed much else.

Social issues, the issue of rights and responsibilities: our judicial system is based on Roman law and in theory there is no crime or offender, until this has been demonstrated. A powerful system, democratic but that is used to get things wrong, and for this reason it doesn't work well.

When the justice system is misused, it can too easily produce results that are contrary to the will of the people. It can transform two ideas, two views and two people, into two opposite issues, where one of them is necessarily destined to win and the other to lose!

There is no chance of meeting in the middle in a way that is fair and respectful of those particles of reason that both issues probably possess.

In a legal case there is no middle ground: the two sides are entrenched and bound to a position; there is no chance of legal compromise: one party must win the other must lose.

The judge and the jury are forced to choose one or the other, against the other. One is right, the other wrong, the judge cannot admit that both sides have at least a percentage of wrong and right.

There is the concept of *mediation* in which both or at least one of the parties, can move from their entrenched position and move to another but this is carefully avoided and constrained. It would speed up the results but would take the hay from the trough.

Advertising and the media visibility, given the long time taken for the trials permitted the magistrates, lawyers, experts and consultants, the same defendants, are certainly not a deterrent but an incentive to increasing the number of cases requested and faced. Naturally quibbling follows and will drag the same cases to infinity with costs and damages for the people and persons in any way involved, exposed without mercy or respect.

The newspapers and the media in general now speak almost exclusively of reporting and possibly of crime reporting: a few isolated cases are held in court for years regularly following one another on the front pages, each time for a few days, providing food to feed the fear and indignation of ordinary people; they do it by diverting attention from the far sadder problem of management for the common good, of political choices in an almost hushed silence, determine the future of entire nations and their populations.

A few isolated cases surge to terrifying generalized problems, instigating fear and insecurity in ordinary people.

Absurdly in the long run the characters who steal, corrupt, trick and cheat large numbers in an apparently non-violent way are all managers politicians, officials ... they rise to the role of innocent victims, or in good faith, of the system. At best they are labeled as smart or incapable (if they got caught). The delinquents, the perpetrators are always poor, immigrants, vagrants, drug addicts, beggars, gypsies.

The good are extracted from average people, rather simple, dedicated to work and family.

All invoke the 'certainty of punishment' for a few, and everyone forgets the priority 'legal certainty', guaranteed for everyone.

The criminal process despite being a more limited category of situations, raises the media to the only category of process, involving and making it known to people. The administrative and civil proceedings only contribute to the statistics of number and duration.

In effect, in this case, the criminal, the sharp contrast between those who proclaim themselves as innocent and those who are accused of the crime is a good way to arrive at asserting the truth.

Also the criminal trial is never all black or all white: there are gray areas corresponding to mitigating or aggravating situations, circumstances, psychological or mental conditions.

The public prosecutor must pretend to blindly believe in the guilt of the accused, defense lawyers must pretend to blindly believe in the innocence of their clients. In order to do this well they must be convinced. The more they are or appear to be convinced, the more the jury will eventually be influenced but in the succession of interrogations cross examinations, arguments and rebuttals of the evidence, the public present will really find themselves in the position of not knowing who or what to believe. It would be very difficult to release a certain and unequivocal sentence to the public: guilty or innocent.

The public would tend to attribute percentages to each of the parties involved: the jury cannot do that, because they shouldn't.

With respect to a normal hearing, the manner of judging, expectations and what ordinary people believe, the judicial system is focused on getting things wrong! Whenever a process is annulled, or the jury's verdict is not unanimous, it is not the result of decisions but of simple failures in the system. The system claims not to be able to carry out the work that it is called upon to do. Judge and juries are forced in any case to decide, for yes or no, sometimes relying on a small number of clues or according to negligible elements, such as behaviors, statements from witnesses or sources of the second level, mediating circumstances, marginal elements. In any case in criminal cases we arrive at a result thanks to a system of contraposition.

It is a very different discourse in civil cases! The line between right and wrong between two contenders who do not get along is very difficult to demonstrate: in a divorce, a case involving work, a case caused by provoked or perceived problems, how do you define exactly who should win and who must lose. The judges are forced to transform the gray, only this color is present, into white or black: an individual cannot be a little guilty and a little innocent; a woman cannot be slightly pregnant, a little beautiful or a bit ugly.

In life there is always a middle ground and so the justice system does not reflect, but instead overlaps with it, of the empire! The judicial system is designed for other purposes and cannot, for example, define what is or is not a human being since it forces you to define different degrees of humanity as well as degrees of reason.

What is the difference between a fetus that is not fully developed and a partially incomplete man and physically substituted as a result of transplants? We must then discuss not what a human being is but what it is to be, to be part of the genera 'human'.

I think that people, as a whole, are generally more generous and tolerant, more correct, than is predicted by the judicial system.

The State, by limiting and not supporting, the people's freedom of decision, its right to attribute correctness or not, and accept or reject different behaviors and situations, does not render the service it is responsible for but, rather, subject to its own ends!

What I believe in is or will become my world!

Horoscopes and fortune-tellers, magicians and group singing: charlatans! People always continue to pay any amount to be deceived, first frightened and then reassured but they won't spend a penny to get back to reality.
If I am reborn I will become very rich writing books on how to become a very rich writer; I will become a professional prophet, making great terrifying prophecies that terrorize people into wanting the reassurance of normality and then making individual reassurances prophecies that promise minor tribulations and then success, happiness and revenge, which will earn money: especially for me.
I might even become an occultist and medium and interpret the spirits, blaming the variability and instability of the universe on the skeptics that mar the perfect picture if things don't work out as predicted.

I don't know if I've already said this, I consider myself a European citizen but educated, cultured and of Italian origin, the country where I live and where I proudly accept and respect the laws and many traditions.

Why have we reached this present geopolitical State?
Most of the current leaders didn't fight in the Great War that determined our social situation.
After every war most people feel it could have been avoided, blaming those who took the earlier decisions and also those who made the sacrifice to bring them to fruition: denying the errors and also the heroes.
After every war there is a period of recovery and economic involvement that requires peace. People go to vote and generally vote for who has never been at war, for those who have never fought or those who would never have fought, hoping to keep the peace as long as possible and perhaps also because they think that the next time it

will be their turn, this time they have survived. Unfortunately, history teaches that the winners write it, that the evil enemies are those who have lost and the two categories although reduced to factions and movements over the years, forget the horror and deepen the differences.

The economic interest of nations protects peace by generating war on the borders of the pacified and economically stronger area. When time passes and the historical positions of the combatants are closer together reducing the taken for granted differences, then it re-creates a uniformity foreseeing new misfortunes.

Rarely has a period of peace lasted more than sixty years: young people are young, impulsive, reactive, they don't have their own memories and what they know is what they are told by winners and losers respectively; history becomes only legend and slowly even in peaceful but more economically depressed areas, skirmishes and small guerrilla wars start between separatist movements and no longer shared governments.

With reduced economic well-being and its staunch defense on the part of those who have, you go from the revolt in the square to a terrorist insurgency, to civil war and then war again: this step is unfortunately too short. I'm worried about the future.

What an effect it had on me to go into a modern hotel, stereotyped, and see a display showing the hotel's history: the lift system, a menu, a napkin holder, a coal holding iron, some vintage pictures with personalities clothed and arranged, as in the late nineteenth century. It was anachronistic with no connection with the actual hotel. Strange there could have been a past in that place. It hadn't survived the passage of all the people over all those years: slowly and completely degenerated.

Honestly I didn't understand the meaning of that exhibition: a historical reminder that's been totally forsaken.

The thought of the past fills me with a strange uneasiness, contorted, pulling me and repulsing me. I'm not interested in reliving the past: I consider it important to know but the only thing that interests me is what I'll be doing in ten minutes time, and mostly what I'm doing, trying to do, now.

Today moving about in the world, leaves the impression of absolute indifference to many things, including life itself; perhaps in the past issues such as politics, patriotism, home, family, business, jobs, weren't considered simple topics of conversation but were subjects of deeply felt beliefs and able to trigger emotional conflicts: unfortunately, we have seen the result.

Recalling a time: I am in the grip of a sudden, uncontrollable tension. I will react, I will find the calm; nobody, not even another part of my brain can completely control me. Relax, there is all the time you need! I know what I'm going to do what I do in front of someone. It is because these people have a good opinion of me and know that I can do it; for this reason they've instructed me to do it and are awaiting the results. The only one who doesn't seem to have this high opinion of me is myself!

Recalling a time: "Relax" I repeat to myself drinking a coffee. Everything will be all right I promise myself: I'll make it! And meanwhile the improvised gardeners have mistreated the hedges with pruning shears. Incompetently they tried to improve their chances. Just thinking about it I stifled a smile but I drove away the apprehension that involved me on a mental and visceral level. I banished the apprehension, I won't be upset, too much, about other people's negative opinions! I move ahead, relaxed and calm and I'm willing to listen without getting hurt.

Recalling a time: sitting on the beach, with a few people around me! The sun is beginning to set, the waves break on a calm sea almost rhythmically with such frequency as to force me to seek this rhythm, which instead I fail to find: only appearance, therefore. This situation and the effort to seek the rhythm of the waves, in this environment, at the end of a normal day but when is a day ever 'normal', made me suddenly acutely aware of an absence of silence in what instead seemed to be a silent world, the passage of time, punctuated by the non-rhythmic rhythm of the waves, aware of groups of people present on the flat beach: suddenly aware, sharply, deeply, intimately aware of everything around me. A strange sensation as though I was not an external observer but was at one with the environment and the moment.

I hit the boards that barred the doors and windows of the bathing kiosks, peeling and rusty, waiting for the summer renovation, some dirt mounds surrounded the grassy spot of the beach. For a moment it seemed that everything was standing still as in a picture: a moment, one moment absolutely profound, before I realized that during this time, apparently motionless, the sun had sunk quickly until it had almost disappeared. It was time to move on and go back to the more ordinary normalcy of daily life. The strangest thing is that I don't remember when this happened, nor where at all. It is a memory, an image, a thought that has arisen from the depths but it is also an end in itself, it gives me no indication. Probably it lasted less time than it took me to write about it.

I returned to Grado, near Trieste, I recently took a walk along the coast: the city is an impossible explosion of hotels and boat docks on the asphyxiated lagoon and fishing vessels on the enormous port channel; absolutely no parking lots at all, already in the winter period certainly not crowded. The beach is virtually absent, there is hardly any trace of the coastline but only a series of swamps and salt marshes that blur with the shallow sea where here and there small strips of land crop up, gray, muddy, while a cold wind blows constantly the tramontane, the north wind also named the 'bora'. There is a pervasive smell of rotting seaweed and decaying fish while myriads of birds fly low in search of food. Everything changes, especially the landscape. And to think that at one time I considered it a beautiful place immersed in nature, the characteristic small village of resident fishers, with high-quality restaurants in the old historic houses where I walk. I never want to go back.

Despite my pragmatism and my cynicism I have to declare my personal devotion to the Madonna: in particular, 'The Madonna of the graces' venerated in Bardi (Parma), where I was born on May 26, who my mother taught me to know.

I believe that the cult of the Virgin Mary or universal mother is common to all peoples, to all civilizations, in all religions past and present. The Virgin Mother, Mother Earth and the Moon Goddess are indivisible, have nothing to do with various bishops priests friars, priests and their representatives on earth.

Mothers, they, have intruded, they... regardless... represent something unique and essential: infantile humanity needs to recognize and engage with their mother, their own nature, their own being insecure, indecisive, suffering or one you can hopefully talk to and confide in, seek support and answers only from their... own Mother!

This is the type of prayer that every man, woman or child addresses to the Virgin Mother. The relationship you have with Her. The fact that she is almost always 'Virgin', has no human significance, it just means she is greater and earlier, she has no sexual association and that is she is different and detached from her 'derived' humanity; produces life as a result of the natural energy that comes from the sun with her essential participation, 'heavenly' by definition, since she definitely resides in the sky: the Moon.

Think of the simple effect of the tide which the moon generates lifting entire oceans for meters and meters (while solar attraction alone fails to move them a few centimeters, as happens more or less in the Caribbean region).

Don't you think that the same effect of the tide should be as unavoidably effective and active, on the least volume such as that of a cell full of water? And on one hundred billion more or less, of cells, that compose a human body collaborating symbiotically and synergistically?

Any farmer knows and also if, a modern agricultural businessman, denies the influence rationally (?); in respect to the lunar cycle, which determines the moments and the times of biological development, and precisely for this reason are affected in any case; that is the cycle of human life, of menstruation and pregnancy and is the one that determines the time and the seasons. Always and everywhere, including the tropics where its action is even reduced.

The native peoples, the American Indians, who had a very special relationship with the 'earth' and nature, with which they felt in symbiosis; defined their age by the number of seasons: the spring of the young or winters the elderly. They were probably right; calendars are just useful rationalizations and in fact they are all different, ancient calculations, the Gregorian or Hebrew, Chinese or Mayan or Hindu whoever, in the service of reason, of the organization of production, and in the end power!

If insects were as large as us, or at least the size of a rat or a squirrel we would realize they too are creatures and inhabitants of the earth, accompanying man in life, for better or worse and not simple presences, often annoying or unknown and ignored, to be hung in the binders of collectors or billions exterminated without posing any problem.

To my knowledge, I don't normally dream, or maybe I do but I don't remember; they say it's a matter of the accumulation of dopamine in specific areas of the brain. In the morning on awaking impressions remain, and sometimes impressions of color. Only one dream, perhaps a nightmare, I remember as recurring but maybe I had it once and it seems to me, as I still remember it, I had it several times, who knows... It happened in winter, because there was the sensation of cold and because of the clear night sky; I was standing on the balcony of the home of my youth in Bardi, a balcony with iron railings; I found myself there looking at the stars, which suddenly began to move, rallying to form what I think were the Christmas figures: I seem to remember the scene of the hut and in particular the central Madonna between the ox and the donkey and the cradle; or at least that's what I seem to remember but certainly I my hands were stuck on the freezing railing, whitened knuckles, terrified and unable to tear myself away, frozen to the bone.
Who knows if it had an intelligible meaning, who knows if it's true it repeated, and who knows why: even remotely today, certainly, around fifty years – since I had to be a child I believe – I remember; as much as it has faded, remembering it consciously I still feel that sensation of terror.
It isn't true, though, thinking now that it was the only dream I remember having; in effect I also remember having dreamed other times of flying or better of gliding over a town but they were induced dreams,

required, evoked: usually I went to bed and began to think of a journey, which regularly began on a motorbike. I wanted to dream of what
I wanted and then in practice, before falling asleep I told myself a story, I created a setting and then maybe I dreamed something connected, who knows what. However the only realistic dreams I remember
date back to when I was a child or perhaps a teenager. Then nothing
more!

A long time ago I read somewhere, probably something in a mytholo-
gical context, a description of the seismic waves, according to me
very poetic but rational: more or less the legend or what or how
much I held, retained, considered the earth silent but not motionless:
I like to think of Gaia, the mother, dozing, snoring slightly. In the seas
and the oceans seismic waves propagate like an angry growl from the
mother, disturbed by the melody... audible or played... of the gods.
Melody that causes the waves of the tide that resonates in the co-
smos and in the oceans and interferes with the vibrations of her snoring. During the concert of the gods, the moon plays her harp with
the waves of the tides: in the Pacific Ocean, immense and deep, raising huge tides along large sections long and deep for hundreds,
thousands of kilometers, but not particularly high on the coast, running from Antarctica to the Arctic. In the smallest and limited Atlantic
Ocean tides are raised and lowered on the coasts with very different
results, from a few centimeters to several meters at a frequency of
twice a day. It must be the low notes of the melody, the violoncello.
Regular harmonic resonances that determine the overall melody.
There are points where the moon doesn't regulate the tides but they
are determined by the attraction of the Sun, far less, that slightly raise at noon and midnight to lower at dawn and dusk: this happens at
points known as resonance nodes, where the waves intersect, rein-
forcing or neutralizing; like physics teaches us, I know it happens in
Tahiti and I know it happens in parts of Norway and maybe who knows where else.
But it's nice to think of this dance of the gods that while the mother
sleeps, sing and play using the seas and oceans as instruments. The
sun god, Apollo or so he was called, the moon goddess, Diana or Isis
or any other name man has given, have fun and men are the fortunate beneficiaries of their enjoyment, or are the victims, sacrificed and

powerless.

Perhaps you are a woman, or a man, you!
Let that person have their freedom, free them from their bonds, un-
tie them and enjoy. You are like someone starving: love isn't alarming,
isn't repellent, it is a wonderful miracle. Don't hold back: love! Cry if
you want, tears indicate letting go, liberation.
Sometimes you meet someone, in one place rather than in another.
In that someone you meet something more than beautiful, the facial
expression perhaps, which will conquer and then persecute. Maybe a
smile, sweet, honest, an ironic smile, a slight smile but always present
so as soon as it is no longer there you feel torn and guilty, full of remorse. It is not necessary that this something is real.
I believe there is love at first sight; actually, I believe there is only love
at first sight at the base of falling in love. Accepting the reality, means
doing something concrete knowing that nothing can guarantee you
won't make your situation worse in that moment: not to accept it
means to have an excuse, a reason to cry for a very long time.

Staying away from you fills me with sadness exactly in conflict with
the serenity I feel when I am near you.
How nice to quarrel and then make peace as if nothing had happened, because nothing has happened! Bizarre behavior, or is this the
simple and banal essence of what is called love, once you take away
the passion?

My dear wife, one thought is able to scare me: I could lose you with
the same ease and simplicity that I sought you, found, possessed
you? A succession of small banalities, is each one lacking in importance? This is my little poem dedicated to you but you've never seen it: I
was ashamed!

For a moment I dreamed of possessing the sea.
For a moment I thought I could have a wave for myself.
I dreamed of a ray of sunshine that lasted a minute

an hour, an infinite time,
while I was playing with the wave.
But maybe it was an illusion and if so there will be no more sea
nor the wave, the sunbeam, tomorrow,
I will not possess the clouds, the wind, the scent of you
and perhaps not even a memory.

Words are things, though often, you would prefer they were not.
Words can trigger anger, which in turn can generate actions or behavior that is not easy to go back on.
It is however always possible to apologize and feel a little humiliation if the true end is to gradually go back to the beginning: to forgive and to be forgiven!

I remember how I once saw the city, full of prospects and vitality, of the opportunity for enjoyment. It made me think that exactly in this moment hundreds of thousands of people live a normal life every day, right next to me, like me: who drive in traffic, who listen to the radio, those on the sofa reading or watching television, who meet at a dinner table, at home or at the restaurant, who cooks, who cleans, who works, who plays, who dances, who laughs who cries, who cackles, who makes love. Adults who participate in meetings or functions or celebrations, kids who celebrate or compete, who are at their friend's house, who is at the movies, who is at the theater; children playing in the street, in courtyards, on the floors; children crying, children sleeping. There are those who love and whose love is returned and those whose is not. There are those who suffer, who are sick at home or in hospitals, who die who are born, who are sad and who are happy, who lost hope and who acquire it, who studies, who makes projects, who speaks, sings or is silent; there are those who telephone or are on the computer, who steal or commit crimes, who are awake, who plot, who impose, who suffer.
Many conversations, mostly about things are that obvious and banal: *what a beautiful day, what a dreadful day, it's raining, what a beautiful sunny day, it's cold, it's hot, tomorrow will be beautiful or bad, you fell off the ladder: did you hurt yourself, do you love me, you don't love me any more, but how much do you love me...* Lit fireplaces and quiet

meetings or cocktails and dinner, disco and wild rock. Everything together, separate, right now.

Increasingly I want my space and the city seems like a trap for human
animals: full of people I don't like, people who behave like a flock of
sheep, people who follow and conform to the common thinking increasingly limited and restricted, although apparently free; people inclined to exploit them like predators, constantly lurking. Walls on walls
they fence you in and subject you to authority, legitimate or not,
shared or not, of other people.

I remember the beginning of a relationship with one of my longtime
friends: it began more or less like this, avoiding a brawl:
"You're bossy and I don't like bullies."
"I don't even like you and I think you're a bully..."
Today I know it was nothing more than typical animal behavior: we faced each other off staring at each other like two male deer preparing
to fight. In the long run there were no battles, neither man was in fact
a bully and now, several years later we are still the best of friends.

Friends belong to two categories: those from childhood who its good
to see after a long time, and these also consider themselves as such
over the years, despite not having had, in fact, nothing in common
with your life. There are those who are more true and real, based on
shared interests and ethical behavior, during real life: I believe these
are the only ones who can be called friends, because they exist, are
current and have something really in common with us.

I was at the theater with my wife, a rare treat that I conceded her,
and I must say I was impressed by the figure of the actress: fragile
body, a cultured voice, cultured as much as it was instinctive, but with
a personality that captivated me. Today the memory of the play is
pretty much the impression only of that slender figure on the stage,
which filled the whole theater.
Life is a path of choices: forks at every instant, for each one only one

of two possible routes can be followed, virtually at random. You can never know what would have happened if at a given moment you had chosen differently. If a person could go back to a few decades ago, they would realize that the path today, had brought them to a point so far from the original, and so it was for all those who met them.

The brain. I believe, given the little respect it has for the body and its extremely faster development times, that the human brain is an autonomous rapidly evolving organism; an organism that uses the symbiotically transiently human body, to later break free and become independent as soon as possible and evolve independently from the worn organic support. Meanwhile it reduces the tendency to deteriorate with medicine and transplants and, why not, cloning and simultaneously designs artificial supports suitable for its exclusive use.
Evolution only needs time, but I don't have it; I'd like to see into the future: who knows if and how much, I have been right...

The act doesn't make the man guilty unless the mind is guilty: it is one of the cardinal principles of our State of law. The judicial system interpreted as *from external acts they would judge the interior thoughts*; that is they need to verify if the accused is in the condition to understand and was therefore able to judge the relevance of his acts by himself.

The greatest magic trick is the one that takes place in full view, apparently declaring there is a trick and openly challenging the public to identify it: apart from conjuring skills, innate and trained, are the words, in general, that distract the public or involve them emotionally. The barker at the market is able to convince you that a parcel containing a declared value, probably less than the asking price may be a good deal. One customer buys, they all buy!

Timing is an example: the sense of the public, that ability to know before what the public would think; a sea of words that can make up infinite phrases without any connection among them and an accomplice that causes the buying mechanism to trigger, or applause, at the right moment.

The power of Voodoo, is that a man who was threatened in a way that involves him, can really be scared to death and live in fear. Or they are the simple application of the principles of physics and chemistry. You will always find meat counters at supermarkets, beautiful-looking, bright red; then you will find vegetable stalls, resplendent with magnificent green tones. It is the lighting, designed to be complementary and enhance the only color perceptible to the eye, which is the one reflected by the illuminated substance. In the light of the sun, white, the true natural color emerges that could also be very different from that of the exhibit. It isn't magic, it is a sales pitch supported not by words but by technology. It isn't even magic that the product most advertised is also the most sold. Independently of the cost of advertising sustained, the product's position on the supermarket shelves, high up, at eye level those that are more expensive and sponsored, low down forcing you to bend down, are the least expensive, on offer or unknown.

Advertising is based loosely on the propagation of the word *miracle* or *miraculous*: people will always be willing to spend to buy a miracle! Man needs something new; he cannot live with boredom, rather he prefers illusion. Shamans and magicians didn't use magic but even they used science; a primitive science they knew traditionally and not from scientific knowledge: they created special effects to support various beliefs. Generally they worked by taking drugs that had absolutely known and foreseeable effects even if the mechanism of action were unknown.

In politics one must never be blunt and direct, you need to be devious or slimy and greasy. People feel resentment toward individuals who live at a level above them, especially of those who haven't done anything to deserve it.

People are usually unable to evaluate, based on their real value, things that should be dearest to them.

The film made in the family, documenting the situation certainly pleasant or exciting, belongs to the system of memories: when we see them again, they always appear too long or tedious. If we submit others to a film of our journey, no matter how beautiful and brief, it will be boring. Memories and dreams are always boring unless the parties we see are ourselves!

If we could slow our rate of metabolism to that of plants, we would see them move at a speed that appears normal to our body and we would see animals move at supernatural speed. Everything is relative! My life seems to proceed in anything but a straight line, rather precisely a spiral: everything changes, moments of suffering, situations, injuries, satisfaction, everything changes constantly as a result of our actions, or at least there is an illusion that everything changes as a result of our actions.

A web of situations is constructed, an intricate network of relationships, and then when you look at it better, you always find yourself almost at square one and we realize that basically nothing has changed, except ourselves.

I like to play chess, sometimes, rarely, go a few rounds with the computer as an opponent but I find it quite boring. Playing chess is a logical game, and also ethically instructive: you think reason, don't shout don't whistle, don't slam the pieces on the chessboard, defeat is obvious and requires a simple admission and acceptance. Playing chess you should learn to be and at least behave like a civilized being is supposed to in a civilized society.

The awareness of the existence of a mystery drives men to two different behaviors: either striving to search for a rational solution, although not believing we can get to the end, or pushing to embrace mysticism and to adopt the mystery as a religious condition; to fill it with dogmas of faith and to limit the search to transcendental meditation and asceticism.

Death despite being a rationally accepted fact, appears to all, especially to young people, as simply impossible; I believe I must get there, however, all of a sudden and surprisingly.

I wonder if all those consciously on their deathbed are affected by the feeling they have never lived.

The summarized life, must appear to all as so short as to have started and finished, ended in an instant, practically the last.

Who knows if comparing two friends and enemies, people close to that point might say, to each other, the other's life was more beautiful than his own?

Who knows what the difference is between a living man and a dead body at the last moment; good question, I remember the attempt at weighing the soul and for some years this filled scientific pages and even films.

What sense does it have to wallow in the thought that something
that is over can or should be given a new life: absurd. One thing's
over it's over and no good for anything!
Lost loves forget it, go back to living and let others live in peace!
It was said *: now is happier; where it is better; some say it's over it no
longer exists.* I prefer to think *: I am not interested in your body but that
you were a part of my universe, whatever that is, as I know and perceive
it. As long as I live my universe will live, and you are part of it, no matter
what you've become, wherever you are.*

The world as we know it ... what banality knowing that as we know it
means only that we don't know it but we would like it to be, certain
and predictable.
Scientists and especially the elusive scientific community, which tend
to exclude individuals or ideas that are not strongly supported, don't
know everything as they would have you understand and often, indeed, they don't even know what they claim to know or who ... really
knows.
I want to trivialize an example: they know the rain and its mechanisms
perfectly well but they don't know how to reproduce it and couldn't
do it without causing planetary disasters if they tried.
They understand and know how to do a weather forecast, on time, in
the short term: they want to expand to the long term and maybe define meteorology as climatology, extending into global space.

The current famine, which substantially affects those who were considered little more than human waste, is not caused by a real lack of
resources, at least for now, but only the poor distribution of the
same.
The continuing demographic increase has reduced the beneficial effects of global economic development to a few companies.
War has always been a very good solution to this problem but now it
appears to be increasingly complicated and dangerous. War is a terrible method and cannot and must not be an end, even in the short
term; it should never be justified. The end should always be peace
and coexistence, tolerance and equality.

I like to travel but I think I wouldn't like it so much if forced to do it too often: I think the habit of constant change would take away the taste of trying it.

I know many people are able to hold forth with sufficient mastery on different aspects of a problem and long enough to show their preparation and determination. When I meet them I can't help but think the only determination they show is they want to talk so they never have to decide anything.

In practice all the water in the world represents a unique and living creature, a unifying factor where all microscopic parts form connections between everything existing, constantly renewing itself in an almost infinite loop, adapting to change and favoring if not provoking it. What matters in sustaining life is available moisture together with available light, virtually nothing else.
The parasites live and reproduce in the flesh and substance of the hosts, integrating into them, blending in and making them believe they are not foreign bodies. The usual swindle!

The climate is changing it goes, for a time, towards hot and, after, to cold it will only determine a different displacement in the resources produced, at least in my lifetime, and perhaps that of my children and grandchildren. Then who is living will see it. There will certainly be those who will be worse off and, by definition, it can only be those who are better off now.
I believe that the habit of the veil and wearing clothing that totally covers women, today belongs almost exclusively to the Eastern traditions, but until yesterday also ours, arising from tradition and religion; like other things based on social regulations for health. I shall explain, pigs, wine, meat are not strictly controlled in hot climates from birth to slaughter, they are elements of certain social harm and of people's health. Religions have adopted the regulation as organs of power and control, aimed at the good of the people and their health. Eating unclean food is potentially very dangerous, possibly harmful.
From religion to tradition is a short step; from tradition to conservati-

ve fanaticism, the step is even shorter.
The above also applies to the veil and full-coverage dress that essentially also applies to men: it is an old tradition that belongs to Western man even from his origins; at the beginning one-piece woven fabrics were the only possible technology for making a tunic for both men and women.
We think of the environment where Western civilization evolved and developed: hot climates near rivers signifying the presence of billions of insects; flowing robes and scarves to cover the nose hair and mouth, would be the first response for anyone protecting themselves from insects as well as from the heat. This certainly applies to the civilizations that developed around the Mediterranean.
Only today, with the technological evolution of the European area, the need for such clothing is less but on the other hand, in the Middle East, or Asia, the lifestyle and the technological conditions are not the same; here is the reason it was required and is still held as necessary, full coverage clothing. And all this absurdly becomes a religious symbol and as usual becomes the instrument of oppression separation difference and war.

Why do people behave as they do? Because they feel they have to. Because they are tied to those who think it is the logical necessity of our work, of our family, also in our own homeland.
These ties are emotional? No!
The closest tie is logic that cannot, is unable, to contradict because it takes strength and will and cultural autonomy, which are not normal human virtues.
I heard an interview with a detainee, now old; who served several years in prison for crimes committed when he was young, fighting against the state. I was struck by his thinking, "I wonder now that I am imprisoned, alone, sick: but why did I do what I did? I did what I had to do, I obeyed orders, I did my job; I had to do it ... Now that I'm alone and I think about it, that logic no longer exists, it is no more, I'm here, you ask me for an account and I don't know how to act, what to think; but now I'm free, I feel free, but I'm not happy."
But what you did was wrong; you knew it!
"Maybe, but those who were pushing us told us: we are here, all of us to fight injustice; we can win if everyone who is part of our group will

be ready to do whatever they are told, or otherwise suffer the consequences. We are professionals not amateurs. They were strong men, powerful or so it seemed. They told us you believe the government is strong and we are weak: it is not like that. The government has its arms tied by religion and morality and mostly by the need to appear as religious moralists and even when authentic morality and true religion must be in a completely different direction. The arms of the government are tied by dirty deals, illegal activities, by corrupt politicians who grasped the areas to be controlled. When the government begins to react and to take action against us we will see just how clumsy and inefficient it will be. We are on the right side. And I believed it, we believed it!"

This present moment, the moment you are experiencing is the most pressing, the most important: the most important of all.
Often it will fly away like this, almost without leaving a mark because in our impatience we see it as a function of future moments.
Yet today, here, now is the time to observe and remember when an hour has past, a year, or a lifetime.
Only when the moment has gone and disappeared can you truly know. I think someone in the past said *Carpe Diem*: Horatius maybe but I'm a little ignorant and don't remember clearly, please check this. Maybe I'm thinking of things you've already thought about. Perhaps, but I'm thinking and that makes the difference.
Take note of this moment of happiness, remember and to remember it better shout it out: *I'm happy! Here right now at this moment I am happy: this moment is beautiful, it's wonderful!*
Later, when you happen to think of everything negatively, you will think back to this memory of being happy at least once and the memory will give you pleasure. If you do it you will find a necklace of radiant instants, resplendent, which will surround your mind and make you smile.

Words are important, words separate things from each other, place them into categories and classes; words connect things to each other, as much as they are distant or different; glue the concepts; the words describe and then compose and render the world around us real: words construct reality.

Forgive me, you, if you find the diary apparently repetitious. It is impossible to re-read and re-write the whole thing, it would detract
from the spontaneity and immediacy of these thoughts.
Many discussions about the fetus and conception, the times – will it
or will it not be a human being? – it is not important to define what 'is
or is not' a human being but rather what it means to 'be' a human
being.
We could sit around a table and establish degrees of humanity, or perhaps they have already done so?
I believe that if God were asked to directly demonstrate his existence
he would refuse, because the foundation of his existence is faith and
a demonstration would deny this. So I ask myself, maybe I don't have
to re-read the Bible?

I always have to explain: one gets tired of explaining!

I saw a documentary on the harvesting of vanilla, those long, dark
pods that we easily break into deserts by buying a little packet with
two or three pods in the supermarket.
Vanilla grows in very special places, marginal areas of strong hydro-
therapy, where the hot water is clear and bubbling in rock pools,
creating a humid, fumigant climate. These pods are processed one by
one, roasted, shelled and cleaned. Nutmeg and mace grow next to
the vanilla plantation. Vanilla trees with yellowish flowers with long
hanging pods like a little finger. The nutmeg, with their seed pods, at
the core is the nutmeg. The seed is covered by an aril, a kind of reddish network: this is the mace, a kind of precious fungus: both must
be harvested very carefully by hand. Just beyond the trees of cloves:
blood-red buds, still closed, gathered one by one using a ladder and
then allowed to dry. And you know who devoted themselves to this
meticulous collection, in this particular environment that resembles
anything but a park? Dozens and dozens of boys and girls with scraped hands, from sunrise to sunset, sitting on the ground or perched
in the trees. The mothers then look after the final treatment. Not a

single man was visible: they said the men were at work in the city.
And we complain if the little bunch of spices costs one euro.
And we who also buy teak or mahogany furniture, which is used exclusively for luxury boats now it is practically extinct, to harvest it the rainforest needs to be deforested or a tribal war funded. We lash out at child exploitation and deforestation that is necessary for the farmers who produce sugar cane in order to survive ... because brown sugar is less harmful than beet sugar ... who knows why! The scientific community tells us.

They always said who makes it for himself makes it for three: you must always rely solely on yourself but perhaps always relying only on yourself you are likely to find yourself on your own. Then one day you get sick, and who will help you? Who will be there to give you a hand?

I realize that even though I knew it and confirm that it is really pleasant to write: many things come to mind when you write on paper: we make discoveries that had previously escaped; events emerge more clearly from the confusion and from the approximation that accompanies them when the events themselves occur.

A long time ago I learned, and tried to teach my children when they were children, that you can decide, roughly, what to dream. At least you can drive the dream towards what we would like to dream: if you focus well enough, you invent or tell a story, just as you do with children, if you are able to direct your dream; although there is always the risk that during the dream it unfolds into a totally different dream than the one wanted, where one forgets oneself and floats prey to visions. Some poignant thoughts dominate your mind beyond the possibility of controlling them.
Humankind clashes with the concept of reality tailored to our limited channels of perception making it subjective and partial: why people try to dream: abstract and distance oneself from reality as far as possible and they do it using various methods, ranging from drug use to meditation sessions, often exaggerating and becoming a slave of this desire to escape, this rejection of the basic simplicity of life; seeking a

more complex reality, it appears less constricting and more satisfactory.

For humans as time passes, the bones become smaller while the cartilage does not: this is why the elderly appear to us always small and
with large ears.

I look around and I think the only solution to the demographic problem and globalization of culture of humanity would be the extinction
of 30% of the existing population. Unfortunately it would mean extin-
guishing about two billion people, and because the solution is also
partially effective, it should be almost instantaneous.
Nature has automatic defense mechanisms, which are brought into
use to exceed the threshold of maintaining life and still more, that of
well-being; behavioral changes that reduce the proliferation of the
species and facilitate the onset of devastating epidemic diseases,
such as abuse of substances that deteriorate and reduce the length
of life, reduce fertility, the development of "sexually, but rewarding,
deviant behavior" in respect to procreation such as gays. It can easily
be checked by studying the community of each animal species to the
wide diffusion and to rats that are our most likely successors in the
distant future.
The priority seems to be to first achieve the possibility of life (multiplying itself) then well-being and reduction of stress, achieved by the
establishment of territory and its defense; thus reducing the birth
rate so as to maintain the highest possible number of elements in
good health. Third and last, the maintenance of the standard of well-
being and equilibrium achieved precisely, with the aforementioned
mechanisms; work naturally and not insignificantly to this end, the increase in personal and social aggression and as a result the use of
wars.

Man is blind and stupid, violent and arrogant. Probably comprising one
species of the ephemeral presence on earth, on a geological scale, in
comparison to sharks scorpions and beetles or to the dinosaurs extinct today.

Every moment somewhere in the world a happy song is raised or one
of a funeral march, the voice of an auctioneer who declaims his
goods, a running child laughs or cries, people conversing or brawling;
at anytime someone is laughing crying dancing killing or making love;
at anytime someone is hopeful someone yearns, someone acts; at
anytime someone takes his or her last breath; at anytime someone
breathes his or her first breath and life goes on in spite of me or you,
and we also live as long as we can, and even when it hurts.
Life could be a dream or simply a shared game, a reality like a computer program, or a quiz competition; a game that is played by all, with
passion and satisfaction disappointment and anger, the pebbles and
the childhood games, first the game of snakes and ladders, checkers
then, chess, card and social games, gambling, racing, betting, lotte-
ries, solitary games, or shared on the network by computer. A set of
games that all have one rule in common: in the end you lose. Not a
single game but games together which in themselves, have no meaning or significance but they are purchased, and are kept functional
by the players, as long as they play; as long as there are players; as
long as they dream of winning.

I'm glad I was born in my era: the more I know about the Middle Ages
and the period of Enlightenment the happier I am. All my useless and
common knowledge is probably superior to that available to the great
medieval era but here I don't need practically anything; what would be
the use of my skills in that world? If I could not use them, I wouldn't
have been much more than an animal but probably if I could have
used them, I would have been burned at the stake. And the future? It
lies ahead or is too fast for me, or is not at all rosy. I was lucky.

I like the cinema, but I prefer to read because it allows me to live lives that are different from mine, to be involved in the imagination and
to construct the faces, environments and situations mentioned, but
not defined which last throughout the duration of the reading. Unfortunately, as the book evolves I am devoured by the desire to advance
in that story and read ever faster and continuously even to the point
of being convulsive. The result is that life is ephemeral, because it
leaves a bitter taste in the mouth when the story, rapidly ends. And

then I start another book and away I go again. (Crisis of withdrawal?) It is how I can live many different lives during mine but it is also like dying, many times over!

Wars serve the economy of rich countries, they serve the rich and powerful, but remain bestial events which find fertile ground in the animal reality where humans, stupid and ignorant, kill rape, massacre torture, other humans who are equally stupid and equally ignorant for even more stupid reasons. The reasons that underlie the war could always be resolved more or less peacefully, without having recourse, if there is not an excess of ignorant people, even educated, but anything but educated, well indoctrinated by the schools for that purpose: to serve as a consumer, intermediaries and/or as soldiers, unable to think things through autonomously thinking freely.

Yesterday I suffered a huge disappointment: my children think I was angry but it wasn't like that; I'm disappointed! It has always been a tradition in my family to dedicate a few hours, only a few hours, on the evening of the first of November to a parody of the 'wake' happy and joyful, in the memory of our dead, and that is based on thousands of years of tradition. Tradition that today is common in Nordic culture. In the south they prefer to pay the mourners and express grief and suffering for longer or shorter times.
At around 20:00, we meet at home, or my sister's, and while the chestnuts cook the rosary is recited to commemorate our dead, our loved ones, friends, people who have left their trace in our life and are here no more. Wherever and however we are there to thank them, because what we are is also the result of what they gave us: a rosary not very dogmatic and in effect rather cheerful; a question of ten minutes and thought flies, the children learn that family ties, blood ties and respect are important and are able to overcome all disagreements and difficulties, using a small gesture of love affection and recognition. The tradition, important for children and the elderly, does not require any sacrifice from the young, in fact after the rosary you sit at the table and eat dinner in company as for a normal festival then, cleared away, you dedicate time while the chestnuts are placed on the table, for a board game called *Pipetta*: a simple game with

amusing implications, based on an old game of chance. Everyone around the table, stocked with a small hoard of old coins of little value no longer in general circulation, specially preserved for the purpose, competitors aim a coin. The dealer, who passes from hand to hand, in sequence, either one of the large or small competitors, distributes the cards one by one. The king pays a coin, the ace takes a coin and the bet is won with the knight of clubs (*Pipette*). Another round and repeat. After a few rounds the winner is the one who has won the most and you return the coins to be kept for the following year. It's funny, you don't have to think, joking and laughing, there isn't a winner and a loser but a lucky one who is contented and happy and some, fewer, sulk. Children learn that gambling, even this simple, is pleasant but it could be extremely dangerous in the absence of strict conditions and of small virtual bets. The whole evening lasts roughly until 23.00 after which all are free to go elsewhere, to bed or to the usual entertainment. You are not asked to give up anything, just take a few happy hours in the memory of our dead, and the family that unites us. Yet last night both my children avoided taking part, they refused. I know they claim they aren't believers, and for this reason they hadn't wanted to come. I know they reject traditions and those they see as an obligation imposed on them by the family, by me in particular. Apart from this dispute that I would find more suitable to eighteen year olds than intelligent and educated adults and it is not worth dwelling on or about it, the disappointment is another: I raised my children hoping to instill in them the concept that tolerance, humility and conscious and voluntary participation, were fundamental to the life of a person; I grew up hoping they would understand thought is free when it is critical, but supported by independent reasoning, based on the highest and most varied knowledge possible; I thought they'd understood that to learn more it is necessary overall to listen and ask the right questions at the appropriate time and place. I hoped they understood that only fools don't change their ideas, simply because they are unable to. I thought they shared the concept of intelligence and scientific method: that the approach of a scholar, in contrast to that of an ignorant, a fanatic, a pompous self-celebrant, was the ability and consciousness to never absolutely deny anything defining it, regardless, impossible.

The disappointment I felt is exactly the realization that I have failed and I overestimated them. They don't realize that, only to have offended me, and what I represent, in their adolescent pride, revealed the most profound arrogance and narrowness of thought.

They didn't take into consideration that as long as the teachings and examples of those who have passed close to me, to us, will remain at the heart of what I and we have become as long as their memory remains closed and protected in our hearts, then and at least until then, they will not actually be dead, dissolved into everything. Returning to the essentials but they will have always really existed, and not only their essence, but their existence, perhaps, will have acquired some sense.

They were not disrespectful to me, something that can still be resolved and easily overcome, they were disrespectful of the concept of family as a fundamental link, higher than simple friendship which evidently they've not understood, but even this can be fixed, we are dealing with human relationships.

That which we can never again remedy and of which we would be ashamed is that with their arrogance – based on the simplest affirmation, not proven nor provable, a declared but not sufficiently thought out belief that God doesn't exist, and nothing derived from religion makes sense to existence – certain of not making a mistake, they were disrespectful to the dead loved ones, the people who obviously were not important enough to them, to the point of denying them, those who are no longer living, a possibility, if that possibility existed even in the remotest possibility, making them miss the help their prayer, their positive thinking, ten minutes of dedication could possibly give them. They excluded a chance that didn't directly concern them. And there is no remedy for this!

You have to contend with the reality not with what we would like it to be! A grain of sand, an ant or a mosquito, I myself individually, we are certainly insignificant compared to everything but just as certainly we are not useless and therefore we are important!

Freedom: is it really worth always having it at the top of our thoughts, to consider the engine of all the threads of the clashes, ambitions? Justifying all wars fought in his name? I don't know what it is really. Yet it is so important for so many, perhaps, but is it really something that is worth wanting and possibly seeking to possess.

Jesus: who was this man really? And God made man, his human aspect and Mary the feminine aspect, the human mother goddess made human to allow for the miracle. Both assumed and ascended to heaven, the seat of divinity after they had conducted their earthly mission. They said and did much good. They have been, and now, they are still the source of inspiration, source of hope for so much of the human race. But who were they really and what changes, if it changes, in accepting to only see them as special people who created a landmark in history?

Jesus was essentially a respectable person, the son of a master carpenter, not a carpenter, craftsperson if not an artist, completely respected at the time. He was able to study, was cultured; was a philosopher, a teacher not a prophet, one known, honored, respected by the people and by the powerful. Probably priestly and philosophical arts in his own community, he was a Nazarene, which also included an introduction to medicine that he didn't fail to exercise for the poor, sometimes with unexpected success creating a legend around him.

He was an orthodox Jew and puritan. He didn't live a retiring life but that of a scholar. Like Moses before him he didn't accept deviations from the law of God, corruption, oppression, idolatry of power, etc. and he never failed to repeat this, everywhere, without false fears; he could afford to.

Like Moses before him he openly lined up to defend the people, not against the powerful but in defense of the most defenseless and exploited people: women, children, the most marginalized, the old and sick who couldn't work productively and against greedy exploiters and the idolaters of money and power. He was equally well received at the table of the rich as that of the poor. He preached justice and fairness, tolerance and generosity in the name of the Jewish God, God the Father, the same one that had dictated the laws and led the people to the Promised Land.

Jesus was, therefore, a person who was respected and respectable and the people who were waiting for a messiah, a leader to guide them to revolution, could not but try to make him their own. Finally the time was ripe. He came to Jerusalem surrounded by his brothers, his family, his court of followers and courtiers, he was welcomed by the crowd celebrated, acclaimed. Camped with them in the grove of olive trees, an armed body guard with swords that only soldiers could afford and not even the royal guards. A commander in all respects, and next to them, for the occasion of the feast of the Jewish people, thousands, perhaps tens of thousands of angry and intolerant Jews, rebels, waiting for an order, a command to start the uprising.

And here is his miracle, his message passed down through history and that history has made and continues to be generated: He gave up! He chose not to fight, he chose non-violence; he was delivered to a handful of guards armed with sticks who arrested him in the midst of his own people, angry and ready to fight because of his attitude. The Messiah renounced being the leader and still chose that of being teacher; nonviolence to lead the people towards the fulfillment of the will of God as he understood it: absolute, not able to be interpreted, true to his teachings which were inspired in Him and by Him. Maybe, like Moses, before him, certainly not like Joshua. Like Gandhi after him; not like Chè. Like Confucius or Buddha, perhaps, not Muhammad. The eternal clash of human nature between the ways of being. Free choice, free will. A teacher, not a prophet, a leader for peace, not a commander for war. And then for the people, an active robber was better than a leader who didn't command and disappoints his supporters; he must be abandoned and punished, he must be destroyed. It's history!

But his teaching, his message, as old as man, had to be reinforced as repeatedly as it has been in human history. Does anything change if he ate, laughed, sweated, thought, played fell in love, and argued with his mother, father and brothers, including James, who was his first successor, powerful among the powerful, a Jew totally, totally observant but less hard. It was necessary to overcome Judaism: Paul, the apostle who didn't know Jesus directly, who wasn't Jewish, does it: Christianity is born. There was a need to move away from the Jewish God to reach the Universal God: a way was needed. Jesus deserved to be assumed into divinity for what he represented and who he was. Does anything change if he was, at least on earth for as much as he lived, only one man? In the end it had to be, no?

And Mary? a young, pure girl, naive, deeply religious, fertile. The Messiah was to have a mother and she had to be a virgin. Mary played her role. The divine Jesus of Christianity had to be God and had to have a mother goddess. They lived, played the role assigned to them by history, they probably deserved respect and honor reserved for them, they were identified and deified, have ascended to heaven, where the gods reside, or the one God; in any case the seat of the gods that cannot be the earth, at least not for long. The legend and the dogma don't detract anything from what they represent: the family, the trinity, the natural principle; goodness and justice, aspiration of the biological helpless child, the furious anger of the father, the intercession of the mother and the forgiveness of everyone and everything. Another possibility, another story. Does anything change if Mary didn't die with Jesus? The world doesn't die with the man. If she had a life full of other children, of joys and sorrows, hopes and disappointments, she lived as a woman, a mother? She played her role on earth as she did and then was made to ascend to heaven. Catholics forget to say when this happened. But does anything change? I don't think so.

The doctor said! For the farmer, even one who is very rich, worth more than 'has been told' the technician, the manager, the president or anyone else and the 'doctor' who wears a tie! If you show up to get a small favor dress as you want, but if you intend to request a bigger favor, then dress elegantly. The outfit does not make the monk but it certainly seems that way!

When you suppose something always consider that your suppositions may be wrong.
Changes often happen so slowly you aren't aware of them or too quickly to get used to; you don't notice them but they happen. Nothing ever stays the same for long; don't hope that this is so not even when you think it's possible.
One thing will never change: who has money always wants more! It has never been given away and will never be and if you're dealing with banks or businessmen then it will be called a loan or commission or some other way, but none of them will ever give you anything.

Colors and art forms are fruit of the knowledge and technology of the moment: once they were minerals, with their crushed and cooked metals, oxides, tin white and white lead also melted and vitrified, green and the blue of copper or turquoise, indigo of flowers for fabrics or manganese for violet; for the blue of stained-glass cobalt and lapis lazuli for the heavens and for the precious cloaks; the gold of the haloes of the great or antimony or cadmium yellow, purple from shells and mercury for red and holy vermilion; the earth irons, red and yellow ocher, conveyed in the white of an egg or blood and then from vegetable oils and then from compounds that first alchemy and then the chemist have made available. Over time all these materials have marked and dated the artistic evolution.

The sun remains constant that lives and gives life and never illuminates the objects it touches with the same intensity and direction. With the light the appearance of the colors change. The arrangement of colors is used to take advantage of the light: green red and yellow profit from direct, intense light, white and blue or even black for the shadow and twilight.

How strange, I have the impression that for most people their defining character is their lack of ambition, what perhaps coincides with the natural man and of inertia. Nature teaches us that matter is lazy, resists and opposes change: it is called inertia and we have all experienced it. Push a stone and it moves easily, it as easily stopped; if you try with a rock it won't move or just a little, but if it rolls it is better to step aside because it is not easy to stop. Matter wants to continue to do what it does without changing, no matter if it moves or is motionless.

Man, his mental and physical organization, form is an integral part of nature and acts according to nature. (By the way, according to Einstein's theory, only matter without mass can move at the speed of light as do photons. To reach a value of zero (inertia) would mean traveling at that speed. At least for now it is impossible even if we can imagine it, at least as far as you can imagine the square root of -1).

What is intelligence? It is a typical manifestation of nature. I am always fascinated by a complex system that takes on unpredictable appearances departing from simple elements.

What is the void? Apparently nothing, in fact it is a seething ocean of interactions and fluctuations, sparkling particles and corpuscles that exist and carry, messages of energy in a continuous and vital flow. The void is the life of nature.

I can take care of it later ... like everything in life ... or forget about it altogether! At the time, one doesn't think... in retrospect it hurts! We are friends, lovers, confidants, but basically we are only intimate with ourselves!

Respect yourself; you need it! Without the deep consciousness of being and representing something important, and worthy of esteem and respect, at least for yourself, without the consciousness that whatever is made, or is being done is still the best possible, for us in that given moment, for us and for all those who are mostly more or less involved, it isn't possible to feel respect for the others, what they are, make, have made.
I have tried to teach my children to respect themselves because without that first, you cannot demand respect from others. I tried to teach them to treat people well and with respect because they are certainly worthy of that. I tried to teach them that they should respect others if they want to be respected themselves.

Keep the mind open as much as possible, don't believe in anything; don't reject anything, unless being satisfied there is irrefutable evidence. Never be certain! What you believe to be established, may be disproved or modified. It has always happened to what we have believed for centuries. *There are more things in heaven and earth...*

There is no limit to the human power of rationalization, which tends to want to always explain everything that you don't know with what is known; the result is the triumph of ignorance.
The result of ignorance is fanatical acceptance or fanatical rejection; believe or not to believe; unambiguous choice. From time to time ab-

solute faith, or its absolute negation and this only in terms of what each knows, or believes to know or what is presented as known.

Intelligence, tolerance, willingness, sensitivity, kindness in relationships, non-judgmental, minimally prejudiced, contrasting with fanaticism, being closed, overpowering, prejudice, intolerance, violence, ignorance.
Can this be linked to the social environment of where the person comes from? To their financial wealth? I believe, rather, in the existing differences between culture and learning.
The world today is filled with specialists, people with much learning but substantially uncultured.

Often it happens that you barely touch reality, almost miraculously, without even realizing it since; simply, we live in a narrow range of ready-made ideas, customs, prejudices, and we tend to relate everything to ourselves and ignore the invisible: because we are simply ignorant of its existence.
The unknown is not a mere hypothesis but a reality, unknown, which exists alongside our normality. Usually it happens that after having carefully observed and studied something that at first glance seemed strange, its strangeness disappears until it become almost common.
It makes you think they're right the ones who believe rationality would always prevail over faith and tradition, over the desire of hope. What is today called the supernatural would be better called the unexplainable. Nevertheless, you can't regardless deny it, exclude it. The objective should be to prove or at least explain it, meanwhile accepting it as a possibility, even very, very unlikely, until proven otherwise.
Bohr the great but particularly powerful Danish physicist who made fundamental contributions to atomic structure and quantum theory (1885 to 1962), at the time, denied three-quarters of the natural world, arrogantly claiming: nothing exists until it has been measured! For example in fact his knowledge, limited given the epoch in which he lived, his will, his intelligence, his arrogance, his vital spirit, his advanced fantastic insights, and not even his atomic model held up to measurement and after a fleeting season of certainty it was relegated to the science museum, as an example of great insight. He'll turn

over in his grave every time he hears the word. Niels Bohr, what he intended, meant that it had to be measured and validated either by himself or by his followers; a very good exercise, as usual, of power.

If it is not a religion it is a scientific community.

Why wasn't this done? I didn't know ... but if we'd spoken, discussed, it's a month that the file has been open ... it isn't possible, you spoke about it with someone else ... I wasn't there ... if I was there I was sleeping ... maybe I wasn't sleeping but I was distracted... I didn't understand ... how I hate this behavior useful only to justify ignorance and the refusal to accept responsibility.

They tell me I have to stay away from knives; in fact I have cut myself so many times but one of these times my father told me to think I was holding a weapon; I realized then that weapons are used exclusively, to make blood or life flow out of men and living creatures. Since then, when I think of a weapon I also think of what it is exclusively used for.

I have my self-sufficiency, my privacy, my freedom, and the capacity to love, to want others to be happy: what else do I need?

Now at least sometimes, I feel free and strong, but I wonder if I had not read so many books, lived so many lives, felt so many emotions, would I have felt this way? Thank God I can read and love it, and in this way I come into contact with the mind and thoughts of others. Writing, as I'm doing now instead I come into contact with my mind.

Be content, therefore, be grateful for what you've got anyway; anyway don't ask for more than you know you cannot have.

It is natural that older men are supplanted, replaced by young people;
the important thing is that they, the old, understand this and do something so as not to obstruct but to select and train the best, the
best young people who will replace them.
A great and useful question to ask the one you are conversing with is:
why are you here and at this time? But it would also be good to ask:
how do you justify your existence?
Ideas run through my head; I'd like to know what's in my head: I
would like to know if, in grave difficulty, would it be worth being helped; if I intend to die or would I want to be helped at all costs to get
out alive!

Society, social relations, institutions are based and hang on hypocrisy,
institutionalized at every level!
Perhaps a little hypocrisy is not even negative; it is like religion, like
coffee sex or liqueurs: a simple lubricant, an anxiolytic, an antidepres-
sant, you need to make civil coexistence acceptable.
Hypocrisy makes you define a man as fortunate if he is reduced to
being a talking vegetable, supported by machinery and expensive facilities; lucky doctors, nurses, technicians and engineers, cooks and se-
cretaries are proud to be part of the team supporting the luck of that
man, not dead, and entrusted to their care for the next many years,
from which they and others, draw such hope for the future and sala-
ries; fortunate especially the father and certainly the mother, for not
having to mourn the dead son; they are allowed to sigh with happiness for every blink of an eye or muscle moved; lucky to enjoy the solidarity of society, fortunate and happy, forced to sell everything they
have, to give up on every project and the future, to transfer their lives
and their home near the hospital that contains their hope and fortune; forced to rely on the social support of those, rather unfortunate,
because they cannot share much luck unless by organizing dinners of
solidarity and fundraising.

Father mother and brothers are believed to have been declared fortunate and have to give up work and their lives to assist their lucky
son twenty-four hours a day and they have to give thanks, because if
their son manages to survive ... who knows... with advances in techno-

logy ... the research produced ... with time ... maybe ... lucky to be able
to take part in and express, their, words of thanks recognition and
hope for the miserable spontaneous support of friends and the solidarity of the participants, making them proud and permitting them to
share their good fortune; lucky and happy to be able to express their
goodness, everyone can take part in the demonstrations of solidarity,
gratified and pleased with the mutual recognition of the good they
are doing.
I certainly don't want to compare the 'luck' stated about this son and
the 'bad luck' of the father of the poor devils forced to steal cats so
as to eat at Christmas time, who escaped war and hunger begging on
the roadside, who are always and in any case sick of 'influence', to
those who have access but do not qualify for health care because
they cannot pay for the prescription or don't have a doctor; of those
who have to wait months and months to have an important medical
exam mostly because they cannot pay. The misfortune of those who
must stand in long queues for access to emergency care and nursing
departments, if not sent by the 'family doctor' for 'the blood test and
the test for blood pressure'. The damn rare misfortune of those who
don't even have a friend who is a doctor or a nurse.
I don't want to consider the 'tough luck' of all those forced to work at
something that is 'unrewarding' and precarious; of those forced to depend on adult parents and the misfortune of those who because of
the crisis, cannot go to a restaurant more than once a week, those
who are forced to eat only pasta and meat and milk every single day,
because look how much fruits and vegetables cost. The misfortune of
farmers who complain about the low value of their production. The
evil misfortune of those who are intolerant of meat, gluten intolerant,
intolerant of shellfish and lobsters... of those who are intolerant!

Then I understand and I know who is more fortunate: it is those who
suffer most obviously. They have more than the others, the public recognition of the hope of improving, here or in the future, even after
death! Only now I understand the meaning of the words: *blessed are
the last* ...

Free will is expressed through 'choice' but it is not true that there are always only two possibilities for each situation either large or small, one needs to make a decision.

Yes – No; I will – I won't! Apparently so, but instead there is a unique possibility of free choice: free, autonomous, independent; a decision exclusively the result of free thought and the willingness to pay the price of the decision taken: rejection! The only alternative is to refuse! To say no.

It's not easy but the decision for the YES, although taken individually, justifiably, fruit of thinking freely about the various circumstances, is nevertheless, unavoidably influenced by the presence of advantages. Do you want a cigarette? To smoke or not? It's a pleasure, I don't intend to stop, at any price; in fact I'm not choosing but justifying a decision imposed by the need, urgent, created by the brain to deal with a sorrow, a discomfort arising from abstinence from nicotine. The brain is cheating, assuming a substance that would facilitate its reaching a state that would otherwise cost it effort and work to achieve. Naturally this applies to all substances: coffee, sugar, alcohol, the wide-variety of drugs with certain substantial and recognized affects (if they didn't work they would be either sought out or imbibed).

The positive choice, thus, was not as free as it seemed.

Doing it you would have followed a primary and powerful impulse, or substantially apparently advantageous, in this case of the animal, chemical physical type. The only choice would be NO, knowing full well what effects it would bring or would result, at least in the short term and being willing to pay the price to achieve future goals (a hypothetical or desired well-being?) or simply to express and affirm their autonomy, even from basic needs.

What you cannot change will have to be unavoidably endured.

There are millions, billions of choices we make every day, but only a few in fact, very few, involve free will.

I am a soldier, armed with orders to shoot and kill. Somehow, choice after choice, I have got here but now, only now, with the enemy in front of me in the same condition I really have to choose freely. Who knows if he will make the same choice as me ... my life is at stake, I can shoot, (to kill intentionally or not, it doesn't matter: to frighten, to injure, etc. are only palliative justifications because, shooting, I may not intentionally kill).

Is it an arbitrary choice? Subjected to the pressure exerted by the survival instinct, the strongest animal instinct, justified by the order to do it for 'just cause', the choice of *yes, I'll do it*, it is definitely easier, probably more useful than the alternative, of refusal, which requires a process of thought and an extremely strong and costly personal conviction. Precisely for this reason, No! is the only real choice!

It applies to all choices but not all have the same value, the same price to pay. The same price tag.

To be cruel or not: is it a real choice? If it was like this masochism and sadism wouldn't be part of human and animal nature: they don't require thought, just action. *Yes, I'll do it*, then it becomes only the easiest choice.

But then does free will exist? It is or isn't?

Free will is understood as a possibility, perhaps, exclusive to thinking man, or maybe just more complicated for him. The lion, deciding on whether to attack and eat you, is in the end, based on the relationship between the balances of hunger, need, fear, survival instinct. Man attacks the lion for completely different reasons, and sometimes, just sometimes, out of fear.

Free will becomes therefore one of the many unpredictable variables that allows nature to maintain the dynamic equilibrium of the system. Equilibrium in the system is crucial and permits you to conserve most of the energy and thus be reduced to the frozen motionlessness of the universe at the end of time (entropy – enthalpy) waiting for a new beginning, a new vibration that will shake the motionless universe.

Free will exists I believe it is a concrete possibility, which though doesn't necessarily involve all choices; only for a few, fundamental, challenging, requiring a huge effort of will and mind to justify the alternative possibility of rejection and the energy required to carry it actuate it generate the results, whatever they may be; the choice is to go against the tide.

We must be certain that the consequences of refusal, will certainly be less predictable than that of consensus and that they will trigger a flow of new choices that will influence the entire whole system. The entire universe will be shaken and everything that is, starting from the implementation of a unique variable, with the least probability of being among all others.

The enemy soldier in front of me, will he make the same choice as I will?

For a while I've asked myself about the sense and the future of the universe: if evolution is the natural way then I imagine even the universe should evolve, and in fact I think it is doing so. But I retain that it is chaos that underlies the universe and nature in dynamic equilibrium, therefore, if it was like this, then the set of individual chaotic elements would make it unpredictable in the sense of its destiny that cannot be determined by any one single moment. That does not take away that in any case the destiny of the universe, of nature, of the living species and of man himself, although not predestined or able to be predestined, it will happen anyway. The answer to the question should arise from within the universe itself, and therefore cannot be either posed or answered; and this to me seems to constitute a paradox.

The cosmic constant describes the reality of the universe, what the hell is that? I've been struggling with this for a while but maybe now I can understand its meaning, or not? Who knows?
Therefore, after the explosion of the big bang or the big bangs, which resulted in the expansion of protomatter, space was created and energy reduced. Gravity originating from the explosion slowed the motion forming first light and then matter. The galaxies formed, etc. each expanding galaxy is followed by another more recent formation; the one that follows has a mass and thus generates a force of gravity, and in this way attracts the one that precedes it slowing it down. In dynamic equilibrium the chain of the expansive force and the slowdown has created the current universe.
The cosmic constant should be if I've understood it, the relationship between the rate of expansion of galaxies (the mean) and the mass of the universe. In fact we don't know at all what the mass of the universe is, because it is likely that a part of it has not yet been transformed into matter. The dark part of the universe. What then is the gravitational equilibrium of the universe? Will there be a time when the expansion will cease and it will start to contract to vary the defined relationship of the cosmic constant? If the mass increases then the

constant will always be smaller and there will first be balance and then maybe contraction; but if the mass is exhausted then the constant will remain the same or increase, and then the galaxies will distance themselves from each other always more so from the center of expansion indefinitely. But if there were more than one big bang? Or if the limited phenomena of contraction that originated the blacks holes gave place to further big bangs? A big bang a universe? Out of phase forward or behind us a few tens of billions of years? If then there were several universes in equilibrium? In the face of what should be the reality described by the so-called cosmic constant.
It is like looking through the bottom of a glass at a bubble for in an aquarium. You see something but what? And we who at the most last one hundred years, what else are we if not a simple unstable point of mass? Oh God does everything, and is always better than nothing' at least we exist and we know it.

Eternity: reading I live, or maybe more appropriately, I live so many lives that they take place and are used up in a book. I make them exist as if I were God, but what happens to the characters in the stories when the book is finished? What remains? Memories of these lives, lived anyway, if not in themselves at least in me. Surely everything will happen again in works by different people who have read them and they will happen again, generating new memories, different emotions. Anyone will tell their story generating their lives, always different but always appearing the same.

I try not to discuss other people's opinions about me: it serves no purpose, but it pleases me if they are positive.

I have come to a conclusion; here, and here I mean anywhere, don't do anything until it's almost too late.

Firefly firefly come to me so I can give you the king's bread, I will give you the queen's bread, firefly firefly come to me. We children saying this rhyme ran after the fireflies swarming in the fields at night in June, trying to catch enough to put them under a glass and make a little living lamp before going to bed. A magic chant that seemed to attract the fireflies and made the task of approaching them to catch them easier. Try and see if it will work ... we children believed and could prove to the adults that it worked.

At Christmas I become extremely nervous. Wishes, greetings, salutations, smiles. But for what? It will get better. But if it has gone well? It will get better. Happy New Year.
Thoughts concentrated in one evening, gifts for one evening, but there's no need. You had a whole year to do it and you will have another to continue if you want. To what end? What beginning?
The most I could do would be wish to find and appreciate a little serenity, I hope it is true at all times of the year.
Come to dinner, let's meet up, let's celebrate. We must close the pending paperwork. End the year, does the world end? I don't believe in good wishes anymore, once when I could I would go and spend Christmas day alone on some mountain. In the evening, with the family. A social duty? Yes, perhaps, but also a great pleasure that I didn't want to forsake.
I like Saint Lucia to pass by and leave something among the many expected and obvious, and however useful: chocolate coins are one thing, also small but surprising.
What annoys me is the relationship with others, the people who all in all I care absolutely nothing about. Formal obligations, exchange of courtesies that might be a real pleasure at any other time. And it costs, how much it costs!
It was beautiful day in the woods alone, in the light, in the rustle of the trees, with pungent scents occasionally of grass or snow. It gave me the strength to return and endure days of Christmas among people.
Maybe on the way back I would stop and have a snack at an inn and watch the people, listen, hear. Two slices of fresh cheese, two slices of salami, a glass of white wine and then return.
I like people, but those of everyday, hello, how are you, all right, hello we meet again.
I like to stroll in the markets, people, colors, smells, contacts and then go home.
I like to go to the bar and have a coffee but standing: good morning, a

coffee without sugar thank you, with a cold cup please. How much? Goodbye. I hate to sit at the bar, something my wife would enjoy a lot. From 2 December I become more nervous every day, closed, intractable, I cannot wait to get to the 6th of January indeed the 15th. In fact I hate Christmas.

I was washing my hands soiled with earth on the seashore; in the waves of the surf. I watched the mud that caked and covered my arms. Slowly it melted and remained near my hand for a few moments then dispersed in the water. A few moments and what remained of that dark, gray, black crust of earth was only an invisible trace that dispersed in the immensity of the sea. Can death be like that?
The earth, the mud is gone, but I remember the feeling of the earth on my arms.
Then immortality, at least on Earth, is made only from genes passed down to posterity and from memory? Heroes are immortal because they are remembered? Like the great criminals! I don't believe it is memory that immortalizes but that of example, of teaching and a profound message, even intended to be dispersed in the immensity of the sea; but the sign it left evolves with the one who received it.

Humans always like to believe in prophecy, in predictions, especially if they are catastrophic! Recently I remembered the Millennium bug, the thousand and no longer thousand at the end of the millennium, the end of the world predicted by the end of the Maya calendar. Earthquakes and volcanoes. Prophecies basically make us feel safe but balanced and therefore better when compared with those who are really the victims of disasters.

Who knows why most individuals who have passed the age of 50 believe that times past were always better than the present? That 'civilization' as they remember it is constantly slowly degrading, and times will get darker and problematic: nostalgia for a time when they were the ones who challenged the state of affairs? Nostalgia for mythologized times, full of fabled righteous heroes who triumphed against the injustice incorporated in their scarce culture they've implemented?

Scarce memory?
I think only of scarce past and present personalities lacking in deep
convictions. Or maybe it's just because yesterday has gone, so it is
more beautiful. To return would be boring. Like home movies.

I'm worried, I'm worried, I'm always worried ... shit.

Revisiting one's life is like traveling to a historic city of art: a jumble, a
succession of ancient buildings, some crumbling, some imposing; the
ancients built to last! Them, they knew how to do it! Indeed. What we
see is all that remains of thousands of years of history; the rest, evidently, had its defects.
We see the mouth of time: a cloister of teeth, some missing, and
others beautifully fake, again others, many, imperfect and consumed,
some decayed. Cavities hidden by restorative fillings, other open cavities and painful ... smells and stenches.
We will look at a mess made up of ultra-modern buildings, old buildings, ruins and monumental statues, fountains, art works worth staying and visiting but remember where life flows every day, noisy, re-
stless, with the unbridled rhythms of today: noises of cars people,
current events, political events, change, change, change ... to become
aware, deeply, to stay there forever, circling around.

Respect: that's what it takes. That's what's missing. It is a magic word:
respect for yourselves and for others; respect for the young and the
elderly, respect for the disabled and for the poor in spirit, for the
most intelligent and the most successful. Respect for their ideas but
also for those of others, for friends and for adversaries.
We must have respect for faith and religion, and for those who have
it. Respect for life and for nature, the environment in which we live.
Respect and fear! Fear thy God, they taught; don't be afraid but fear
him. Then certainly you will respect him. This applies to everything, for
animals and humans or machines. Have fear of them because you
don't know them and therefore respect them, don't be afraid.
Unfortunately I am unable to respect fanatics!

After all, despite all my skepticism and cynicism, my rationality and pragmatism, my hostility to the exercise made up of all religions: I will not be a good Christian and certainly not a good Catholic, but I say this forcefully: I have faith. After having written my book, manual, collected scientific data *There is life and life*, only one observation was made, "It's beautiful, or rather it's interesting but where is God? And I answered, "Who said there is no God? He could be there or not since God was not a question to be proved, but to choose with faith. A matter of faith, not of science. Why not? Have faith, not be faithful, doesn't do anyone any harm indeed it can do good to many."

I'm devoted to the Madonna delle Grazie (Our Lady of Grace), who is venerated at the Shrine in Bardi (Parma) my home town, whose image is typically fifteenth century, the mother nursing her son. Specifically this particular icon has a characteristic, different from others, at least from what I've seen, of keeping the Child on her left arm freeing the right. I feel very close to her, to the mother, I have entrusted my family and my children, my loved ones and I pray for strength and patience. And then Saint Anthony of Padua is dear to me because he is the saint who protects the search for lost things; my mother and the elders told me, that if you lost something you had to ask him to find it: I ask him to help me to try to find and keep calm. Not often, but every now and then! A particular saint that of my name day, on 13 June of each year, one of the conclusions, the end of school exams. In fact I also don't give up celebrating the second Saint Anthony, 17 January, the one with the pig. In June I celebrate and honor my intellectual part, in January my animal; so as to be covered. Among other things, the icon of this saint with the pig and the fire, identified for some reason as the protector of animals, symbolizes the privilege of the Franciscans who managed the hospitals, breeding pigs for health reasons. They needed the fat for poultices and ointments required for various medications for the evils of the time including cuts, burns, skin diseases and 'shingles'. A little more about the common 'protector of animals' or the traditional date for salami: the suitable time for slaughter and processing, in the cold, of pork in agricultural homes.

The paradox of waging war to obtain peace!
Wars or their perception, the choice of war, are not generally appre-

ciated by people, they are not appreciated or desired by those who fight but are liked and extremely useful to the lords who command, create the conditions and impose them: the only ones who make a profit. Peace is achieved by avoiding and refusing to make wars! We must be firm and resolute in this belief.

I look at my wife and it moves me how she likes to take care of the grown children and the well weaned: she likes to take care of them as if they were still little children. It's a feeling that I share. We know that every day that passes takes us further away from them, and that while they will no longer need us; we will however increasingly need to feel their caresses and their look that simply asks to confirm our affection. We can no longer protect them, reassure them, but we can always guarantee that we will be there whenever they ask and they need us.

Sometimes I think all the gods have always been only likenesses that are useful to justify man's folly. Even before himself when he beco-mes aware.

The talent of the artist is the ability to find and describe not what you see but what you feel inside. As for the ability to fall in love, you lose slipping into the habit.
Habits protect us from the uncertainties of life like traveling to a new place, seeing different views, meeting new people, facing new ideas, taking risks; they protect us from the excitement, joy of exultation from disappointment, from pain. Comfortably abstracting taking walks at dawn and dusk, insisting in the nostalgia, persisting in the bitter-ness. With habit the spirit slowly withers. To limit oneself to mental fatigue is lack of courage, unjustifiable but an irresistible temptation.

Governments, banks, institutions exist because they should serve the people, to address and ensure the requirements and the needs of ordinary human beings. As with everything only governments can, occasionally, make gestures of justice. What in the end do they care

about the populace? About the populace? They are and remain rational cold forces, hard, which can break up and destroy people's lives
without remorse or any afterthought. And money is everything!
Scientists should always be at the service of a commercial activity. A
scientist who tries to do everything on his owe, to cure both the business and the development of his science is a disaster, he would live
his whole life in the courts. All governments, all companies and banks
agree with this. A scientist should receive his salary and feel comfor-
table, do research, handing over his inventions and discoveries to
companies and proceed with his work. For this there are universities,
the scientific community: everything is organized like this.
A craftsperson is different producing and processing: if he produces
well he sells and earns and then is bought out and his idea yields
more from the system. If the idea proves to be good but isn't feasible
the craftsperson earns little to cover the cost. He fails and doesn't
get any help. Then the bank buys the idea and improves it, optimizing
and manufacturing and of course earning. Something can also be left
for him.
Only talent is always on sale, it is the soul of business.

The heart and soul of business, as if all that can destroy people in the
name of profit and interest in opportunity could have a soul and a
heart, like banks institutions and governments could have a soul and
a heart.
A secular world, (also one governed by the church) a mixture of conflicting egos, voted to interest, to business, to the cult of personality,
indifferent to major general issues, the needs of the masses who are
just tools, to be used to solicit feelings, cheap labor, slaves to the global economy. Any type of unity can be possible; no kind of global economy can be possible with parity between the components: the system works as long as there is someone to be exploited, or if there
aren't or are insufficient, they are created.
Today, though it happens periodically, the economies are in pieces.
These gentlemen who are part of it, deep down are dependent on
war to support or save their economies and their regimes. They sit
there clinging to their privileges and their prejudices, to the arrogance
of their opinions sowing confusion, fomenting hysteria to distract
people while remaining secure in their position: sooner or later they

will find a pretext, throw good sense overboard they will govern the economic chaos and will benefit from some war.
Wars avoid revolutions: revolutions undermine the consolidated balance of power, are dangerous for them, for the money oligarchy.
In all ages and historically noted epochs and in all countries, the Jews handled money, in the service of the government in power. Collectors of money then burdened with exorbitant taxes. When government debts became excessive they created racial laws. Jews were driven out and welcomed back by almost everyone. Every possession was sequestered and removed over and over again. Their only competition was the Catholic Church, which was split and divided when in the Middle Ages it was forbidden to lend at interest (which although removed from the individual in first person, did not however prevent the creation of the state bank) and, again, in the Middle Ages, in the community of Lombardy and Tuscany. But as talent is always for sale they have always taken up again in the service of some other government.
After a war, most of the population thinks it could have been avoided. They blame everyone: anyone who formerly took the decisions and anyone who made every possible sacrifice to humor or save them. They even blame the people and the soldiers and the fighters: all those who have in fact taken part, fought suffered as a result of these decisions. People will always deny and elect to power anyone who makes them hope it won't affect them this time. Anyone promising drastic change to restore and maintain peace.
But when the First World War was declared and then also the Second, the streets were full of fervent supporters. Even for them it should have meant that... if this time goes well hopefully there won't be another. But history teaches us that a long war is always won by the rich and that peace does not last because the new generations forget; at most the war will be far from our home, possibly near other people's homes: we sell and gain they die and suffer.

Anything is possible, often very unlikely, sometimes downright unwise.

A man contains billions of creatures. Even the cells contain organisms that were once independent. Yet all these organisms would be extre-

mely boring, unable to surprise and amuse.
Machines are basically even more stupid. Maybe that's why man welcomes everything unsettling invasive, disturbing with pleasure, anything that would engage him in an attempt to eliminate it but which nevertheless doesn't permit him to control it (... for this reason it must be eliminated!).

The certainty of punishment: but does finding the culprit of a crime restore the disturbed equilibrium? Resurrect the dead or heal the victim? Does it restore dignity to the offended stability and security to the tricked and duped victims of burglaries or muggings? Righteousness, which is based on the certainty of being punished, is perhaps something different than revenge without great satisfaction?
The punishment can never be equal to the guilt.
Is it more important to punish the guilty or discourage the crime?
Is it more important to have the certainty of punishment or the law?
To know for sure when you can be right or wrong, to know quickly if it creates a dispute, wouldn't it be more useful and productive to be forced to read and listen to news broadcasts where you proclaim the horror and scandal of a crime or misuse of injustice and then demonstrate, on the sidelines, quietly asking relatives or winners and those who having reason ... after five, ten or twenty years are you satisfied? Invariably the answer is: no.
The journalist who is asking the question seems, to me, to be an idiot. Like the one who asks how much the mother of the dead man is suffering or the desperate person who has lost home and family in the earthquake!

Most of our life runs parallel to us, someone or something, independently of us, defines our immediate and subsequent future, changes the course of events and influences what we are or will become.

The church after having encoded the word of the father and son, the Old and New Testament, closed the door to the Holy Spirit, protector of free thought of the word itself, the gift of God. It closed with the prophets and with the word. Whatever had to be said has been said

what had to change has been changed.
It seems that the new Pope Francis has reopened its doors to humility and listening and then to discussion as indicated by the saint whose name he took. Who knows?

The allure of the megalithic circles: male and female, light and dark,
the basic seasons, summer and winter with the sun and the solstice
moon respectively coming from one side to the other in the circle,
opposite and complementary: in fact so as not to create a difference
with the other solstice it appears on opposite sides.
Every 19 years the moon is located at exactly the same point in its
periodic oscillation. This means that observed from a single point the
moon reappears exactly in that identical position every nineteen
years representing a lunar cycle. Again every nineteen years, the time
marked by the movement of the sun and the moon coincides. One
year cannot be divided into only 29 lunar days (lunar month) but nineteen years yes.
Common astronomical coincidences in everything having a cyclical
movement: sooner or later go into phase or into opposition. Knowing
the periods of motion are enough to solve simple calculations. But it
is exciting to observe the application, and admire the intent of the effort to document it and to think it dates back over many thousands of
years. It has been a very costly search. It required the necessary and
indispensable creation of the first religions and churches. How many
dead were sacrificed to the research. Even today there are those
who follow cults.

The pantheon of ancient Roman represented perhaps the greatest
result of use and integration of religions in the power system of an
immense multiracial multi-ethnic and multi-religious empire. There
were a profusion of gods, for all and protection of all. Gods overlapped each other without prejudice. A local deity became imperial simply by changing the name to the Roman one. For the more extreme
laity, there was always the emperor. Even he rose to the status of divinity as it was for the pharaohs. A good servant would acquire
rewards in heaven. All the gods had human attributes or were recognizable in nature, plants, animals.

The God of the Christians was uncomfortable at first because without a face without attributes, unique and unknowable, invisible and unassailable even the emperor could be called into question. This is also why I believe, Constantine favorably welcomed the figure of Christ, as he brought to earth a recognizable God, the Father (of the Jews), and the son of God was born and died. The Holy Spirit would also be there, no longer gave so much trouble: no more oracles or prophets, the wise men and seers. Christianity certainly did not disdain the unifying symbols such as the east-west orientation of graves in cemeteries, with the path of the sun. Self-discipline and ritual sacrifice, came from the cult of Mithras and is common to Freemasonry. Devotion to the Virgin Mary or Isis, the Moon and the Earth, mother and children. Roman gods are parts, attributes of the divine, and as such worshiping you also worship the same idea of the divine spark in every human, represented by the invisible, unknowable, elusive, insubstantial, soul.

The Romans were not fanatics, they were observant of shared principles, patriotism, courage, Roman honor; the Christians were, have been and still are (although more nuanced) fanatics. They have often demonstrated this, going to martyrdom or disputing Pelagius who claimed that a man had to freely and spontaneously select the God he wanted to guide him on the path to heaven, a little like what happened for the pagans but instead in the body and in the teachings of the church. Every man is a separate entity against the universality of the church. Free will beyond the control exercised by the Holy Spirit. If God created the universe, the universe belongs to him; if God wanted the Church to represent him then the Church is the representative (and exercises) the power of God over the entire universe! Or you're with me or you're against me! If you don't obey the voice of the Lord (the Bible) you will be cursed ... The list of divine curses (taken from the book of Moses, Deuteronomy) is infinite for those who step out of line by sinning.

Talking about the Bible in any case it is not the Christians' *book* but *a book* of the Christians; rather it is the book of the Jews. Christians read the Gospels or should do so.

The book of Leviticus highlights a number of unclean animals and therefore not edible: ruminants without cloven hooves (for example rabbit or hare) or those that crawl. The ferret, the lizard weasels and rats all animals that are carriers of rabies, plague and disease that caused 'biblical' massacres in their time. The Bible contains a lot of scientific information by translating them into myths and parables and fairy tales. Some of its advice may be useful in particular conditions but certainly only for the fanatics, they can open it to read the signs of the day, or compare their own judgment with that of God. Everyone has direct access to the word of God and should not submit to church dogma.

Baptists, Calvinists Puritans, Anabaptists, Quakers, all subject to direct inspiration without the mediation of the church, at least not the one in Rome.

Catholic popes were right to want to prevent the vernacular translation, printing and wide dissemination of the Bible.

Transubstantiation, the great magic behind the Catholic rite: the Catholic must be deeply convinced, must blindly believe that the priest has the divine power to transform the host and wine into the body and blood of Jesus. And not symbolically. To not accept it and believe it simply means not being Catholic. Possibly you may be Protestant or Puritan. These however even though they are good Christians, hate everything that brings joy and happiness, from hair to clothing to music, to art.

At no time in the Bible is happiness spoken about, least of all as an objective. Fortunately, in the American community there is the tradition of allowing young people, while heavily indoctrinated and educated, as in an initiation rite, to travel without supervision or almost, in a real way, to accept all the dictates of their faith without reserve once and for all.

I prefer the Catholic view, the present, of the works required of the church: at least there is no doubt about siding with peace and solidarity; for tolerance and mercy, for the sharing of resources and for the correct use of the environment. If they didn't come from her, they would be almost unknown words and very little spoken in our society. I have no problem in accepting the dogma, like the constitution that states that the Italian state is 'right', 'social equality', 'founded on work', etc. Believe me it costs me more effort, perhaps excessive, but... everything is possible... and then the important thing is the effect of magic: if it is positive, why not?

I noticed that politicians who aspire to be elected don't really like to flaunt luxury, regardless of the money they have. People believe what they think they see. There are ways to enjoy luxury more efficiently and less visibly. Who permits it be seen and demonstrates it sees that it is appropriate for personal reasons to provide that image, not for policies requiring trust; perhaps to facilitate the identification of the attainable aspirations of ordinary people.

On the streets, at home, in shopping malls the sound of advertising fills the ears with music and words: *eat at this guy's...drink this... use this toothbrush... this other toothpaste is made for you, take advantage of the discount, go to the gym, test the car... people come in, come into the one place where you can see and enjoy all the wonders of the world...* In all this jumble of lies perhaps there is just one tiny truth, a little information to bring down the entire building. And instead it seems to me that people are mostly trusting. Also it seems to me that I am surrounded by people that basically, care about me.

Sometimes in order to obtain something good you must lie to people.

Logic permits the development of science fiction although often it would often meet with a paradox.

A paradox is a proposition that contradicts the real or more often alleged, logical mechanism. It is only an exercise in logic, which can be solved by applying a self-referential reasoning mechanism.

This statement is a lie! But is it true or false? I have called it true, so I assume it is true, then it is true. Don't be obsessed by the possible consequences of an unique action.

One thing is certain: the present, the here and now, right now in this exact way, it is safe and proven practical and real whatever that means. No butterfly trampled in Sydney or New York or Rome can change this. Maybe you can change the future but certainly not the present of this real and concrete world in all its nuances and dimensions.

The pure creationists (and I mean extremists, fundamentalists and fa-

natics) will never be interested in paleontology. For creationists who derive and take everything back to the Bible, dinosaurs should have been the animals drowned in the deluge but no later than 6 to 7,000 years ago. Only if there were at least one human skeleton in the middle of the dinosaur fossils it could prove they could be right.
I saw the movie *Jurassic Park*. I only made this observation: The upper Triassic was a damp, warm environment, full of insects that were excluded from the film. And it's not true that all dinosaurs became extinct, some have adapted by becoming birds. Maybe just all others were drowned in the universal flood.
The main difference between the Mesozoic and the Cenozoic period is not the absence of the dinosaurs but the presence of grass. With respect to the plants, grass has changed everything with its ability to quickly recover, which allowed for the extended grazing of mammals.
The Fundamentalists believe in violence. They kill people. For Presbyterians predestination is a dogma... they can however still be good people.

In my years of teaching I've noticed a curious thing: the best guys, the most well-liked by the teachers in their final years of high school, never break through. They collapse.
Instead, the wacky, eccentrics, misfits, loners, the peripheral elements of a good class have a serious chance of success in the various fields and sectors: singers, actors, scientists, doctors politicians, etc.
As for evolution, the least successful organisms don't thrive. They remain present and inconspicuous until everyone else suffers a meltdown because their conformity disallows adaptation to change. These are extinguished; others gradually come out and fill the world occupying the empty spaces left.
The experimental and provisional method of science should make sure students are not certain about anything rather than providing cement for some. The teacher learns from the students, their questions, sometimes even from their misunderstandings or from the deliberately idiotic rambling and interpretations made in jest or provocation.

The White Cliffs of Dover or the Dolomites are the result of the work of billions and billions of fossilized creatures that lived over generations monotonous and organized: we could call them conformists. They are not extinct. They are organisms that still thrive in the same way as always but elsewhere. The Dolomites are the durable and residual legacy of those lives. The human race with all its technology doesn't seem capable of leaving a lasting legacy that is comparable to these (and if they existed, not even the aliens who would have visited the earth).

A military parade, as an aerobatic demonstration is not real war but simple displays of force, such as for the Olympic athletes and do not guarantee high military performance.

Animals that inhabit inhospitable semi-arid areas do so in a smart way: they never hang out together on pastureland but they do it in small groups. They graze continually on the shoots but never shave the pasture to zero; when they are a few too many some distance themselves, so as not to change the balance that sustains them and the area itself. Any ecosystem is like a dance with a choreography that develops in a complicated way, a ballet of needs, a balance of appetites.
How do these beasts without a thinking brain maintain this balance when intelligent beings such as humans are unable to? Evolution is not an arrow flying straight from the dinosaurs to the penguins: it is a kind of radiation out in all directions from innovations in search of free spaces. Normally in a healthy ecosystem there are none since all the available niches are occupied by specialized species and novelty does not take root. In step with evolution though extinction continues; sometimes it is a mass phenomenon that leaves many empty niches. This fact determines the distortion, radical change, the evolution of the entire ecosystem, in the space of a few tens of millions of years. Science should work methodically, gathering evidence and data and then analyzing them only after expressing hypotheses of falsification in the field. If the hypothesis is resistant to attempts to prove its unreliability then it is good and solid and can become a theory. A good scientist should avoid hasty conclusions. But no conclusions do not get funding.

That all germs carry diseases is not even a theory: it is absolutely unproven and only the best explanation available to date on which the
goodness of people bet their life. Surely it is valid, for most of many
diseases.
Yet it is a fact that scientists are continually in search of glory, they
jump out with more or less stupid ideas and try to demonstrate in an
inverse process. Yet the evolution of science shows that all are needed: the acrobats, the drudges, visionaries and the investigators. People who prefer elegance, or the affirmation of the idea, the correctness of the contents.
Take for example commonly held information: the dinosaurs were
cold-blooded animals that died of cold. The body temperature can be
constant or variable, it can be adjusted from inside or outside according to the metabolism at rest. Homeothermy maintains a constant
temperature (humans). Eterothermy depends on the external environment: (hibernating animals). Then there may be variations in the
resting metabolism. The animals, in different physical and environmental conditions can change from one state to another characteristic, may even change sex if necessary or with age. And it is far more
complicated than that, in the face of those who own and spread certainties validated by the scientific community. But the dinosaurs what
kind were they? Who knows! At least I don't know for sure.

If you request something from a bureaucratic structure, and they
don't want to concede, relax, pretend you believe they haven't understood the request and start all over again from the beginning of the
speech: repeat all the points and important issues with maddening
precision. Then eventually begin again: stress and take them out of
their boredom, as do the vendors, sooner or later they will give up.
Hide your anger and humiliation, keep your cool.
Easier said than done!

As long as I'm alive I want to know, simply know, continue to learn; I'm
happy when I get home at night and I can say: today I learned something new.

I wonder what God was like before man, and admitted, not conceding there weren't and are not yet, other forms of life.

It was without sensory organs, thus perceived the universe as its own emanation. It was devoid of language, however, omniscient and therefore expert in celestial mechanics in chemical biology and anything else that was created and took form little my little as it existed. Expanding or breathing in cycles, it created the universe. He did not age, because he had not created time. Could not know emotions because he had not yet created them. God didn't even know good and evil until he created man and woman to define them. Could not feel alone because he was everything. Could not even know the concept of loneliness having always lacked company. He was a unique being, nature being nature, that had to however evolve, but could do so only by increasing his awareness that is by creating things that would allow self-awareness. He did not need science, but had to measure his omniscience. Thus he created it.
After billions and billions of years finally, he decided or it happened, he created man... and became GOD.

Nature is never man's friend, and moreover of any other living thing! Our beloved planet is teeming with life forms and they are all, always, committed to killing each other.
It is disconcerting that this simple reality is knowingly ignored by man and never willingly admitted.
Tradition teaches but cannot be taught. Traditional knowledge is learned from the masters of life that come his way.
A master doesn't fill the mind of children, pupils, with notions but stimulates them to seek their own path and find their own truth. Everyone tries and must learn to develop and use critical thinking that will allow them to judge for themselves what is said and written, and what is reasonable and acceptable, and if, you must instead blindly accept, delegating and leaving the so-called 'wise' to decide what is true and right.
The religious have always despised the world and the way they lived and at the same time feared, which is why they needed a God who absolved them after they've been judged, however, good. And for

each of them their own God is supreme and cannot, of course, be otherwise.

How many divinities are there on the earth? Is it necessary that the gods have a gender? And therefore a limited role? Is it required that the gods have an image that permits us to identify with them and love them as humans? You can love with human feeling, with passion, even though he understands, he cannot be defined, seen, touched, imagined? And since for humans, love and passion are feelings that are anything but stable and durable, can any GOD represented be loved infinitely and indefinitely?

The philosophers of ancient Greece and all civilizations, of all times, have tried and continually try to transcend the real world so as not to be involved and to master it, judging, misleading and lying about all the schools that were not, their own.

If the common and ultimate good is the flourishing of humanity and all its components, if the divinity needs to be worshiped and propitiated, then it must be right that everyone is free to interpret the deity in their own way and according to their ability, all free to follow their own religion or philosophy of letting individual thought vanish and evolve as a contribution to the common purpose.

Ordinary people think about the world they live in as a real place, visible, perceptible, full of unpredictable powers that constantly need to be propitiated in some way. And usually we always only think of ourselves. Everyone sees the world as an imperfect reflection of an ideal simple world they yearn, building billions of individual truths that everyone seeks, and finds, beneath the surface of the world where we exist simultaneously, the truths of all cults and all philosophies. To learn to think should be part of everyone's education like learning to control hunger, ambition and instinct.

Each student should be stimulated to personally want to find their own way, in the privacy of their own selves. You learn from books and studies but free thought must go beyond the limits of what is already constructed and accepted. Imposed teachings can never be part of our being until they have been rediscovered within our consciousness and awareness. Every one experiences the world differently.

I think all religions and all philosophies are useful guides but wrong, simply because they are partial and incomplete. They are brilliant facets of a single diamond. Wrong every time they suppose there is no other truth but their own.

I think that beyond my strength only my need exists. I want my freedom.

Memory is a mechanism of simple accumulation: memories may comprise a witness but they can never directly produce the results of intuition, typically female abilities in which our genes are impregnated. All human designers, of any existing mechanism didn't have to invent anything: it was and is already present in nature, from the wings of birds for aircraft, the woodpecker's reinforced skull for submarines to every other 'invention' arising simply from careful observation and intuition.

An idea may lead to a procedure. Rationality and logic, used in institutional instruction has the scope of containing independence and maintaining ignorance since this creates dependence, from which the power of authority is derived.

Orthodoxy presupposes the citation a priori of the norms established by authorities who are the self-appointed custodians of truth such as the religious and the so-called scientific community that move within dogmatic patterns.

The man who believes himself the apotheosis of nature does not agree to become a simply part but thinks he should be able to adapt it to himself twisting and degrading it to a simple tool: no longer *man in the world*, but *the world of man*.

Our mind is used to working schematically, rationally observing phenomena to explain, often it prevents us from grasping the essence of reality.

I wonder how to explain, beyond the complex chemical and physical mechanisms expressed as complicated equations, mechanistic approximations, sensory experiences such as the sensitive highs of drugs or ecstasy, more or less mystical.

The official scientists still refuse to accept their irrational side; they don't consider it important, a simple personal complication. But the irrational side of personality exists and is part of humanity, present and unpredictable it escapes any attempt at rationalization. For example, the propensity for violence, or the uncontrolled response to stimuli. The human brain permits imagination. Science is therefore nothing but an arbitrary conception of the universe.

My cultural journey has evolved in the opposite way: from real and rational values of learned chemistry, and those of the environment, which are still partially rational and of nature studied and directly experimented on, to finally seeking the symbolic value that originally produced alchemy. Alchemy: science in evolution where the symbolic overlapping of natural facts, where man was one of the many expressions, was the stimulus for research and experimentation, tending to demonstrate that man and nature were basically the same thing, like all things that exist.

Alchemy: research of the identification of man with the entire universe. The earth is not enough! But man is still at the center and must be. Even today, aliens and ghosts, angels, supernatural beings, though intelligent and good are imagined as similar to man, anthropomorphic. Only if the aliens are bad, ferocious beyond human ferocity, unpredictable, primitive, essentially demons, then they are identified as monsters, and still today as in the days of the Babylonians, or in the Middle Ages, often with horns, similar to insects, however, natural unknown and formidable.

Man changes, man is made of matter; matter changes.

Natural laws, invisible and therefore spiritual govern man and matter.

In seeking them we were looking for a better interpretation of the unifying message of God. The attempt was not blasphemous but certainly not manageable and thus free thought, which affirmed the uniqueness of natural things, has been artificially guided towards division and incompatibility. Between the rationalism and theology of the two faces of Janus or rationally every coin, both denying the supernatural, that is, the unknown or rather what is inexplicable at the time, because it has not been adequately subjected to 'human' superiority.

Blind is he who is unable to embrace the whole, basking in the contemplation and admiration of his perfect and thorough knowledge of one part. Generally he neglects giving evidence of the marginal details, the shadow areas that he couldn't have failed to notice appearing as if that knowledge was truly complete.

During a trip to the city that I love, Venice, I remember thinking there were over 400 bridges but tourists knew and visited the three on the Grand Canal and perhaps some other and that's it. The whole is much larger than apparent knowledge.

Proudly the scientist or religious man would not risk a bath of humility, if not of humiliation, faced with a society that exalts and supports him and to which he belongs.

The man in question would think: why give up reporting on my own shortcomings; if others are so smart, at least as much as I am, make them work and find them. Such is the way of the world!

The ethical methods of the scientific community are basically founded on dishonesty. Espionage, plagiarism, theft of ideas, exploitation of the insights of young scholars, appropriation of merits and especially funding without which the ideas and prestige cannot be translated into the concrete.

I smile thinking of horoscopes, magicians, sorcerers, witches and the like, of the occult sciences; charlatans whose achievements are supported by the naive! Nonetheless you can't deny that for thousands of years they have attracted the gullible that "say they don't believe", that they don't know the rules and science, but will seek confirmation and possibly immediate benefits. Obviously it isn't science. It's an approach not even opposed, despite being fundamentally heretical: only slightly marginalized, because it doesn't in fact place the 'system' in doubt or in crisis. Social psychology, generally positive, generally at low costs in the service of those seeking their identity, and their own advantage, in the interactive mechanisms of the universe, attributing a privileged place: the universe cannot ignore them!

When the earth's crust melts then the iron particles begin to rotate to align with the magnetic field; when magma cools, then they stop, magnetically oriented, in the position they've assumed.

By analyzing the magnetic alignment in a rock core, you can perform geological dating. It is like counting the rings of a tree. A magnetic inversion corresponds to about 26,000 years: the poles switch places, the north becomes south and vice versa.

Every body absorbs the light that invests it or partly reflects or refracts it, or does all three things at once.

If you see red it is because the organism absorbs everything and reflects red. If it absorbs energy, consequently it will emit energy in a different form. If it doesn't do these things it would be invisible to the eye and to instruments.

The stars are studied using spectrographs that make an 'electrocardiogram', for example by recording the peaks of light emitted: when a material is ionized, for example because of the heat, it emits light at different wavelengths. Different materials at equal conditions emit different wave spectra, characteristics and specifics. The result, applied for example to a star, analyzed in the cosmic vacuum without interference of absorption, permits you to understand exactly what materials it is composed.

A diamond absorbs little light and reflects a lot from the outside surface where the surfaces of internal planes are at favorable angles, the absorbed light is then both reflected and refracted, causing the sparkle that makes it valuable.

Glass absorbs little, reflects and refracts little because it is not a crystal: if we crumble it then it becomes more visible because the absorptive and reflective surfaces increase; if we put it in water which has an equivalent or higher refractive index (a thicker liquid) then the glass disappears, literally, from sight.

Most natural materials are composed of fibers that are visible only as a result of mutual optical interference. Paper tissues, linen, cotton are normally white: if we put them in oil they disappear or almost because the oil fills the gaps between the fibers and reduces the surface area. Except of course unless they are impregnated with colored pigments. Even meat is red or pink, just because of the iron that colors the blood that permeates it; jellyfish and krill are transparent.

A game of mirrors can make something appear or disappear from the point it is found to make it perceptible to someone else's eyes who observes and receives the light.

The magic of illusionists always fishes in the natural laws and exploits them, and demonstrates the effects; skillfully arranging them in shows where they are not expected or predicted.

I ask myself if knowledge has never really satisfied anyone? Or rather is it necessarily a source of dissatisfaction, to demonstrate our ignorance and our limitations?

When a result, the goal, is almost achieved "when the feast day" approaches, then one realizes how the efforts appear to be inconclusive; when the stress and adrenaline no longer sustain you, when the wait is nearing its conclusion, you find yourself apathetic and without motivation.

On long awaited Saturday or Sunday you are sick and tired. Leopardi was right (Italian poet and philosopher, 1798 to 1837).

I'm getting old, slowly but surely: I notice because sometimes I pause surprised that I'm attempting to remember things. I make an effort to remember the details of my life, to track down the first memory: the rooster as large as I am who looks at me, swinging on the branch of the fig tree above the bench (I had to have been very light); gooseberries at the well (before I was four years-old. I know because then I moved house). Then games in the snow in short trousers, my mother massaged my legs, purple from the cold, in front of the kerosene stove. One way to school in the morning, in the snow going by way of the hotel Pavone shortcut. One evening at the music school Saint Catherine, questions and prizes in sandwiches. A nightmare linked to the cold, at Christmas, in the winter, the Orion constellation: I have never been able to perceive whether it is recurring or only fixed in memory. Before I was ten to twelve years old, a memorable trip with the Seicento, camping in Bled, fishing and the rain, the car won't start and the attempt at communication; in one or more unknown and strange tongues to buy replacement gas ... Another trip before 14 to16 years old with the 1100R the overloaded roof lost the load after fifteen kilometers it had to be rebuilt. College? A game of tennis on cement, a red-skinned Superior, irritable and perfectly unlikable and false, who had something against me because I had no respect for authority. The friend who stole the money and, like Pinocchio, buried it.
There are few memories that appear without effort: A key argument with my father when I was 18 years old. There are few that can also be easily recalled. Before the age of 25 I remember very little even though these were my formation years: I left home at 14 and returned at 25. My mother was happy with my return, she had suffered as a result of my absence and would not take her eyes off me. And she didn't ever again. With hindsight, it means that everything flowed, was momentarily important but not really meaningful.
Over 60 years of life and very few powerful moments. At the entrance to a church on my wedding day, forced by a slap on the shoulder from my cousin Fausto: the last doubt. My wife tells me she is pregnant two hours after sex, the waiting and the birth of my daughter, but without wanting to know the sex; the first image in the delivery room, seemed like ET. On leaving the hospital, the immaculate snow, 22 °C

below zero. My son at three months, nighttime preparation of the
baby bottle with the 'glue' to help him keep the milk.
Twenty in all? Events that seemed impossible to forget took place
while, smells flavors of things tasted, the excitement of things heard,
sudden revelations, thoughts also actions, motivations and hopes.
I don't fear the world or even disdain it! I became a man who burns
with passion: indignation, revolt, pride. Without being either a saint or
being strongly balanced in my convictions I never really understood
what others expected of me until the responsibility towards my children clarified every doubt imposing choice, forging me day after day.
No memory, truly strong deviates from their presence, my children
and my wife! Faded memories even about my parents. Yet now I try,
with intensity, to reconstruct the path of my memories and I know it
is a futile effort.
The old stuff is taken to landfills and left there, it shouldn't be allowed
to over-clutter the site of present life, the everyday.

The simple fact that a man speaks in the name of a god doesn't mean
he's telling the truth.
The tragedy of a liar proven wrong even only once, is enormous: if a
man knows or doubts, deep inside, to have been or to be a liar or an
imposter, he will spend a lifetime wishing he was believed certain that
a minimum of doubt will reign anyway. Even worse they will attribute
the same ability to lie to others out of interest and they will never
completely trust anyone anymore.
All men lie a little or a lot, all interpret a role and we only judge others
by our standards, attributing them our ambitions exclusively, our ve-
nality, our ways of being and our own passions. Perhaps this is the
reason, rational if not instinctive, there are so many wars and abuses
of power.
I thought of the strange situation of women worldwide, forced by
their state to always give strength and comfort to men, to give birth
to them, feed them, raise them, teach them, always the stronger of
the two sexes increasingly forced by their nature to give; always being
forced to move, seamlessly, from the state of daughters to mothers
from needing their mother until being or representing, the mother
herself.
Children think of their parents only in relation to themselves and not

as people. Only advanced maturity succeeds in making them glimpse them as ordinary people.

Sometimes I feel tired, I think I've had enough... but tomorrow... tomorrow... Something new... interesting...

If the elderly never let go, how do the young ever get a chance?

I don't do a lot of charity work, only a few concrete interventions that are of some immediate use, but I never refuse to answer whoever asks me for donations, with the little that I can, very little because they are many and not all are truthful. I don't care whether it is true or false; those who have the courage to ask must be answered not judged, at least not by me. Poverty should be defeated by the intervention of justice and equity with no social marginalization.

I was different once; maybe I was an asshole or at least considered as such looking at myself today. Today I've learned to assume the responsibilities that exceed myself, but I haven't changed, I've always made the choices that made sense to me; have changed my behavior, not me, and today a few choices make sense to me that are different than those of that time; that's all.

I've long since ceased to listen to the end of the news or so-called programs that go deeper: of the twenty minutes five will be reserved for the political situation among others submitted exclusively by the 'power' currently in place whatever it is; three minutes are reserved for the opposition especially if they don't pose a serious threat to the established order. All the rest is commentary, or sensationalism, presented in order to create the expected and predictable, well conducted, alarmism in the ignorant population unaware or at least uninvolved.
But who really cares to know that in a remote village, as a rule in southern Italy, a couple of elderly people were kidnapped or a girl was ra-

ped by an immigrant or gypsy of the moment? And again immediately
after to lessen the impact, if Belen or the actress who is unknown to
most people, whose image is to be launched, has changed boyfriend
or has remade her tits?
The journalists' salary and that of the newspaper editors, the success
of contemporary artists of every time, depends on who pays them
and nothing should interfere.
The opinions that really should have an impact on current morals are
reduced censored and condemned to oblivion.
All certainly know that the memory of the news presented with emphasis will be that guy or Caius has been investigated and therefore
potentially is not honest. The subsequent denials or claims of innocence will be worth nothing. People don't notice. The news won't
have the same relevance. I'm surprised that the Catholic Pope is left
outside, this Pope Francis, who punches at the system loudly affirming his dissent. He cannot be totally held hostage, now in the present, and therefore finds many apparent, supporters but it is certain
that he too will sooner or later be reduced to oblivion.

Business: produces gains for the self at any cost, to the detriment of
the earnings of others who would be at our expense. And ethics? I'm
unable, not cynical enough. I'd sell everything and start again to fight
to reaffirm myself?

The powers that govern global commerce, if they can, absorb and use
the church or, not being able to, oppose or make them clash and the
people who identify them, generate wars of reduction and productive
investment, a long way from home.

The function of the press and of the masters of life today but maybe
always, from time to time have been able to take along the mass of
the people, it is a matter of putting up with the state of affairs, existing in a given period, manipulating and misinforming or giving biased
information from the pulpit, public opinion.
Once it was heresy to oppose the power and absolute knowledge of
the Catholic Church, today a heretic doesn't conform to the will of the

new financial and economic powers that are often managers of the
various existing churches.
The big question is: who pays their salary permitting their lifestyle?
Omission or alteration, like emphasizing facts and reality comprise
the stories, now briefly summarized in titles and subtitles. Today, it is
a method, a constant of the corporation, totally dependent and submissive, of journalists and writers, of radio and television authors (it
isn't understood why in Italy there is still a registry of journalists, fascism created it to control information, and what is it used for if not always for that reason). The result is the spread of information, biased
and partial images, often only partly and not completely truthful, of
reality.
The fourth power! Illusions created on purpose to prevent people
from perceiving, knowing, seeking the truth of things or to push the
evolution of the situation in a certain way.
The process is the initial statement of half-truths that then, with time,
will be reduced again and again from passage to passage, with the result that the public is provided a pleasing story on the top layers, in
fact replacing the real story, misinforming instead of *informing*.
I checked each thought in contrast to mine and therefore to yours, it
seems it can be presented as false or malicious.
The communicators are at the service of the owners, even if they
themselves, certainly many, in good faith don't even realize this; they
don't recognize it as such; they consider themselves serious professionals and are convinced of having integrity being free and autonomous ...
Power, its priorities, its goals, objectives, statements, dogmas and
slogans are, as always, at all times, supported by science and the
scientific community and disseminated by various schools of thought,
scientific, artistic, environmentalist, etc. useful at the time; that is
they must let people know of the future long-term objective what is
today considered useful to know and who has the job of confirming it.
All our claims of freedom, democracy, are only an illusion; nothing is
as it seems and even, it seems, America, the historic symbol of freedom of thought and action, the new world for a new era, appears to
be a totalitarian state like any other.

One day I was sitting on the riverbank, rather to be truthful a fairly impetuous stream, which is called Corsenna, near Bardi in the province of Parma, the town I come from. That day, I had climbed up to try to capture the nervous and delicious Fario trout, as I did when I was a boy, admitting that I'm still able to fish them, today it seems they are no more; at that time they populated those places together with small shrimp that inhabited the various pools and waterfalls; I paused to enjoy the silence broken occasionally by the sounds from the distant road, which didn't conflict with the natural sounds of the environment.

Perhaps it is precisely then that I developed one of the first approaches to this diary that only now, with the memory, I can define as important. Maybe then it seemed like this but apparently, the thought has never left me, and the seed was deeply rooted in me.

I watched the water flowing and I told myself that what was below me had gone for good, I couldn't do anything about it; in another place, and in another time it would have comprised the present, eroded and washed out, but here no more. Only pools directly in front of me on my path had some importance, in fact it is there that I could bathe and find the fish I sought. If the fish had found it, then they'd no longer be there and in the flowing water beyond, everything would be changed.

I thought these waters and these pools represented my difficult present and yet they were full of possibilities and feasible actions but at that precise moment, neither before nor after.

Looking up at the pools and waterfalls higher up I saw them full of water, perhaps fish, maybe shrimp, full of hypothesis and activity but at that time they were not within my reach; they would be so when the water reached me, time passing, in the pools in front of me or if I had moved towards them to reach them.

Perhaps those waters represented a future that would change my present defining my past, as I would have changed the present and the future of someone else as soon as the water had run before and beyond me, if I had only and simply observed. Who knows if even higher up another fisher wouldn't have been deprived of the fish I sought in the waters that reached me, or would have polluted my possible swim, by urinating and contaminating the clear, cool natural waters, awaited and admired. It would still be natural, but even to think about it, not very pleasant. However I hadn't hesitated to wash my flushed face. The waters seemed, I wanted them to be, clean.

I'm not a humanist, a philosopher; my foundation is technical and scientific and I have a pragmatic, empirical and experimental character. For this reason, perhaps, at some point, I felt the need to make use of my cultural background with that part I realized I lacked. I needed to think, to learn, to look deeper.

As a child I was always very curious, I wanted to know everything and I thought I could do this by taking apart alarm clocks and watches that I could no longer put back together. I realized that behind science and its different almost watertight parts, there had to be a unifying path.

I've read so much, everything, without prejudice and so I thought it is because I don't like nonsense, and mostly fools and I don't want to feel I'm the same.

I have always found points of profound thinking, in every reading even in the most fanciful, also in novels other than essays and even in men's and women's magazines, although I've sometimes become aware of it only much later, when in fact I began to think. Out of the habit of spending time with humanistic thoughts-philosophic-socializing I realized that now instead, in practice, I'm forgetting the scientific basis underpinning my cultural background: I have to force myself to retrieve it also for you who will perhaps be reading me one day without boring myself and boring you and to go over everything, selecting a few concepts.

I'm a chemist and geologist: a good geologist, despite being specialized in petrography and thus substantially still a chemist: I became a geochemist and from industry to the environment and to mingling and interaction between the two sectors, the pace was quick and automatic. My professional career developed in this sector, well ahead of its time.

My technical training leads me to rational thought that always needs concrete and real demonstration, which is obtained in the research laboratory, testing and experimentation. Geology has taught me to see the whole in different time scales. Instead, my personal and humanistic self-study allows me to glimpse and evaluate the philosophical aspects at the foundation of the evolution of critical and scientific thinking and to accept the theories to be tested, as possible until proven contrary.

I have taught science for a lifetime and I have come to doubt that I
ever managed to convey the basic concepts.
Here below I intend to try to re propose them but, hell, come to think
of it there are so many: where would I begin? Yet they are the basis
of my free thought! Perhaps they could also become part of yours. A
good student always overtakes a good teacher! One also teaches and
mostly to be able to continue learning; first you learn to teach better
then to continue to learn from those who, having learned, have developed new knowledge beyond ours.

Who knows if when an amoeba dies another remembers it, at least a
little about it?
It is not simple to summarize sixty-odd years of life experiences of
ideas and reasoning: it would take sixty or more years to speak about
the reality you are attempting to express and to suggest the contents. And if I try to summarize everything in this way?
The association is stronger than an individual and rivalry.
A large association is more powerful than a small one.
From bacteria to higher animals, the caveman to industrial globalization, even for man the animal, the law of nature has been proven to
be confirmed. Interaction (between active parameters in space and
time) exchange of energy with formation and evolution of dynamic
equilibrium comprises nature, therefore everything!!!
For the principle of action and reaction and the law of universal gravitation every body in space attracts all others with equal force, proportional to the mass and function of the square of the distance and in
fact pushes them away as well; the equilibrium of these forces defines the mutual position on the surface of present reality.
In the long run a few million billion years it will all be melted into a big
black hole, and a new big bang will begin. The attraction and the reaction provoking differentials in pressure and temperature between two
points, which are at the origin of the movement. The End.
I believe that's everything. A little too simplistic? Maybe it's like when
the environmentalists (sui generis) speak of the world or of man, as if
the same was in a measurable cube with few interfering parameters
and perhaps moreover a closed system and in perfect immutable
equilibrium! A little too simplistic to be adequate.
When you study something you should always impose three condi-

tions: if I hold something firm and vary something else, what happens to the third thing that depends on these two? Applied to life assuming this symbolic meaning of the number three: every time I make a choice I have to ask myself where I have come from, where I want to go and what would happen if I went in the other direction, to the other arm of the Y.

My training in chemical and thermodynamics and then geology and partly naturalistic, has familiarized me and permits me to consider individual events but also to place them, the events, on a large-scale with ease and then to exceed the limit and regardless of the limitations of the details that instead constrain observers.

I must teach you how to do it like this: it's like looking at a picture with a scene of the city, full of places, plants, animals, people, market stalls, signs and shops, sky, clouds, splashes of sunlight, foregrounds and backgrounds. Lacking however smells scents and stinks and the sensation of heat. Here it is, though, that from here you can go down and enlarge, study and improve every visible detail, probably hundreds, in turn composed of details that appear only after isolation and magnification of the figure.

But we must never forget that the whole picture, a whole that now appears complex and on an ample scale in turn represents only a detail of the world that it wants to represent: to appreciate the whole observing the many pictures represented in small pieces, at least one picture gallery is needed and all the art galleries and collections and markets and all the paintings that exist in the world, aligned. All these could only give an idea of the universe and, therefore, the nature and details that compose it. However, all in all it is absolute simplicity.

The basic components of the painting are always the same: a surface, of pigments, diluents, brushes. It is the relationship between their interactive combinations but mostly it is the observer who makes the difference. Nature is based on simple basic principles, endlessly repeated mechanisms create the complexity of things.

Try with any sign, a V for example, repeated endlessly, and you will draw the world around us: it is mathematics known as fractals. I have never been a good mathematician; I always lacked the extreme imagination required.

Man is part of nature and follows the same universal schemes: its cities grow like cells, his brain, communications, its technologies, the network of links between the information and the direct and rapid in-

tuitive paths through it, they function like the entire universe.
Man and all things interact with each other between the present and active factors, exchanging energy, forming precarious situations of equilibrium, dynamic that is continuously changing.
All that is ecology, the entire system of relations in equilibrium and also the sum of the science that studies this equilibrium.
Einstein (we are at the end of the 1800s) in his theory of relativity set out as far as it is incomplete, when he stated that energy can, variably, have mass, even packets of luminous waves, the photons are like particles. After which all that exists, attracts all that exists! It's called gravity and depends on the mass and distance (squared) of bodies that attract each other: the larger they are the more they attract, the more distant they are the less they attract.
So how does the universe work then and thus nature?
Everything attracts everything else, generating differentials of pressure and temperature between two points. Reality is nothing other than a surface, which is defined moment by moment; the surface is the plane of the points where the interactive forces are in equilibrium, all forces and existing variables, an area of unstable form, of variable equilibriums continually, constantly changing to maintain constant equilibrium under changing conditions. A constant is always and only a relationship.
Take a flat piece of paper, manipulate it and equal to the surface of its reality, its concreteness, what you see and perceive, will change shape over time and as a result of the pressure you've exerted, from a flat sheet to a curved, waving, to a ball. But that sheet always remains.
Open and close your eyes on a seemingly stable scene: you will see it change every time, and perhaps you will not realize it until the change has become so obvious, it is impossible to miss.
Note a portion of an embankment as you pass by in the car: you will see its reality day by day, pebble for pebble, the bank will change shape and appearance, sliding from steep embankment to gentle slope.

At school I often used a visual representation of everything: a simple plastic mesh, white packaging. Seventeen m ^{2} of coiled net, wrapped and wound up to give it a hemispherical shape. Inside some long skewer sticks were inserted, red or blue. An excellent representation of the brain, the thick knots and the wires as neurons, axons, synapses; like the universe, stars and galaxies, atoms and electrons; of the Internet, of interactivity, of the concept of surface, space, time, of the contact between two distant points. The immense vacuum that separates the lumps of matter. The sticks indicated the rapid connections between two points in the network, the ways of intuitive thinking in respect to the rational, from node to node. Simple, light, you could play with it, crush it, pulling it the substance didn't change. I liked it a lot.

Biology? It is the most immediate method of comparison we have to study the world. Biology follows the same rules for the entire universe: like the human body or others, are composed of hundreds of billions of cells, so the universe is made up of hundreds of billions of galaxies.

So let's start with the molecule: the smallest part of matter, which retains its overall characteristics and allows it to be identified as such. We come to the cell: not the smallest (the ostrich egg, goose or chicken, are certainly not small) but the minimum vital structure, organized and structured to live, able to deliberately decide, though with simple, instinctive mechanisms, by way of sequences of choices of the type *on-off/yes-no*, the most suitable mechanisms of life, survival and reproduction, that permit identification at the species level, in the context of an environment, defined chemically and physically.

Hell, it's beginning to get difficult!

Nothing can be said of a single organism that exists or has existed, in a context of an instant or brief time, which cannot be identified using the characteristics of species; nothing lacking the capacity for ecological evolution, genetics and environment, which allows it to be identified repeatedly in time and space; no one can say either it is or was even alive for a moment, or that instead we are dealing with a simple organized organic structure, it existed maybe but without history; a soap bubble.

Unicellular and complex organisms exist and have existed, aggregates of two or more cells, similar or different. A cell may be a living organism, or simply viable. What then is the difference between living a organism and a viable organism? Thus between life and the simplest 'possibility' of life?

The single cell can be alive, living, (unicellular organisms) if they are able to feed themselves, grow, survive and reproduce, as a species, within its own ecological niche, of its own habitat, identifiable in time and space.

An egg is a cell, and nevertheless a simple organized structure. If you leave it for a while on its own it will rot. If it isn't fertilized it is unable to live as an autonomous body, that is if it doesn't become part of a more complex organism, able, to live.

An organism may thus be single-celled or complex (aggregate) alive and living in harmony with its environment, or simply viable, that is structurally predisposed to live but unable to do so on its own. These organisms were in the so-called primordial soup, and still are, individually viable, interacting, the basis for the development of even the most complex and evolved living things that exist today.

The time has come for evolution: It works a bit like the computer: today no computer would use only the DOS operating system, but it's part of the current systems that have evolved and like all the programs developed through the continuous updates. If something goes wrong you can always resort to the restoration of a previous state, less updated, and start over. Nothing stops an old inefficient and slow computer from working with its diskettes, it can still work effectively even if in a far more limited context. The punched cards could also work again.

Man, the elephant and the birds are up to date in respect to bacteria but yet they still exist and they work very well; even the simplest organisms, either autonomous or integrated within the larger bodies, govern limited functions: single-celled algae and bacteria that also live very well without light and oxygen in the fumaroles of the deep ocean, at unimaginable temperatures and pressures and feeding on sulfur as they did three billion years ago.

If conditions change, nature has an alternative backup. You can always start with a previous functionality even if it is less efficient. Evolution, therefore, is a mechanism of incrementing biological capacities (always by summation of existing capacity) that allow new organisms to exist and persist and grow and develop, and eventually reproduce more or less in extensive environmental contexts, depending on the genetic exchange, and environmental conditions created. The ulterior skills acquired provide greater efficiency and effectiveness, but do not involve the disappearance of the pre-existing. Only the collectivity of living organisms survives that are most capable of evolving but even these are more developed, in the ecosystem, as a function of their evolutionary capacity.

The determining factor for the development of a complex ecosystem, is the time the environmental changes occur, and the times (specifics and linked to the characteristics of each species) required for the modification and adaptation of the genetic traits. *Biodiversity* originates in this variability of conditions; the difference between the biological ability of all living organisms that comprise the whole of the specialized collective of living organisms, that are similar in their biological capacity for life and survival.

Species that are identifiable in time, adapted to limited environmental systems, chemically and physically defined, which are called *ecological niches*. The set of ecological niches make up the *ecosystem* and the equilibrium between systems, *ecological sustainability*.

This was difficult to pull out! But try explaining the living world. Each of these characteristic living collectives, represent the potential for evolutionary and biological capacity able to develop, modify itself to the environmental conditions, in function of the times of this change.

In the context of the current ecosystem, evolved to varying degrees, they are limited by specialization and thus, by the same factors, exposed to the risk of extinction.

The greater the evolution, the specialization is so much greater and therefore the capacity for adaptation to variations in the environment in which it lives is greatly limited but may change (it happens constantly) too quickly to allow for adaptation.

We think of the panda or the koala bear, not to mention the monkeys, primarily tree dwellers: they evolved to the highest degree that is fully integrated and symbiotic with their environment: if their range of life is reduced, the trees disappear or forests or there are fewer eucalyptus, or bamboo that pandas eat, they would certainly have the chance to remember they are still bears and thus potentially omnivorous but before their bodies readjust to the new environmental conditions, a sufficiently long time can pass and cause them to become extinct. Even coral reefs that formed the Dolomites for example, can only grow if they have light in the depths of a warm sea at the most 60 to 100 m. They are now rocks and towering mountains, but have a biological origin and grew up in an environment similar to that present in the Caribbean: life and death for entire ages, until the final death is caused by changes in the environment. The corals, however, still exist although in other places.

It should be almost immediate to deduce that man is far from advanced, at least from this point of view; certainly not the most evolved living organism; only this permits him to be present and occupy almost all ecological niches; his speed of reproduction is sufficient to guarantee him adaptability to change, also rapid.

The animal man thus doesn't seem to be naturally destined to extinction, although he'll always have to compare himself to rats, for example, who are direct competitors in the same habitat, equally adaptable genetically but extremely fast at reproduction and at modifying their genetic heritage and the characteristics of their species.

If over the long term and in the presence of large, radical and disturbing environmental changes, if I had to bet between the survival of men or rats I would certainly point to the latter. Not a penny for most other living species, whether plants or animals. Probably you could only count on the bacteria.

There are terms, used and existing, which describe the total sum of the mass of living organisms on the earth, in any species they belong to, like the term *biomass*. The term is generally used, reductively, to define the use for energy purposes, renewable, useful to man. Man is actually a supreme species on the planet by virtue of a special feature: the instinct for survival and aggression and also, the hugely evolved evolutionary force of the organism, probably autonomous, I believe, his symbiont: the brain. I believe that man as an animal is not particularly advanced, but it is basically just a means for another autonomous organism, independent and strongly evolving: the brain. Symbiotic (they need each other) and synergistic (provides instructions and support to the carrier body to evolve in a manner corresponding to its ends), sooner or later, the brain will manage to do without the enslaved body, which, moreover, shows it little respect. At this time you may have a radical change in the concept of humanity.

Biology is built on the basis of the chemistry of the elements, which were formed separated and aggregated in the depths of the universe when radiation slowed the rate of expansion, attracting one to the other, with ever increasing mass.

Biological times, however, are extremely more rapid than chemical reactions and this is possible because of the presence of enzymes, which are capable of catalyzing biological reactions.

Also here nature has reserved a number of possibilities: for example all living species (or almost) use just and only levorotatory (molecules with angular chains, mirrored like hands, deviate the light that strikes towards the right or left) of sugary substances. That is using only half of those available.

The other half? Is there and it transforms, thus serving however for something in the ecosystem: someone and something uses it.

Don't ask me what or who they serve; it would be too partial, limited, defined, detailed and difficult. You will have to study a little chemistry. I don't feel like answering.

It is always increasingly difficult: at the base of chemistry, of nature and of biology, there are certainly water and carbon dioxide; derived from cellular respiration that is, from the life mechanism, which occurs in the mitochondria, organelles present in animal cells and in those of plants, factories deputed to the regularization of exchanges with the external environment.

Breathing doesn't need light to occur, as we don't have it we breathe the breath of billions of microbes and organisms that compose us, they are symbiotic (dependent and provide) or synergistic (they support). Some people mistakenly believe that water and CO_2 is the product of photosynthesis, an activity exclusively (or almost) vegetative, which takes place in daylight in the chloroplasts, the organelles in plant cells that produce the synthesis of glucose and oxygen. That is not the case.

In practice during the day plants produce sugars and oxygen and water and carbon dioxide at night. All of nature and its biological children utilize them. The alternation of day and night allows life for all existing species.

Water is an organic compound that isn't derived from life. And fortunately it was initially here! It seems to have been brought, largely, by the comets that fell attracted by the earth.

Oxygen is a combustible that allows everything it touches to 'burn' easily, oxidizing; therefore if it had been present early in life it would have been destroyed immediately. So luckily it was not.

Oxygen is a 'waste product' of life that, by increasing this it is increased accordingly, serving however as a brake, until it was possible for living organisms to adapt, conform, and learn to use it as a highly efficient source of energy. Certainly a damn and very radical environmental change, which took two billion years (three of life and four and a half of the Earth's) to near current conditions.

In the beginning life developed in a toxic environment and we have taken billions of years, accelerating ever faster.

Fortunately there was so much iron in the planet that it rapidly oxidized subtracting the nascent oxygen out to the atmosphere: this is the reason why you can't find elemental iron but only in the form of colored oxides in rocks.

The process of adaptation called for the development of a cell membrane comprised of phospholipids (fats) and proteins: it is this that allows cellular respiration; traversing water, oxygen and carbon dioxide, entering and exiting freely in the cell and they are the products, which are then useful for photosynthesis.

It was also necessary to develop enzymes that speed up biological reactions otherwise relegated to the speed of simple chemical reactions that require seconds, minutes, hours and thus making it impossible for the 'energetic and productive collaboration' between all the organic and inorganic components of living things. Everything that is from balls of twenty amino acids, non-living but essential constituents of proteins, produced by cells having ATP. Hydrogen, carbon, sulfur, oxygen, and from here to fats, to special sugars to proteins. All in all not much at first but now transformed and changed into so many and different, for the evolution and the development of the one at the beginning.

Now relax; you will also have time to digest the summary as I have myself. Of course I've forgotten something, indeed a lot, but basically this is it. It took a long, long time. And so much energy in the form of heat and radiation, especially ultraviolet that even today it continues to do its mutagenic work.

One thing that unites the universal mechanisms to human life is the aspiration, the tendency to rest, to quiet. But at the same time the amount of stimuli constantly changes the energy balance and therefore man must continue to make and do.

My mother always told me that it is always better to do than not do!

And besides, if you don't try, how can you know for sure what is going on? How could you learn?

We've come to the chromosomes: all animals have them; they're cal-

led the genetic heritage. Not all animals have the same number of chromosomes but only each individual different species and for this reason they cannot reproduce different species between them.
We shall disclaim a common racist misunderstanding: there are no races, let alone those that are higher or white. The different somatic types of one species (the look, the 'race') are just variations in that one species that facilitating survival in different environments.

Characteristics of living beings are the ability to respond to stimuli and the fact of having a life cycle: birth, feed selectively, to grow larger, survive, reproduce, then finally die and return to a simple substance and useful energy for the future, leaving traces of themselves and of their evolution in the generations that follow.
The first viable organisms were absolutely simple: the prokaryotes that naturally still happily prolifically exist, that don't have a nucleus and therefore they don't have DNA but only raw genetic material, the chromatin, which is present during normal cellular activity in the cytoplasm that exists in each cell. Little balls filled with chromosomes.
The GMOs are genetically modified organisms that act on the chromosomes, because they prove to be more adaptable. They are part of the future of the world. They were created to adapt to environments and usually adverse growing conditions, to meet the growing demand for food and to be able to move productive agricultural economies spatially in the world.
But we are speaking of economics thus these 'should not' be used where the economy and the environment are, for now, stable and sufficient where abundance and luxury are sold and consumed. A demonstration that the government of needs is not of man but controlled by those who induce and impose these needs, financial oligarchies that control the technological innovations, their development and use through carpet-bombing positive or negative advertising.
Then come bacteria that are not yet multicellular organisms; they are the most abundant and widespread form of life and they are also the favorite food of the white blood cells that can perform phagocytosis and eat them, destroying them and releasing the infected organism as their excess. It's called the immune system and increases the chances of survival of the complex organism, which needs to use them.

The cell is the fundamental unit, structural and functional, of every living organism. Not all cells have microscopic dimensions. Not all have
a round shape and often possess pseudopodia (like feet) that are
protrusions, cytoplasmic extensions, used for movement.
DNA is the (complicated) molecule a spiral protein, fat and sugar, on
which chromosomes are organized; following this organization they
define and differentiate genetic characteristics.
Cellulose is a complex sugar, virtually indigestible as such; it is contained in the cell wall, and gives added strength to the cell (in fact plants
have bark).
Vacuoles are empty spaces in the cells, they are the dumps and
warehouses that slowly fill, increasing the cell volume, and then are
emptied with use and disposal.
Then there are the ribosomes, organelles present in bacteria: they
are the factories for protein synthesis in every cell.
As we see the same organization of our cities: roads, inputs, outputs,
stores, food warehouses, raw materials, products and waste, and
control of trade areas, factories and processors, hospitals and resi-
dential areas.
There are only twenty amino acids in nature, which are polymers (that
is, more or less long repetitive chains of minimal elements), and only
these are the basis of the construction of thousands of possible proteins.
The proteins are themselves constituents of all physical structures of
living organisms (other than bone) from DNA to animal muscles. Think
about how many different words can be formed with 21 letters of the
alphabet. We are talking about trillions. How many books can be written.
All known creatures have been subdivided by scholars and grouped
according to similarities and obvious differences, into *five kingdoms of
living beings*; they are still subject to some ongoing disputes: animals,
plants, fungi, protists, and Monera and already this is becoming complicated, then as always, nature maintains a transversal possibility.
There are, in fact, viruses that aren't always living; they behave normally like crystalline minerals but in the right environmental conditions are activated and acquire the characteristics of the living.
Here again, and the demonstration of why a real scientists cannot exclude any possibility is not philosophical, at best they regard it as highly or barely probably and only in a certain context.

If anyone doubts the rational schematics we use to face the unknown may exclude the impossible can explain this virus to me! Or if you would like to limit nature for our own convenience.

The observation for small systems and classification are however required to study mechanisms for man; alternatively there is dogmatic faith: *I don't know, I don't understand, I can't explain, I'm not sure* and then believe it or not, affirming or denying both, without concrete reasons.

Thanks to the endless achievements of the evolution of life and time past, man can rely on the biomass, in fact, sugars, fats, proteins, are all organic compounds based on carbon and may be industrially derived from petroleum, which is also derived, like coal and biogas (a mixture of methane CH_4 and carbon dioxide CO_2), from life.

I forgot, every animal that eats protein, then decomposes it thanks to bacteria and emits smelly gases, biogas, which causes flatulence and intestinal bloating and even the major greenhouse gases in the atmosphere; and many beings eat a lot; the same bacteria that also allows you to make humus and beer.

Because of this the atmosphere has changed, over more than four and a half billion years. If you want to do it before and change the atmosphere, then just burn organic substances, plants and animals, and the result is the same: water and gas (CO_2). Of course a result consists of local, rapid climate change, and for being too fast it can be detrimental to the economy of certain areas of the earth and thus to people's quality of life in these areas.

Only man can knowingly realize the alteration of the equilibrium in many points, forcing the entire planet to re-balance everything with greater speed to the natural.

Even man, however, is a natural variable and is what he is, behaving like this, without adapting but adapting the environment to his needs, quickly and effectively creating the conditions for his extinction; certainly not the end of the world or of life, which will continue to generate and release carbon dioxide, or reaching thermal equilibrium, remove it, the CO_2 in the air, with geologic time, will be reabsorbed into the rainwater eroding rocks, segregating, favoring and building new animals with calcareous shells and then when they're dead, dissolving them in the oceans; and then starting again.

But then, if everything is so complementary and interactive, how do we poor humans rationally understand the phenomena associated

with "how things work"? Or applied, or if they should follow it, the *scientific method* of Galileo Galilei, at least for what you can actually do, first and foremost observe!
You must locate and possibly try to observe a 'surface', the points of the plane where the interactive forces are in equilibrium, that is a limited and defined reality that is within our reach; it should be a precisely defined environment for study in these three characteristics: *Space, Time*, number of *Parameters* actively present and interactive; therefore observe and make objective observations, non-personal and subjective assessments.
Observe possibly placing yourself outside; it is necessary not to be part of the observed system so as not to affect it.
An objective affirmation must be: *Measurable, Reproducible, Verifiable, Deductive* (*is it hot*: a subjective statement, *it is 22 °C*, objective observation). The unit of measurement, the system of comparison and reference required is conventional that is can be shared. To make an objective observation it is necessary to find yourself outside, not involved in the system of study; an alternative is required to proceed by means of deductions that are often contaminated by subjectivity, may only be prejudices. In this case, to observe from the inside, it is necessary to break down the problem being studied into many small separate pieces to distance oneself and so reduce, for everyone, the personal approach.
Deductive: the scientific method must also be applicable to situations where it isn't possible to objectify everything and therefore must allow for making deductions (better *inducing questions*), starting with the most objective basis possible.
The reconstruction of the whole, is decidedly more laborious and demanding, it should then be more objective but takes place following a path full of judgments, prejudices, valuations, affirmations of pride and feeling and therefore errors.

I'm told the new vegan fashion dates its theory to the realization that monkeys eat only vegetables and don't suffer as a result. That the first humans were gatherers, and they lived well.
I believe that justification is unscientific because it is partial: monkeys are vegetarian? Yes, some monkeys but not all. Many are omnivorous and powerful carnivorous predators.

Monkeys don't suffer because of this? It may be but certainly I suffer less than they do and live better and however I don't know monkeys that are raised to a human level for their adaptability and capacity. Primitive man did what they could but they certainly didn't live well, healthily like their successors do more and more.

Today can you live well in the world of abundance, only eating vegetables? Probably, thanks to globalization that has multiplied and seasonally adjusted what there is on offer. The primitive Indians, however, cooked bones (of animals and perhaps other primitive beasts) to be consumed ritually in drinks, the ash contained phosphorus: they had no supplements and pharmaceuticals. Nothing to object to, everyone does what he or she wants and in this space and time and geographical location, can also be a vegan but certainly not primitive.

I don't like fanatics, especially those who don't eat meat from slaughtered animals (poor things) and condemn others, but buy pate de *fois gras* for the cat or similar delicacies, as if the animal providing the liver and other components hadn't been butchered... poor thing...

Elvia has been my wife since 11/09/1982 I met her the evening of 29/07/1979. After some time this thought appeared on my sheets of paper: *And Life Begins, Antonio*.

I think it's a good example of how falling in love works: acceptance of a simple fact that I'm in love. And from that moment the mind and heart leaps freely and uncontrollably.

It started like this and in many years occasionally I've also had regrets, and she too, but both doing it, now me now her, always one step behind when it was necessary, we are still here, and we have lived together most of our time.

Perhaps we are no longer 'in love' but certainly we still care for each other and always more.

As you see I also believed in the sentiment like everyone.

My wife, don't get angry: also this little poem I found was for you and this I never gave you... Shame, Reserve? Terror? Who knows, I don't remember but now, perhaps, if and when you read it, it will definitely become yours like it has always been mine, from the first moment I met you.

Why do I love you? because I care for you!
Because I love you.
Why do I love you?
Because you're stimulating.
Why do I love you?
Because you're amazing.
I love you,
you are fascinating,
because I love you.
you are inaccessible
because I love you
willing
I love you.
you are affectionate
perturbing,
reassuring?
Why do I love you? I don't know!

Who is content enjoys... what others leave!
I now gladly leave to others but without giving up, the desire and the
possibility of falling in love, the opportunity and the responsibility of
enjoyment and much suffering from the emotions, both positive and
negative which from time to time gives meaning to life; from time to
time and sometimes perhaps for some, forever.

Love and falling in love: I will quote some excerpts from novels.

Both were in the grip of a kind of frenzy. They arrived at the hotel, the
doorman in red raised the curtain and they entered. They wanted to
make love to exhaust the feelings they felt for each other....

... only to laugh, the bright glance, ready to joke. Curvaceous, appeti-
zing, intriguing, with a constant smile, the expression that promises
who know ... It was she who decided the rhythm of the conversation...

You had to be willing to die for him if need be. However it was not very difficult not even staying away from him for the Christmas holidays, attending parties with friends, laughing and joking having fun ... The man you care for so much ... The man you love? But is it true love?

His wife always knew what he thought, what he believed, he had no real need to express his opinion, his guidance, even if she simply took it into account at all times, to please him or to counter him. It was a certain certainty, like love and affection they felt for each other, but that took away the gratification of the moment...

... away from her, in that place he felt like a tycoon and forgot the panic, despair and at the same time the anger, but the will to live also eluded him and to triumph at all costs...

Amelia believed she could read the mind. Goodness! She had gone to the doctor for a precise reason and he was asking her exactly that. He was handsome man, cultured and admired and had courted her forever. She blushed as she had expected, but held his gaze rewarding it however with an expression of admiration, just as she had wanted. There was nothing romantic in the approach between the doctor and his patient... the liniment would create a sense of well being that she would attribute to him because that was what she wanted.

She didn't love her husband, and this was a serious sin, maybe God wanted to punish her: had given a draft that contained a strong dose of digitalis. She couldn't now, only now, notice she was expecting a child by him; it wasn't possible now that he was dead, to have a child by him. It was not acceptable!

... he, correct and respectful of the laws and conventions, a decent

man, with a family and so many interests, sometimes sought comfort in the imagination of this false environment.
It was the theater of life that he had never had or maybe, he could no longer have. It was enough to pay....

...That dense and doughy sensuality that emanates from all the popular neighborhoods... subject to the general chaos of life: the bells ringing all at once and making the flocks of screaming birds fly up and remain in flight and the people who stare at the sky seeking to follow their movement.

He remembered his wife. He realized that he was missing her simplicity, her normality....
He turned towards home and only then remembered why he had spent a crazy night.

His wife had left threatening not to return if he had not changed the way he was, but he couldn't give up the attentions of that attractive young woman in her thirties, fresh, seemingly naive who made him feel important, even if he was aware he was only dealing with a comedy, an evening of theater where he was not an extra but the protagonist....

She wanted to solve everything by being a nun... missionary... in India.
...

It was not simple desire for sex or for adventure...

... he wanted to see her, wanted to surprise her...

... all of a sudden he stopped and picked up a bouquet of wildflowers for Her ... hoping she would like them...

She constantly questioned herself torn between guilt and dissatisfaction. But was it true love? It was to be with him, live with him, have a family, a common purpose, was having a child her true, 'true' desire? She wondered about her deepest desires and nothing came to mind. It is true, she wanted to cuddle him and also protect him to be with him but was it true love? She loved him but love should give a poignant feeling, exhilarating when she was with him...

Love love is the easiest thing in the world, the fear of living and sharing it instead makes the love of one alone, the easiest, simplest and most satisfying, gratifying.
Much better than love between two people requires that one or the other has the tenacity of stray dogs, always hopeful, continuously returning to the charge, just chased away, never tiring each time...

And you what do you think?
... and it rains rains... on our loooove ...

We have come to the main questions adolescents have, to the motor that conducts life: ah... sex! How beautiful it is to make love from Trieste down... with whomever you want...
But what is sex? A source of joy, pain and suffering and motivation of the greatest proportion of actions is simply a mechanism, cellular, for the exchange of genetic resources; different between all living species to allow reproduction and life; it organizes and rebalances the genetic capacity for adaptation to the environment, the capacity for selective nutrition for growth; growth for the longest possible survival; survival to ensure the maximum possibility of reproduction of the various species.
Chromatin contains proteins, tubules and membranes and also mostly DNA, comprising long sequences of simple proteins, closed in the cytoplasm by a membrane that is present in all cells with or without a nucleus; if the DNA is localized in the nucleus the cells are Eukaryotic; Prokaryote is without the nucleus where the DNA is in the cytoplasm.

Sex is a simple functional expedient of most eukaryotic cells (multi-cellular organisms). Sexual reproduction is more efficient than asexual (usually by prokaryotes) since it allows for the combination of several variables.

Sex and the mechanisms of differentiation are related to the environment and its energy conditions (from climate to the abundance of food to the amount of people present). To explain how it works, it's a nice problem: two meet, sniff each other, the pheromones send signals, the body sends signals, hormones go into circulation, the brain doesn't understand anything: the two are in love, cuddle and make love, they exchange a lot of cells of all types including those needed to make a baby. *Pouf*, it's done, the mother will transfer her love exclusively to the child, and the two may also fall out of love to start all over again.

The baby? Here it is difficult to say, however, because of the abundance of scientific names to remember, but basically what for? When one has figured out how it works... Well I'll try.

Humans have 46 chromosomes, that is 23 homologous pairs. The egg and sperm are called gametes; fusion of the egg with the sperm forms the zygote. The cell with the full number of chromosomes (mother) is called diploid. When division takes place of the mother's cytoplasm into two identical daughter cells, cytokinesis, duplication of the DNA; takes place in all cells, even plant.

Mitosis produces two cells that are identical to the mother; children of the mother even if the mother is the father; thus meiosis halves the number of chromosomes giving rise to cells (daughters) with half the number of chromosomes, which are all called haploid.

Not very imaginative but as I've said, nature prefers simplicity and being lazy and in any case always pursues the maximum results with the least effort. However this happens both for the father and for the mother.

After love everything proceeds automatically; you don't see or hear anything, but who knows how, the mother notices it almost immediately: she knows that's all.

At the end of meiosis four daughters are formed, the haploid sisters, each with half the chromosomes of the parent cell. The two halved starting cells, in the end recombine to form new, complete, each with the whole amount of chromosomes half from the father and half from the mother: the new human, male or female, intended for reproduction or anyway and in every case, sequences that are useful for all the rest functional.

This applies to all cells and the position of the point the chromosomes connect, in the middle or a little to the side, determine the form of the paired and the sex of the unborn child.

(XX-XY and the Y is in fact only one X that came out badly, a little twisted).

In case you haven't understood there are no males only females more or less knockoffs.

In the multicellular organisms the mechanism also guarantees replacement of dead cells.

Many animals can safely change sex with changing environmental conditions.

The evolved organism is similar not to its parents but more easily to its grandparents, because it takes time to assert the predominance of some characters!

I forgot: the genetic heritage of the cells is exchanged and is modified from individual to individual, but there are two DNA; what is contained within the mitochondria, the organelles within the cells don't undergo any variations, if not occasionally over thousands of years; they come from the mother and only from her and can take us back through the generations, exclusively through the female and back in time until Eve and before that, by rebuilding the fundamental episodes.

So there are no males but only females with varying characteristics from totally manly, people with % of femininity among a little less than 100% to just over 0%. Thus all racial and sexual states are merely natural, just maybe, you will find at the extremes of the Gaussian curve the average normal.

I mean a man or a woman 'statistically normal' have 50 and 50 of one and of the other character. If they have 60 or 70, etc. in respect to the other, they leave the average 'normal'. According to the prevailing interest of society (common sense, for what it's worth) or rather one temporarily imposed by whoever is guiding and commanding, from time to time they will be accepted or marginalized.

Also in nature, here metaphorically in the molecular aggregation and then also in that of the cell, finally in that of the organisms, there is in turn a disturbance. An 'element' that creates some unrest, continuously undermining the internal, causes a dis-equilibrium within the 'social' group.

The molecular aggregation that occurs according to strict chemical and physical form sometimes imbalanced, threaten cohesion (like disharmony in human society) than at any time they can become 'explosive' when they arrive at some critical threshold of endurance.

In analogy being all naturally natural that is that exist, a universal law wants nothing to be created and nothing to be destroyed; it happens in all the 'families' (in an atom), in a group (molecules), in a town (cell), in a city (multicellular organism), in a nation (population of organisms) and is the radical change until the existing has been destroyed and thus often, leads to the construction of a new 'order' and a new 'society'.

However evolution continues over time, driven by the case and circumstances: among thousands of variables, changed by the effects of the environment and of ultraviolet radiation from the sun and anything else can interfere, some solutions are successful and evolve becoming predominant, in a particular context; others die out, others remain still limited spatially and functionally, totally willing, in waiting.

GEA, Mother Earth meets the SUN one day and falls in love with its energy: its empty shell is ready to accept it and provide its seeds.

From their meeting GAIA is born, the living planet, the family of their biological children.

The divine trinity of the holy family: the invisible and omnipotent Father from the angry demonstrations, the strictly virgin mother and protective, the son sustains their essence.

The scientific method: the study conditions of a system or of an environment is exploited by the great writers of science fiction, generally true scholars in one or more fields or supported by scientists: to create a different world you start with a condition of error in respect to reality or impose a different convention and study and describe, imagine, its consequences and implications.

Once at school I proposed a science fiction theme: it tells a story in a maximum of 15 lines in which the world you live in, white is not white but blue; the result was poor, but still interesting.

I've already said that to study something you must always: define the field (system) under study relative to the observer who is outside and does not interact with the field (system), but can observe it; space, or where something is done; time, when something is done. There must also be interactive parameters, how and by whom? (who does what and how is it done, how does it influence the other parameters). Finally the reference systems should be defined (certainly compared and defined if not, preferably, shared) it is necessary to compare and therefore objectively measure the observations. Multiples and sub-multiples of the reference unit.

I'm taller than her and shorter than you are, it's the least indicator possible, where the unit of measurement or reference will probably become her, because she is the smallest and they contain her.

But what is a system to be studied? A system to be studied (an environment) is the context in which you study, compare, verify, test, experiment, reproduce, a fact, a theory, etc. You study a fact in its context, in a defined reference system (of which the conditions are known) and unique (uniquely defined – unique – that and nothing else) because it is an objective system (in which the comparison, reference, among the measurable parameters permits the results to be reproduced).

Because a system is uniquely defined (in which there are necessary and sufficient conditions) conventions are required (recognized arrangements that enable a comparison (to compare) and define the characteristics of a thing compared (in comparison) to those known and defined: for example, the system measurement, of the shapes, capacity, of the colors. etc.

A black and white marker is therefore the system: Observations: it is not of any color other than white and black (so it can be white, black, or black and white). Black is different from white (hence the marker can only be two-tone and not all white or not all black). To define white (or black), however, we need to define the characteristics of one of the two or else you end up with nothing. Black defined, for the hypothesis presented, the other part, being different, may not be anything but white! (necessary and sufficient conditions). Same reasoning for vice versa.

If you are observers and for example don't define the specific characteristics and reproducibility, objective, of the color black, then you
cannot even define those of the color white or any other color; doesn't matter what they are, since they are shared.

In the absence of conventions (which define the interactive parameters and the type of comparison system) it isn't possible to characterize the system of comparison objectively and then define the *conditions* that are *necessary and sufficient* to make objective statements
(white for example is not and cannot be white if black has not been
defined first as black in its measurable and reproducible characteristics). Failing that, if you are not sure that black is black, by definition,
even then the white that you see may be black and you are immersed in a sea of uncertainty.

I've talked about the importance of the reference system that to be
such and complies with the scientific method, in respect to the observer must be: uniquely defined, in which the conditions are known,
and they are necessary and sufficient. In which the interacting parameters are known and defined! I reiterate the importance of the observer who in studying a system must not interact (possibly), or however must interact in a minimal or in the most controlled way possible, with the observed system.

The observation must be verifiable, reproducible, referring to a defined and unique system, on equal terms, it cannot be variable according to the subject that makes the analysis; it cannot be derived from
observations that are variable based on the views or emotions or
characteristics of the subject.

It's the only way that we can draw inferences from observations with
a high probability of their being acceptable.

Obviously the system can then be closed, with limited parameters
and defined or open where the interacting parameters cannot all be
uniquely defined (if not restricting the observation time to a single instant).

Imagine a room with a window closed and open: in this case the external will act on the internal.

Under normal conditions the observer cannot compare the two types
of systems, and then the observations made in one are not necessa-

rily also applicable to the other; they would not be objective.
If the system for comparison is not defined (reference) in its characteristic parameters, if it is in the range of incertitude of the uncertainty.
If, until some features have not been examined and classified and defined with certainty, it is not possible to define the specific parameters, then everything is possible in these systems and the opposite of everything; you are dealing with indeterminate systems.

There is a nice very informative story about Heisenberg's Uncertainty Principle, Scrodinger's cat (Nobel prize).
A closed box on the table contains a silent and motionless cat: it is not possible to determine, without getting closer and opening it if the cat inside is dead or alive. In this indeterminate state, it is therefore possible that the cat is alive (not dead), or that the cat is dead (not alive) and it is also possible that it is in both situations simultaneously; from the point of view of the observer who is outside, in fact, it may be simultaneously in both situations, at the same instant and without possibility of contradiction.
Are there ghosts? Are there other dimensions that overlap and intersect our four normally known?
Today it isn't possible for us to define time except as a difference between two certain moments; since (at least in our normal universe, known and more or less defined) two bodies cannot occupy the same space at the same time; in this other system, strange and not determined, it can however deduce, that this condition is possible because the two alternatives cannot be demonstrated.
The condition that it could be possible that two bodies can occupy the same space at the same time, different to our world would be defined as: if space is unique (as defined in the measurement systems) time does not have a single dimension but at least two, parallel, two real states that brush up against each other without or at least with little, interaction. If time had only one-dimension then it would be space that would have more dimensions.
The observation makes me think that if the cat is simultaneously not alive and not dead, then it is a ghost that cannot exist in our reality and thus, if it exists, it has to exist in a different reality, in a different area of equilibrium, that intersects at least at one point and for a mo-

ment our area of reality, in a different dimension.
Then if you open the box then the cat is either certainly alive or certainly dead! Definitely or rather very likely, it will not be a ghost.
The system is determined when you examine it, and then what happens within it becomes true and real, here and now, and can be studied in defined conditions.
Bohr said that nothing is true unless it can be measured: evidently he was never in love, was not religious and didn't believe in ghosts, just the opposite of Newton who though said the same things.
But we who are within nature can we study ecology, the huge system of our planet and the universe around us, in an objective and rational way?
We have in effect a few instruments at our disposal: for example the magnetic field and the interactions of mass-energy or better temperature-pressure, classification for common properties and different properties that permit the decomposition of the system studied and overall applied to specific, limited phenomena, the method of observation, external objective.
Mostly communication allows scholars of different individual sectors, to compare with those of other sectors on common aspects and themes or that involves them equally, or differently, than the sectors in each study.
Unfortunately, in the midst of these are interposed a welter of pseudo scholars anxious for notoriety, fame and money and they propose their own unique version of the truth, no matter how partial and sectorial it might be, at least until they are proven wrong and brought back to their place in history.

You need to take great care with observations since one same observation can lead to different deductions. *A ball is round* is an objective statement (because it refers to geometry, which is a reference system of forms); *a cable is one meter long* is an objective affirmation (because it is related to the system of measurement, at defined conditions of temperature and pressure); *the sweater is warm, two iron balls are heavy* are instead subjective affirmations because they cannot be demonstrated independently of the observer not having been referred to a certain system of comparison.

The complex observation of a feather and two iron spheres of different sizes that fall together and come to earth together (the spheres) and then the feather, all stopping on arrival at the surface is objective: it shows that they are heavier than air and less than the earth (comparison); that the feather is lighter than the iron spheres; that there is a force that acts in the same way, proportional to the mass, on the bodies attracting them to the earth; but it does not prove that the force of gravity exists.
Leonardo, Galileo, Newton, have taught us to be wary of easy interpretations.
First the philosophers had ingenuity and intuition, but much more difficult to discern since they did not have the precisely applied knowledge of the scientific method.

I don't agree with the method of those who interpret their own emotions, feelings, moods, to look for answers to their questions and formed by impressions and opinions, arrogantly or superficially turning to the encoded thought of classical philosophy.
We are dealing with schematically classified thought, statistics, drawn up by philosophers, sociologists, mathematicians, etc. well-established, settled, consolidated, exceeded, only endorsed today by the identifiable scientific community, that preceding our reality and mostly composed of silent deaths.

To resort to the full reading of the philosophers to find ideas, phrases extrapolated from the historical context in which the whole thought was worked out without having developed a thorough overall knowledge, shows no willingness to express and develop free-thinking, autonomous and critical but nonetheless seek identification through sharing, consensus, belonging, integration, of a socially gratifying endorsement.
I recognize the need to know. I can appreciate it, while detecting the final identity of recognition by a social system, anything but disputed, the study (the research of values while extremely valid and profound, of layered and recognized concepts, to review them, approve them or challenge them, growing personally in accordance with this study.

Forfeiting these values yes but then I believe that the thought that results should be autonomous, developed as a result of the interaction with their own experience, through introspection. Only in this way will a thought be free-thinking, right or wrong (is there a codification of this kind? Certainly yes, among philosophers of the past and of all men in power: whatever power!).

I cannot overlook the opinion and the valuation of the ignorant drunkard, the ascetic monk, the 'master of life' giver of good advice, of the communist proletarian sculptor who has produced over a hundred copies of his most requested work and paid for, of the night dancer recounting her sadness suffering and need; of the Junoesque woman hero and the medal of red resistance who married a skinny and cultured former fascist and defended him against everyone; but doesn't talk about politics if he is present while not hesitating to express herself in any other moment, as indeed he does. Most of all the ideas, those of the artist who sees what I am unable to perceive.
All of them are so many characters that I've come across in many different places and moments of my life and who have contaminated me. They weren't educated and mostly rich or powerful like Plato, Socrates, Marx, Espinoza, Nietzsche
or Sartre among many, but certainly their thinking is not worth less, in forming my own.
Proposals, certainly not recipes such as those that are certainly not made to pray, their great, to provide. The meaning of things, of life, the sense of happiness, the big questions so common that they don't provide answers but only interpretations, suggestions and hypotheses!

The blatant cheat who angers me: who would not find it absurd to treat a disease that you don't have because you might have it in the future?
If the question were to be raised like this, one would answer that the drugs are to cure the illness when it exists and is manifested. Instead the information, manipulated by the scientific community and accredited by science that this time, interpreted by me I find I am in agreement, affirm that only with the preventive care and information, heal-

thy men or normally injured, will become the assiduous clients of doctors and pharmacies; potential patients, very profitable. Instill the need to cure the illness and its effect preventively. It is the purpose of the 'leaflets' that accompany any medication, even the most known and used: to inform and to justify! Make the disease known, spread the worst features, make the side effects of the drugs known that you use to treat it doubling the fear and multiplying the profits!

Gathering together the memories again until they stay with me and I attempt to make a more concise summary of my life! Will I succeed? The lesson perhaps I wanted to construct a base to have my students develop it. Over sixty years but this, this content is me, not what I know but exactly who I am.

Definition of *nature*: Interaction exchange of energy formation of dynamic equilibriums. The *electromagnetic spectrum* is the measurement of the *available energy* the units are *wave lengths and frequency* and each radiation arises in a precise area of the electromagnetic spectrum since it has a unique frequency and specific wavelength which is inversely proportional: that is if one increases, the other decreases. *Matter*, formed of *particles*, gravity attracts light in the form of *photons*. The energy can travel in the interstellar vacuum and also in mass, in the form of *waves* (by changing the frequency and velocity).
Like every other animal we are equipped with detectors capable of perceiving part of the spectrum: eyes, ears, skin, nose and mouth. Why don't we see the x-rays? This is simply because they are beyond the limits of the capacity of our specialized sense organs and therefore are imperceptible. Not by the eye the instrument that is sensitive to the light of the human body not by the skin that senses heat, not by the ears that can hear noise, etc.
Absolute zero is minus 273 °C (0 °K) it can never be reached; the system would be static motionless reality would be frozen, if variation ended time would end which in fact is one of these, that between two successive moments.
The energy that determines movement is *heat* or rather it is the difference between two points.
The Sun attracts the Earth and the planets the Moon attracts the

Sun and the Earth and the planets, as well as the water of the seas and in the cells; creating pressure and temperature differences between points attracted differently and accordingly on Earth there are the *tides* but especially the *wind* and then *water* or *ice* that are the agents, the principal perpetrators of erosion and of the renewal of the surface.

The Moon, but also the Sun, and even less and with evidence only locally in a few areas of the planet, influence the ocean tides, marine, lakes and rivers and also the cellular tides; the cells are like little worlds filled with water. They also influence life cycles. The coral reefs grow if they have light, so they are of biological origin.

Nature and life depends on the mutual interaction of two fundamental parameters: the *availability of light* and *humidity*; only these parameters define the climatic zones of the *Earth* and their vegetation and therefore the kind of life you'll find.

There are four s *easons*, or two depends on where you are on earth, more or less distant from the equator and closer to the poles, the two *solstices*, the periods the day (available light) lasts longer than the dark of night and the other two are the equinoxes when the day is approximately equal to the night, because the earth revolves around the sun in an elliptical orbit regularly moving away and approaching. The oceanic islands are of volcanic origin arising from the difference in pressure and temperature between the center and the surface of the Earth; they are on *fault lines* or along crustal *fractures* where magma rises or where earthquakes originate, on ocean ridges and continental edges, where *subduction* occurs suction phenomenon and destruction of the old crust (what is hot, matter and gases, salt, then cools and then falls and is heated again, changing and forming new matter).

The *convective currents* are the way to move either the energy in the form of heat or that of matter; they originated in the hot material that rises creating more high pressure points that push, the material releases heat by moving physically to a different point because of the Earth's rotations and then cold, where the pressure has become lower, descends. A continuous ballet at all levels, from the center of the earth to the sky and back, this can also be verified in a pot of boiling water.

From the rotation of the metallic solid core (NiFe) at about 6000 °C inside the metal mantle, fluid at those pressures and temperatures, is derived the Earth's *magnetic field*; the *polarity* (of the iron molecules) is reversed every 26,000 years or so (for this reason you can measure the age of the Earth's crust from the dorsal area of production – to the boundary of the subduction zone).
Nature is always cyclical: its phenomenal manifestations are always cyclical that is begin to develop, they are exhausted for certain periods and then they are repeated.

It is possible to make many more observations: all parameters interact with each other, in perpetual, precarious, unstable, momentary equilibrium.
The lithosphere is the sphere of all the rocks: they are formed by all solid materials that together form dry land and the seabed. The rock plates that make up the Earth's surface, on or under the sea, moving to the effect of convection currents in the mantle, clash; their movement is called *Plate Tectonics*.
At the continental limits – between an oceanic plate and continental – this movement creates pressures and temperatures that allow the growth of the mountains on that side. It's called orogeny. Or on the other side, in subduction, depressions are formed that draw matter toward the mantle to melt and start to develop new rocky material from mixtures of the existing.
The *fumaroles, geysers, thermal springs*, are found at the margins of the plutonic and volcanic areas because this is the area that is still hot which heats the water in underground pockets, increasing its pressure.
The *continents* float on the *mantle* because they are less dense than it is otherwise they would sink; they are composed of silicates of magnesium and carbonates, while the mantle is composed of nickel and iron.
The *pressure* increases if it is equal to the *volume*, the *temperature* increases while the *density* of a body, that is the quantity of matter contained in the volume is lower at a higher temperature. It is easy to see with a simple balloon that if it is heated it gets bigger, becomes lighter and rises then cools, becomes smaller and falls, although it always contains the same amount of air.

Increasing the density of the medium through the energy propagated, you gain in *wavelength* and lose *frequency* and of course vice versa, and so, earthquakes and the stars can be studied by reading the time the waves travel.

Everything to be studied should be observed classified, and cataloged observing the common features and the differences. A simple example of classification that permits us to separate humans and birds, could be:

– *Birds*: living species, animal kingdom, not the human race: in fact they are completely different for example they can fly and humans cannot but also some birds don't fly, however, we all know that humans are not birds, or do we? Other features common to birds: wings, beak, ovoviviparous, hollow bones, the nest, have feathers, all have legs and three-toes plus the spur, have tails are bipeds. Some differences: flightless, long nose (limivore), short, curved beak (birds of prey), a short and thick (granivores), long or short legs. Other animals with few common characteristics and many differences are not birds: bats have wings, octopuses have a beak, the crocodiles are ovoviviparous, etc.

– *Man*: living species, animal kingdom, the human race: the same race the following type and subtype: according to the amount of melanin: whitish, reddish, yellowish, dark, black, Creole, olive, etc.; according to the color of the hair: blonde brown black red, albino; according to the origin and physiognomy: Eurasian, Asian, African American, Indo-Asiatic, etc. So on and so forth. The different types somatic (races) are variants of a single species.

Colors (colors by definition): the computer identifies 65 million shades, not less than 16 million, we about 7 colors and dozens of shades, but what differentiates the color blue from white? They are not the same color! And so what, certainly, does the color white have in common with the color blue? It's not the same or similar to any other color that isn't white or blue (they are both different from all the other colors, red, green, yellow, black, purple, etc.).

Or again for the *natural elements*: solids, liquids and gaseous, metals, (electrically conductive) or non-metal (non-conductive). Naturally there are exceptions to the rule; there are always exceptions.

The *Earth's orbit* is an *ellipsoid* and the plane, the surface described by its perimeter is called *ecliptical* and is the plane where the *motion of revolution* takes place. The duration of the day is about half of 24 hours; the rest is night.

By the way, the perfect shape for scientists is that round, spherical but in nature it is a rare and random shape: the natural form is generally elliptical, you can easily check this. Perhaps nature is imperfect! We need to change it...

The Earth is in *perihelion*, the closest point to the Sun on 3-4 July while aphelion (the farthest point from the sun) is six months later. Halfway between perihelion and *aphelion*, the earth touches the points where the day is about the same as the night (*equinoxes*); this is where the polar ice caps are completely illuminated. The *equator* is the parallel where the sun's rays are perpendicular on September 23. On September 23, the *Arctic ice cap* is fully illuminated the year (*revolution*) lasts 365 days and 6 hours and a few minutes. The phenomenon of seasons is the result of the motion of revolution and the Earth's *inclination* on its *axis*. Italy is in the temperate boreal astronomical region. In Parma the sun's rays never fall perpendicular.

The *parallels* are conventionally 180 of which 90 boreal and 90 austral. The *latitude* is the distance, angle of a point from the equator (N–S), (distance drawn on a spherical surface along a meridian); *longitude* (E–W) is the angular distance from the meridian of London numbered as meridian '0'. The *Tropic of Capricorn* is latitude: 23 ° 27' south; that of *Cancer* 23°27' north. Between the *tropics* and the equator extends the tropical zone; between the tropics and the polar circles the *temperate zone*.

Classification is a fundamental and basic process without which you cannot face serious study of a system that is, a set of interrelated elements that react with each other to achieve a given end.

In a closed system nothing is exchanged with the external environment neither matter nor energy. The *Earth's system* is not closed because matter and energy are exchanged with the space that surrounds it.

All the water present on the Earth's surface makes up the *hydrosphere*. Each molecule of water is composed of two atoms of H and one of

O: H2O. Water is present on land in all three states of aggregation based on the area the seasonal period and the climate. Water evaporates at all temperatures above 0 °C it boils at 100 °C and changes state, becoming steam.

Matter is all that surrounds us, has mass and energy: the basic structure is the *molecule*.
Atoms: an atom is neutral because it has no free electric charges. The number of *neutrons* makes them only larger, increasing the mass. If there was one *electron* more or one less, then we would be dealing with ions. The electrons revolve around the nucleus and are particles having *mass and a negative charge*. A *proton* is an atom that is missing one electron making it neutral; it is just one atomic particle that has a *positive charge* therefore it is an ion.

The *elements* are materials composed of only one type of atom. When matter is formed by equal atoms we speak of the elements; the *compounds* (H2O - NaCl) are formed by associations of more different atoms.

The *void* fills the enormous spaces (to scale) between elementary particles, like for the universe between planets, stars and galaxies.

The symbols of the fundamental elements are Calcium Ca, Sodium Na, Nitrogen N, Oxygen O, Hydrogen H, Carbon C, Silicon Si.
The *internal molecular bonds* (intramolecular) between the atoms that compose them, are forces that hold the atoms together to form the molecules and therefore matter; they break or become weak during transition from one state, an ordered form to a more disorderly form, for example, taking energy, warming and thus dispersing the heat gained.
Density (*weight of volume*) is the ratio between mass and volume.
Being a ratio it is a constant and is specific to a specific substance under certain conditions. Ice has a lower density than water in its liquid state; equal in mass the ice occupies a greater volume than wa-

ter and therefore at the same volume ice weighs less.
Ice has a volume 9 times greater than the same amount of liquid water therefore it is lighter and when it forms splits everything that contains it.
The air is a homogeneous mixture because it is simply not possible, to separate the phases (liquid solid gaseous). Air is not a single gas, but a mixture of different gases; air has weight and its weight is the atmospheric pressure therefore the pressure decreases when you rise in altitude. The *barometer* is a tool that measures air pressure.

The *states of matter*: in the *solid* state particles are rigidly fixed by intra-molecular bonds and have no chance of running over each other. Therefore, solids have a volume and their own shape while *fluids* take the shape depending on the receptacle containing it.
The changes of state imply the breaking of the links and the increase in the disorder of the particles causes them to release heat. The change in reverse (*reorganization*) absorbs heat.
Changes in state:
solid   liquid = *fusion*
liquid   gas = *evaporation*
gas   solid = *freezing*
gas   liquid = *condensation*
liquid   solid = *solidification*

At the base of life is the simplest instinct: to *feed and grow* larger because it is easier to survive.
The second basic instinct that unites the individual cells to larger and more complicated beings is *survival at all costs*. If there is energy (nourishment) it can grow and if it grows it can survive more easily!
To use energy and to survive consumes the organism, which cannot therefore live forever not even humans. Since individually you don't live forever, therefore it is necessary to reproduce, multiplying to exist longer, at least as a species!
The fourth instinct: to *feel pleasure*. Pushes the living organisms to strive to live. Man most of all.
Two cells or ten or one million who know how to feed themselves, grow, reproduce, make up the entirety of living species reproducing

and transmitting the sum of their abilities to their children who consequently evolve.

If it helps, everything is done better and therefore the simplest organisms cooperate and survive, feed and reproduce better faster and more efficiently than those that do so on their own account.

I give you a hand and you help me; we combine our limited capacities: here then is the *symbiosis* (an organism cannot live without help from another) and the *synergy* (mutual aid for a single purpose), which multiply the forces and capabilities.

It takes place between *simple cells* (two cells without a nucleus form a *nucleated cell*); it takes place between billions of cells that form large organisms; takes place again between large and small: these and the fungi and the roots of plants or intestinal bacteria, which work together in symbiosis.

What pushes the living organisms to strive to live? The fourth instinct: to feel pleasure. Living life causes pleasure, death causes suffering: there is enough for the first brain: *on-off, yes-no; 0-1*: a computer! that operates in binary language.

I will do it = pleasure – I won't do it = suffering: one must choose.

It has grown from the cell to man's brain but the common basis of all living beings remains the same: an aggregate of cells capable of choosing stimulated by pleasure.

I need energy = I'm hungry! (before eating there is the suffering of hunger – after eating the pleasure of satiation).

I must survive = I'm afraid! (be careful = cells of the body provide adrenaline!) then, safely, the euphoria and the pleasure of relaxing (cells of the body provide dopamine to make me feel pleasantly tense and euphoric and then serotonin to relax) two pleasures for the price of one, in exchange for survival.

I must reproduce = I need sex, which is known to be a pleasant and satisfying activity.

The fourth instinct is an end in itself: I want to feel pleasure! An evolved biological computer working in binary language has fun existing and therefore chooses to continue, as much as possible.

The fourth instinct involves the *brain* in humans and the larger animals. Living life causes pleasure, dying becoming sick, causing suffering.

The brain has changed, grown, evolved, but the common basis of all living beings remains the same: to be an aggregate of cells capable of choosing to be stimulated by pleasure or by its absence.

The human brain has exceeded during evolution pure instinctive need and thus if not for necessity, hunger, sex or survival, works for the sheer need and taste for pleasure.

Games, sudoku, crossword puzzles and riddles, mathematics and philosophy, art and science, concrete or abstract works, are used only to provide pleasure to the brain that the more it has to choose, the more complicated the sequence required, the more fun it has and it grows and develops. LIVES!

The human brain is slowly making itself independent of the body, evolving as an individual organism in its own right, freeing itself from the symbiosis that binds its own needs to those of the body, which it oversees.

Gaia is the living planet, born from the union between the physical structure of Earth matter and energy from the Sun.

According to the most ancient cultures, the gods corresponding to the earth Gea (the female principle of fertility) and the Sun with many names in each time the male principle of energy and life, united in marriage, and the planet Gaia was born filled with life.

This is true for about at least 3 billion years while the Earth existed as a planet formed more than 4.5 billion years ago. At that time about 4.5 billion years ago, a large planet more or less like Mars collided with the Earth peeling away a piece that went on to form the Moon permanently defining the particular characteristics of the system. Comets collided several times with the Earth in formation and provided almost all the water that exists that began to evaporate and fall cooling and solidifying it. The planet continued heating and cooling on the surface for about 2 billion years, moving from being an arid furnace to a ball of ice, until it became a hot sphere inside, with a surface formed by land and water on which, then, developed life in all its forms.

Gaia is therefore the ECOSYSTEM! as large as possible, bounded by space and time, not closed but with some outside interference from the sun and the moon, from the universe. They're evidently fairly obvious interferences but with so many and such interactive parameters involved that you can't study all of them together. One can only attempt to observe small portions (niches) and then attempt to put them next to each other to try to understand what is happening.

The main living system, the Ecosystem Gaia is regulated in its macroscopic behavior, in its dynamic equilibriums by large cycles; that is repetitive situations.

If this is so for the ecosystem, then also the interactive parameters are influenced by those same cycles more or less evident. The cycles can have very variable durations, very short or very long and influence, interact on each other affecting all the minor systems like those that are living.

Ecology: is the science that studies the equilibrium, dynamic, that regulates the ecosystems that is the interactions between the various parameters (the reciprocal influences) and the effects of these interactions on the multiple equilibria for this, in the ecosystems, that are continuously creating and destroying (dynamic equilibrium) by which the systems themselves are altered accordingly, adapting to new conditions, defined in time and space.

Nothing much to do with the environmentalism of the bar and the daily news.

Again making you aware that I'm writing on the wave of memories and my own elaborations and assessments, and that we are dealing with a travel diary, first of all useful to me and maybe, just maybe to someone else, it is certainly not a scientific treatise everything but exhaustive and formally correct, I invite you to read and study and investigate, hoping that you've been stimulated.

To summarize seven points are fundamental, I believe, for the study of nature:

1. in nature static equilibrium does not exist;

2. at every alteration of an equilibrium (pollution) as small as it may be correspond to a variation in the entire ecosystem;

3. the Earth doesn't belong to man but man to the Earth! Everything that happens to the Earth (even to man's work) returns and happens to man who undergoes it for better or for worse;

4. all evolved living species have been given the more or less complex brain or at least systems that permits them to sense and respond to environmental stimuli and everything until extinction, they evolve and adapt to their environment, exploiting their specific intelligence;

5. the scientific method permits objective measurement and evalua-

tion, that is, to consolidate the experience (to learn), but this is its limit. Imagination, intuition and practical intelligence allow you to break away from the scientific method and to make inferences and choices which, while subjective, are not necessarily wrong or unnecessary but on the contrary, valuable for the fast advancement of knowledge and consequently along the scale of adaptation and the evolution of the species;

6. evolution is a radiative mechanism. That is the continuously produced new radiates seeking spaces, niches, a place to grow. Normally they are found occupied but sometimes since evolution is accompanied by extinction and sometimes mass extinctions, then they find it and start the change.

7. nothing is unnatural and abnormal in nature. Everything is only the expression of a possibility being tested.

Nature is always cyclical. The manifestations of phenomenon are always cyclical that is they begin, they develop, they are exhausted for certain periods and then repeat.

There are cycles of minutes, hours, days or months, years, that regulate the oceanic currents and help or hinder fishing in the Gulf of Mexico and in the oceans, rebalancing the temperature and salinity and relative density, that is, acting on the stratification of ocean water; cycles of tens of years or hundreds of years, but also volcanic eruptions, earthquakes, record floods, magnetic and radioactive storms. These cycles correspond to the missed adaptations of living species and continuous mass extinctions of entire species.

Lets look at a few cycles:

Lunar cycle: 28 days, approximately monthly, its gravitational pull directly influences the tides (every 6 hours 4 times a day) and all the cycles that have to do with water in containers from the seas to lakes to the cells. Influencing the tides it also affects fertility by stimulating or hindering the growth and development of life as farmers well know and nurses in maternity wards even though no scientist, so-called serious, will ever admit it. The lunar cycle has the same duration as the female menstrual cycle and coincides with the fertility of the human species (like every other living species) the animal cycle is also affected by size and environment.

Circadian cycles: are reproduced in about a day. Day and night, light

and dark 2 times per day equal in duration, however, only the solstices (2) and equinoxes (2) sleep-waking 2 times a day for about 8
hours of sleep and 16 of wakefulness (1:3) The body temperature rises and falls 4 times daily. Natural hunger about 4 times a day.
Annual cycles: The revolution of the Earth around the Sun: 1 year of
about 365 days to make a complete turn. Earth around the Sun and
Moon interacting with each other with peaks at the equinoxes and
solstices where day and night are approximately equal but then, the
relative duration of the day (or night) increases gradually as the Seasons advance (for us 4 a year of about 3 months each; in other parts
of the globe 2 times a year the rainy season or monsoon and dry season) and you change the temperature (and the rainy or dry seasons)
in an annual period. This is possible because the Earth's axis is tilted
(angled) with respect to the sun.
Different cycles: The Sun does it on its own with the temperature and
density of its plasma (gas at millions of degrees) and explosive and
nuclear activity waxes and wanes approximately every 11 years (with
the maximum sunspot every eleven and super approximately every
150) invading the earth with electromagnetic storms that can disrupt
even radio and television broadcasts and create exposure to higher
or lower amounts of radiation of all kinds (mutagenic) of living beings.
Every 26,000 years or so the Earth's axis (angled relative to the sun)
completes its tour and reverses the polarity of the Earth's magnetic
field and its action of orientation of each molecule, containing iron.
El Nino (5-7 years and La Nina (9-11 years) are phenomena that affect
the temperature and salinity of the Gulf Stream (a river caused by
pressure and temperature differences between the various points
leading into the hot ocean water from the equatorial zone – Gulf of
Mexico – to England influencing the climate: the ocean in fact evaporates producing the rains the wind, monsoons or hurricanes that go
up and down (roughly but not exactly, to the north or south) or towards the hot or cold according to the air that is a component of
both, relatively, warmer or cooler.
The cyclical effects influence and determine the climate in many parts
of the world and therefore the harvest (famines or floods) heating or
cooling relevant parts of the earth (repetitive cycles of tens or hundreds of thousands of years) and every variation modifies the conditions and modifies the foreseen changes.
Imagine if the current slows down or is diluted with fresh water mel-

ted from glaciers: the tides would be higher and higher changing the level and position of the coast, the climate in England would become arid and cold, the desert would become green and temperate. The facts demonstrate that the model doesn't work like this and the seas rise much less than expected.

If the Greenhouse Effect produced by carbon dioxide and by the other gases as well as from volcanoes, fires and man's pollution, made the temperature rise over a certain limit, it would melt glaciers and it could happen that at first, the heat would increase: our summers would be drier, the seasons would be longer and longer and less distinct; the rains would be more plentiful and there would be flooding when it rains. In this situation the crops would be destroyed by the heat and the rains, so there would be famine; then probably from the north in our latitudes, lacking the warm water current but mostly the evaporation from the oceans, caused by the immense cloud cover that would intercept sunlight the warming greenhouse effect would be offset, it would begin to spread more and more cold and slowly. It would trigger a new ice age. All this would last from about ten and a hundred thousand years and then, the last cloud precipitated, the sun will start again to dissolve everything and we would more or less start back all over again, year after year, full moon after full moon. It has happened in this way for hundreds of millions of years!

We don't live millions or hundreds of thousands of years and we suffer or enjoy what is there or what we expected there will be, in a matter of more or less 50 to 100 years. We have little information, traces of legends, myths, about civilization that maybe existed, before the last ice age that is over 10-15,000 years ago.

The time scales: *years – months – day – hour – minute – second*, are what we perceive and know. In the system of the cellular or atomic world they don't exist, the times are too long! There are *microseconds, nanoseconds, picoseconds, the Armstrong*: are too short for us. In the system of the cosmic world there are *thousands* of kilometers and years, *mega and giga*, (you know them from the hard drive of the computer and Internet costs), eras million kilometers and years, *light years, eons, parsecs* (measuring angles on the magnitude of distances): are too long for us.

Space: nature organizes itself on essentially microscopic scales and minimally then, replicates and multiplies constituting the visible struc-

tures, bodies, trees, mountains; all that exists is the pile of replicas of minimal and basic geometric shapes and structures that are reproduced indefinitely (in mathematics they are called *fractals*) going from the infinitely small to the infinitely large.
At each microscopic structure features correspond to skills that multiply, defining the characteristics of matter, inert or living.
If an atom had a nucleus as large as one centimeter, the closest electrons, at any time, would be approximately 100,000 cm, that is, a kilometer, at the nearest point. Matter is in fact full of emptiness. The same empty space that makes up our universe where the stars correspond to the atomic nuclei and the planets to the electrons.

The events: a child is born every second, men die per second; every minute someone gets married or has a car accident; in Italy a car is stolen every three minutes; in every moment, continuously, someone is crying or laughing or crying or eating or sleeping or making love.
Every year there are about 40 volcanic eruptions; each year about 300 large earthquakes, tens of thousands of thunder storms, millions and millions of lightning strikes, tens of thousands of devastating fires and dozens of disasters that impact on the environment.
Today there are about 7 billion people but since man has existed more than 90 billion have been born lived and died
The human species is made up of a set of billions of people who live an average of about 50 years (on a global scale and statistically).

The vital functions and related social mechanisms: the *metabolism* is the mechanism by which living organisms are able to chemically transform substances into others and more again; to reduce them to extract a simple energy of the type most useful for survival and used by cells that make up the various organs. (The chemical transformation that takes place directly or through the action of *enzymes*).

Active substances: all substances that give us pleasure or comfort are active or else why would we continually consume them? They are the so-called drugs, which are strong or weak. Since they alter the delicate balance upon which the lives of billions of cells that work symbiotically and in collaboration within our body over the long term, more or less, these substances pollute and therefore, come to modify the organism until they destroy it! Some may have hallucinogenic effects that make you dream (or have nightmares) with open eyes abstracting us from reality, especially if we don't like it.

The active substances from the point of view of the effects are divided substantially into two families: *stimulants* (sugar, caffeine, tannin, adrenaline, amphetamines, ecstasy, cocaine, LSD, hashish, alcohol, pharmaceuticals); *relaxants* (nicotine, opiates, morphine, heroin, anesthetic gases, marijuana, alcohol, pharmaceuticals).

They work, the brain knows them and knows their effects: asks for them. To provide them saves it the trouble of making the body make an effort thus wasting energy.

Then there are *doping substances* that are or simulate the effect of *hormones*; fundamental mediators of vital functions, able to develop body mass or to increase the amount of oxygen present and retained in the blood, EPO; used for doping in sports to enhance physical performance, alter the sleep-wake rhythms, etc.; they do not act directly on the brain but in the long term, in excess and imbalance, take the action of control from the brain and destroys the vital organs.

The brain: being an aggregate of cells that work like so many tiny chemical factories, producing or consuming the chemicals needed to provide useful energy and provoke choices, is able to experience pleasure (or suffering) through its external biological sensors but also from the effect of chemicals, not produced on request, but taken directly (for example the stimulating adrenaline produced by fear and tension, stress or relaxing serotonin, produced by enjoyment and relaxation that make you drowsy or dopamine, euphoria that keeps the alive, the love molecule, which it asks the body to produce or consume).

In man, the un-evolved animal because it is not very specialized and adaptable but extremely complex, the brain is highly developed, overpowering the instinctive level (living it feels pleasure, in feeding it feels pleasure, reproducing it feels pleasure or to die and then it feels no more and knows or thinks).

The brain always has the primitive function of choosing between two alternatives; *yes–no, to do–not to do, pleasure–pain, life–death* and in doing so it feels pleasure! If it is determined like this the evolution of the human brain to achieve pleasure as an end in itself, however being constrained to support the body in its function of control always coinciding with the priority of survival as a function of the environment (in hardship situations, hunting, cultivating, sacrifice; of conservation and refinement of the instinctive and passionate factor; the steady increase in the number of expendable individuals). Or in the situation of wellbeing: development of philosophy and the arts, or of social distraction with reduction of passion and research of alternative pleasures in an attempt to reduce the number of individuals to maintain it.

I noticed there are alternative conditions when space and the available resources decrease.

Ability and the end point for the brain is to feel pleasure and realizes them thinking and ordering activities and production or transformation of this or that substance whose action leads to an increase in the stimuli of well-being and pleasure (for example fear, pain, passion, anger, love, sex, feeding).

Unfortunately, to follow through to do this end, if it is allowed to easily enjoy it does, it will however do so even at the expense of the body that contains it and which it should oversee: drugs, improper nutrition, etc. simple by alternating choice of stimuli, pleasure-abstinence, pleasure-suffering, that are agreeable.

The brain is able to sacrifice the body for itself, for its pleasure (I'll parachute jump or drive fast in the car to feel excitement even though I know I could kill my body, or reduce it to a semi vegetative larva).

Hence the use and dangers of drugs, capable of making the brain react (stimulating – relaxing) without it making any choice but the two most simple: *I want a stimulus – I want to sleep.*

Feeling almost all the pleasure it needs with this simple choice, the brain, in an attempt to evolve independently in accelerated time, becomes able to sacrifice the body to itself and to its pleasure and substantially burns and kills itself, enjoying itself while doing it, without there being any use for man and for the human species.

Sooner or later it is able to get rid of this body, currently needed animal burden, so delicate and limited!

For the same reason, limiting the need for cerebral functions, the drugs are legalized or prohibited, like faith and religion a powerful instrument of control for social organization and order, in the hands of those in power who never appreciate free choice since it corresponds to the normal attitude of man and, if anything, would lead to the exclusion of individuals, rather than to their commercial exploitation, at times criminal and violent that the current conventions, prohibition mostly, permit and indeed impose.

It speaks in favor of prohibition listing the health care costs of managing illness, they don't count the social costs of prevention and protection, and nor those of necessary repression. They don't count the possible savings, also in terms of energy needed to impose and maintain unnatural prohibitions, rather than regulations. Everything that regards pleasure in our current social organization represents an exploitable business and it is exploited everywhere you look.

Man, arrogant monument, evolved like all other beings but created... by himself or rather by his symbiont brain, made and interpreted in the image and likeness of the deity, which of course is the maximum expression of the power attributed to man himself: omnipotence, able to meet his every need!

Man is an organism composed of an aggregate of other interactive organisms of smaller dimensions, composed in turn of aggregates of more simple interacting organisms: the cells.

All living species more or less large are composed in the same way (naturally excluding unicellular beings compounds from a single cell).

All species react and obey the same fundamental imperatives to the same needs also called instincts.

Man is just an animal species among others! The human species applies the species mechanisms that apply to all other species.

Concrete thinking: man can manipulate nature and so, really change the world, especially his world! The place and the conditions that allow him to live acceptably as a species, possibly the most healthy and pleasant.

This is the world that the 'environmentalists' at least the scholars of the 'environment' are trying to protect, manage and 'save'. They realize perfectly well that the message coming from the study of the geological eras and previous inhabitants of the planet is absolutely clear and unequivocal: alteration of biodiversity, its reduction, consequently reduces the conditions for survival of the dominant species in that period, renders them unstable and delicate. Even slight changes in the

relationships produce conditions for the substitution of one dominant species by another, more adaptable to the new context.
As has already happened to the dinosaurs, the weakening of the food chain and the reduction of the interactive parameters of the ecosystem renders the dominant species more susceptible to a rapid extinction (rapid in geological time, thousands, tens of thousands of years) in the case events are truly catastrophic, or generators of rapid changes on relevant areas of the planet.
I want to send a message to the gentlemen in the busy crowd of environmentalists at the bar, rich and civilized, gentlemen of abundance and waste: take heed of the scholars, slowly change your lifestyle, make it sustainable without huge upheavals: save the world, but don't think of saving the earth, think of your world, that is the ecosystem that allowed you to get here and be in the position you are; otherwise you may find yourself suffering the consequences along with the whole human race that today results as being too crowded. Breathing heavily polluted air in big cities, walking in a dirty park, drinking polluted water and eating useless rubbish is stupid, as well as detrimental. A more balanced distribution of resources and a reduction in excessive abundance in some areas, could be an imposed solution and not chosen in the next ten thousand years.
But anyway I won't be here, we won't be there then, so who cares? The ones who think of it will have the problem! Or no?

Evolution and adaptation: we like to say that man is the highest expression of nature, the highest point of evolution, the most evolved organism. That's all nonsense! Man is just an animal species among others!
Biological mechanisms and species behavior are applied to the human species as they are equally to all other species. An organism is much more evolved as far as it is more specialized and therefore more fragile and near extinction. Man is much else than specialized and is still capable of multiple adjustments, and then, still backwards on the scale of evolution (fortunately).
Adaptation Lamark theory: in brief, living things develop differently according to the environment they live in adapting to it and those that survive always demonstrate and prove they are better adapted. Giraffes would have the longest neck to eat the leaves of the trees where

there are no bushes and the trees of the savanna are tall and survive
when short giraffes would die of hunger; if they had grown where there were always bushes they would not have developed such a long
neck because it would not have been needed. So there are giraffes
(or animals of the same species) with a progressively longer neck based on the environment in which they have developed or elephants
that are larger or smaller, etc. Over time if they have not become extinct, and are in different environments, all varieties are found.
Evolution (*Darwin's theory*): in short the animal species including humans develop and genetically total, that is, through the repeated exchanges of genetic material in the chromosomes that is, at the cellular level, the biological skills required to improve and increase their
ability to survive. They evolve according to the environment and the
necessary abilities; develop through random mutations of the original
species.
By cutting a leg off mosquitoes, they are no longer able to pierce the
stinger and die because they cannot feed themselves; but if out of
many thousands, millions, two learn to do it by changing the point of
equilibrium and couple and reproduce, their successors will always be
able to feed both with four and with three legs, even if they have never done or seen it done before, if and when they have the need to
do so.
Clearly, neither of these theories (about a century of scientific knowledge between them) is sufficient to explain the immense variability
of living species of all kinds of shapes and sizes and in any environment, but both together, can provide most of the explanations.
Living species evolve by sum of the basic biological abilities that they
acquire stably by genetic crosses and modification through the errors
of genetic transcription, except random interventions resulting from
environmental mutagens. Existing species then use these skills when
necessary, without losing the lesser and simpler abilities. The modifications permit them to adapt to a larger number of environments and
situations able to use a greater number of skills, to exploit and dominate nature for their own benefit, in a greater number of situations.
The greater the number of possible crossings, the greater the possibility of evolution and adaptation of the species
Evolution comprises genetic adaptation to the environment of the
species (reaction to environmental stimuli) that can have greater or
lesser possibilities of asserting itself in a given context. The environ-

mental conditions ultraviolet radiation, the components of the earth, of water of air, of food, initiate further random genetic mutations in the individuals exposed. Random mutations induced by the environment, radiation, pollution, extreme conditions, constantly introduce new factors that nature has put to the test: errors also occur in billions of continuous transcriptions of the genetic code; in any case if they have any chance of being successful, they are integrated and developed by favoring those that have them, or are abandoned because of extinction or again, set aside and held in reserve in gene pools. The panda bear is specialized, that is it has reached its maximum level of evolution in that form. It lives in a small geographical distribution area because it only eats buds from a kind of bamboo and nothing else. Since its environment, where it has adapted and specialized has been reduced and the bamboo is in short supply, its instinct for reproduction is very much reduced (because if there are two in a km2 there cannot be three or therefore either the area of bamboo is enlarged or one is born, practically, only when another dies). This lack of incentive to reproduce is a common mechanism for species that don't improve, despite the veterinarians in the zoos trying in every way. Evolved, specialized, at risk of becoming extinct if something changes in its environment. So what does the Panda do? It remembers being a bear (the bear is omnivorous) and begins to eat other things than bamboo (that is turning back on the evolutionary scale) to become more adaptable. If it has enough time maybe it will succeed but if it has taken thousands of years to evolve to adapt to specialization, perhaps a few tens or hundreds of years will not be enough to go through the reversal!

All species increase the population if the available resources are abundant and peacefully coexist (it is a euphemism), increasing their well being. If resources are falling then secondary mechanisms come into play for maintaining the healthy conditions achieved: such as food specialization, reduction of the population through adoption and spread of deviant behavior, reduction of reproductive stimulation, infertility, or the decidedly most effective method, war.

Man evolved from the apes: generalization and common places far from being demonstrable. The monkeys are in fact more specialized than man (they don't live in all environments, hot cold humid and or arid like man) therefore they are more evolved. If they are more evolved in respect to man, man cannot descend directly from the monkey, but he must have developed from an earlier originator of both (those currently present). For man, his evolution as a primate diverges simply following a different and more effective path.

In effect man's biological and genetic (DNA) is not very different from the fly although he certainly resembles it less than the monkey! Different species do not mate and reproduce in the wild (in the laboratory working on the genes in the DNA though you can create new cross-species).

And in this way all the immense nonsense is debunked once and for all, affirmations sustained over time by 'science' and the community, from time to time scientific, useful to the European economy have been held up for centuries: the principle that human races, diversified by somatic characteristics induced by environmental adaptation, have different origins and dignity or the affirmations, still in vogue, that in nature there is something defined as different, different or not normal.

The evolution of cellular development is a mechanism that resulted from the first cell to complex organisms through a series of steps that are common to all living organisms, which involves the use of and increasing requirement for more functional energy.

What does evolution consist of? In the genetic and environmental adaptation of species that use, primarily among the common biological capacities, the most profitable in terms of energy to guarantee the minimum action to have an organism live: 1) feed selectively that is in the best way; 2) grow to survive and to do it; and finally 3) to reproduce as an identifiable species, occupying the greatest number of environmental niches possible.

As a result evolution, substantial and competitive, has produced random mutations and adaptations to the conditions existing in time and space, cells without a nucleus; cells with a nucleus; mono-celled organisms; multicellular organisms; fish; amphibians; fungi, plants and everything that exists; various animal species (dinosaurs, monkeys, mice, bears, panda, many flies and lots of mosquitoes) among which man.

For man, the point of diversification and of different development is placed much before the monkey, at the level of definition and aggregation of multicellular organisms or however after the fish and amphibians, when the first mammal primates evolved.

During the formation of the body of the child in the womb, it quickly retraces the whole cycle of evolution, going from the egg cell that joins the sperm, to more cells that multiply up to the formation of the cardiovascular system and the primary structure of the instinctive brain, of the nervous system, of the cartilage structure, the bony skeleton, the various organs and lungs. Oversimplifying, it repeats evolutionary transition going from egg to tadpole to frog to mammal. For example, teeth are the evolution of the dorsal ridge still present in sharks.

Man therefore is not derived from the monkey but is the result, in a specific chain (sequence), of a different substantial evolution added to adaptation. Man is another species of primate and not evolved from the monkey species.

Question: how big is a cell? Have you ever seen one? Answer: the egg is a cell! How many eggs do you know? Certainly many and very few are microscopic.

Because an observation or a measurement is objective they need to be compared to each other in a *reference system, comparison of size, conventional and shared* (through international agreements or shared conventions).

It seems to me obvious that there are no static equilibriums in nature. To every alteration to an equilibrium, however small, corresponds to variations across the entire ecosystem. The variation corresponds to a contamination, positive or negative, in the perceived effects.

I believe that now we can, thus, easily define pollution comprehensively in only three words: *alteration of existing environmental parameters*, known and cataloged. Pollution is a process in constant evolution inseparable from life. Man living, in every way, place and condition, influences singularly and overall the equilibrium of the Earth as it is as the Earth and its ecosystem influences the evolution of man himself and of all other living beings.

A very important concept I believe is that of *surfaces* analyzing beyond the elementary geometric definition that we all know.

A surface is the unique plane of all points, in energetic equilibrium: energetically dynamic, which is modified by interactions in time and space. It is the plane of points where all the interactive forces are in equilibrium in a given instant.

The universe, universal space, is an immense surface crumpled and folded in on itself by the same natural equilibriums.

Imagine a sheet of paper which may be stretched or compressed and laid out again and folded and refolded, its surface area would be unchanged, although completely different in the volume occupied by its mass and in the apparent form, the overall surface.

Time, in the human eye, is what is required to move physically from one point to another, along the space separating them, moving within the path bound and defined by these equilibriums, forcing one step at a time.

If the two points on the surface that contains them are distant from each other, the time needed for the transfer will be long but if the surface is crumpled, they may approach until they are almost in contact.

Imagine if we had the necessary energy to exit the binding surface, to pass from one to another or to create a new fold in the same surface, to put them in contact: the transfer could be almost instantaneous. The forces at stake in the universe at times seem to succeed naturally. We don't know enough!

We know that at the base of everything there are some constants. A relationship always represents and indicates a constant value (but, usually, in time and in space and under equal conditions). For every point in a determined instant, a strong relationship/surfaces is directly proportional to the temperature and inversely to the volume. This relationship is the pressure exercised; it is a constant value for every point and maybe expressed by the gravitational waves. It is easy to slip from science into science fiction supposing we know, that is, instead, we don't know anything.

Heat and *energy* are transferred more or less, in fluids from a warm body to a cold through convection mechanisms; conduction in solids; radiation across the void.

The motion of convection is the mechanism that transfers heat between the inside and the outside of the earth and between the various points on its surface up into the atmosphere. The climate in the various points of the planet is influenced more by the winds than by sea currents. The wind comes from the heat exchange between the various points in space of different pressure and temperature between two contiguous points, from where it is more to where it is less. This differential determines the movement and, combined with the Earth's rotation, the transfer and relapse of masses of air and moisture in different places, happens in a more or less relatively short time. The wind permits the transfer of large masses of air and water vapor, and various chemical components and thus influences the climate and the environmental conditions in the areas occupied by the living beings.

Since the air masses are moving at different speeds in respect to the surface going further away because of the effect of heat, they generate because of the effect of rotation, spiral movements and therefore thunderstorms, hurricanes, cyclones and anticyclones: depending on the energy in play.

There are four large terrestrial climatic zones, determined by the available *light, humidity* and available *temperature: Arctic, temperate, tropical and equatorial*. The temperature increases from the Poles to the Equator, but essentially as a result of the available humidity that increases from the Poles to the Equator and even more with the available light in time also increases from the Poles to the Equator.

The type and spread of life depends on these parameters. The plant species follow and differ from one another from the poles to the equator depending on the available amount of light and humidity.

The borders between the climatic zones is not defined by the classical geographical circles and learned at school but by the vegetation present. In areas with rainy seasons and dry seasons, grasses grow and not plants (or few) since they lack the time and the conditions necessary to complete their development, or they are barely sufficient.

Herbivores characterize savannas, steppes and taiga; eating sowing and fertilizing the vegetation cycle.

The only truly arid environment is the polar where, temperatures are always below zero, it isn't possible for water to be present and available in its liquid state: mostly arid and less strongly illuminated. Then moving onto the continental type, cold, not very bright and humid with steppe and taiga: grasslands conifers, coniferous forests, lichens and mosses. Following the marine lacustrine and temperate with bush undergrowth, forest, permanent meadows. Still the temperate zones, hot continental with deciduous trees, grasslands (savannah). Again the tropical continental areas: desert, where the daily temperature swing is greater; warm and bright but still moist night condensation: lichens and mosses, cacti, conifers, grasslands (savannah, steppe, taiga), deciduous. Finally, the ever-wet rainforest areas, with deciduous forests near the Equator. Mosses and lichens that have basic needs always define the limits of the arid and dark areas. The clouds form in tropical marine areas.

Biomes are climate ecosystems, characterized by the dominance of one or more plant species. They define the climate and the dominant plant species. The main difference between a general ecosystem and biome is in the e number of interactive characterizing parameters that in this case are few, they repeat and characterize the climatic zones: lichens and mosses on the edge of the cold zone and in the warm shaded zone, where moisture and a little light begin to be available; grasses, (steppe and taiga cold, hot savannas) because they have a rapid life cycle that allows them to develop completely from seed to seed, rapidly compatible with wet seasons at intermediate temperatures. The symbiosis between grasses and animals permits the perpetuation of the cycle: the grass grows the animals eat it, they disperse and fertilize the seeds and continue the transhumance along the rim of the seasonal cycle. Forests: in the cold coniferous trees, many leaves for the maximum photosynthesis possible with low light, small to withstand the cold and so as not to loose water; in the temperate deciduous broad-leaved; warm and light and moisture, are easily available; equatorial forest: lots of light, very warm, plenty of water available there are the broadleaved plants, really very large they compete with plants that grow tall, for the light.
Also the *geomorphology* of the places (the form of landscape) is determined over time by the elements: ice, rain and wind. The mechanisms of actions that form the landscape: rupture and transportation for ice; erosion and transportation for water; transport and abrasion for the wind.

The past climate determined the shape of the current landscape. The equilibrium of the climate that is established, will determine the future landscape.

I want to give an example of the complexity of an ecosystem and the difficulties facing those involved in studying ecology.

The field needs to be at least narrowed down to a limited area, and regardless of the equilibrium established between the living organisms in constant evolution and adaptation and therefore it is not possible regardless of the fact that energy is exchanged always and only between what has more towards what has less. It isn't possible for those who have less or nothing, to give to others! (social implication). Heat is the energy that determines the movement of the crust and mantle and the atmosphere. In nature, in the universe, there will always be two points with different pressure and temperature. Temperature and pressure are directly proportional: if T increases also P increases in the same volume. Variations of T and P, uncontrollable, however permit reaching temporary states of dynamic equilibrium that can be studied.

The convective motions originated in the hot material that rises, releases heat, and then colder descends: a convective cell defines the climate in a restricted area of land, for a limited time.

A high-pressure area (hot air will rise from the earth to the sky) will draw in cold air at the base, towards the ground. An area of low pressure will draw in hot and humid air towards the summit (the hot air is on top).

On a large plain it can be simple but if the topography is complex the effects of the interaction are also complex. A warmer and dry land area will be a source of high-pressure, with hourly variations.

The mountain rocks heat up more quickly than seawater; in the day they are a high-pressure area, the air goes from the sea to the base of the mountain. The sea at night cools down more slowly and becomes a low-pressure area; the air comes down from the mountains over the sea. The breeze is a moderate wind and variable ranging from mountain to sea and vice versa, according to the period of day: by day from the sea to the mountains and at night from the mountains to the sea.

Temperature, pressure, state of transition, rotation of the Earth, relative position in space to the Sun, position relative in space to the Moon, light, convection, radiation, conduction, flora, fauna are particular conditions in space and time constraints.

As I seem to have clarified, all these parameters, agents and mechanisms, determine, interact continuously, in a dynamic equilibrium between them, the type and form of the landscape and climate and therefore types of life present and resistant that they in turn participate
in concretely. To all those who would spread information, inductions,
while legitimate and derived deductions, as certainties, face value to
be taken literally.
At the most you can build a model on a statistical basis (although
adaptable and incremental because of the collaboration of several actors) and make a forecast about a small area, spatially and temporally.

A natural system is really a complex of equilibriums, energetically dynamic, defined in space and time, of physical, chemical, biological parameters that minimally interact with each other; a system that tends
overall to the least possible total energy consumption.
Every interaction is both cause and effect of further interactions and
variations particular to the energy balance and the overall modifications of the system itself.
To study a natural system it should be subdivided, classified and defined in space, in time and into the characteristic interactive parameters, do it in small pieces, study them individually and then compare
the results to try to establish the uniformity of small areas adjacent
to each other, trying to put together a giant jigsaw puzzle that however is never still and the overall picture is constantly changing.

The entire global scientific community, intending official and non-offi-
cial together, if they really collaborated, swapping and sharing objectives and results exclusively with a view to study and analysis, it would
be the only human reality that could address the problem

As always nature uses simple, effective mechanisms, repeating them
billions of times and leaving the result to itself.
The atmosphere filters and acts as a shield against ultraviolet rays
and high-energy cosmic radiation capable of damaging or better changing, heavily mutating, the genetic heritage and also causing tumors
and cancer in humans. Modifying itself, it permits the effect of irradia-

tion and gradual releases into the equilibrium of the ecosystem, mutagenic elements and new active factors with which to come to terms with the complex equation that could describe it.

The atmosphere is a mixture of gases; 20.9% O2 oxygen 78% N2 nitrogen 0.03% CO2 Carbon dioxide; other gases among which CH4 methane, ozone, argon, H2O water vapor; of these the ones with the most influence on the greenhouse effect and global warming in order: water H2O, methane CH4, carbon dioxide CO2.

The gas Freon and halogenated refrigerants influence the formation and maintenance of the protective ozone shield, as they persist over time for many months and years.

The air is filled with lots and lots of dust: PM10, which loads bacteria and falls with the rain, PM 2.5, pollen spores that are too small, remain suspended. Each of these grains becomes the nucleus of condensation for the drops of water that will give us the rain, mist. Each one will be inspired or breathed. Each one spreads and carries its bacterial cargo or its properties to the bronchi or lungs. It is called the greenhouse effect that allows heat from the earth to add to heat from the sun without leaving the atmosphere and being dispersed into space. A greenhouse made of walls of air instead of glass or transparent plastic. That is the cause of global warming.

By changing the parameters, change, in time and in terrestrial space, the kind the quality and quantity of heating, differently in the various areas of the planet.

Warming, ocean water evaporates and forms clouds that block the arrival of sunlight: if we exclude the acceleration imposed by the eruption of some volcano, as soon as the balance periodically roughly stabilizes lasting tens and tens of thousands of years it would be overcome, it will happen predictably: flooding or the rise in humidity in the currently temperate and arid areas and desertification of the intermediate zones that would follow or have occurred at the same time (at least on a geological scale) with perceptible effects on survival and human adaptation in the order of tens, hundreds and thousands of years, the glaciation of temperate zones; tropical zones would become temperate.

No component of nature can act independently of any other part of nature itself. The effects may be intuited on the productive economies, settlements, and for the survival of most of the present or future human population.

The great Einstein, distant and unpopular with the scientific community and trade in vogue at that time, (his interpretations have always been well-defined by a few) pursuing his passion as a hobby, he had, the intuition that E = MC2, being mass and energy proportional to the square of the speed of light meaning that mass can, under certain conditions, be transformed into energy and vice versa; that to measure something a reference system is needed; also that nothing is created or destroyed but is transformed; also that everything is relative that everything can only be described with respect to the precise conditions of space time and also that these are interconnected and in dynamic and energetic equilibrium. And again that in nature there are no static and permanent equilibriums. And even that can never be one situation of one instant that is equal to another. And finally that absolute zero is worth -273 °C (0 °K) which can never be reached; the system would be static, but it would be punctual, reduced to a single point, since everything attracts everything with a force that is proportional to the mass and the square of the distance. Not bad for a mathematical hobbyist excluded from the scientific and social scene and reduced to continue working as a clerk in a patent office.

The Earth is full of water. While it is true it has become, and will become more and more precious, more, much more than oil: of that there is more than enough, is easily substituted for energy purposes. Water no, water is scarce; there is little that is useful. It is not difficult to imagine a future world where huge factories on the pack ice, fed by nuclear power if not the sun and wind, melt and boil billion cubic meters of ice to sell drinking water to the whole world, and transporting it with the repurposed supertankers of today.

The well-designed and built nuclear plant, without speculation, won't cause emissions of any kind and provides massive amounts of cheap energy. You may sacrifice a few islets to the storage of radioactive waste which constitute the only dangerous residual slag, those damaged by the launching of bombs in the sixties and seventies, of course after having appropriately secured containers, very secure, pending further technological solutions. It doesn't need that much space. Science fiction? Well! You'll be here to see (you think or your children and grandchildren).

In the study of an ecosystem like the earth you cannot do it regardless of classifying the characteristics of water to see how it may or could interact. And we do not yet know everything today, since they are always finding other new and unexpected conditions that are different than the 'normal'.

On the earth water H2O with the atoms connected at an angle of about 120° is present in all three states of aggregation based on the area the seasonal period and the climate. Water evaporates at all temperatures above 0 °C it boils at 100 °C and changes state, becoming vapor.

The highest percentage of water present on the earth is the sea, salt, about 97%. That represented by fresh water is only a small percentage stored mainly in ice, is unusable or almost.

Water that is effectively available for life, usable, drinkable or able to be drunk, does not exceed 1% of the total. Seven billion or more people need to use it.

The only exchange possible comes from evaporation from the seas, which condenses into clouds and falls on the mountains or in any case on the ground. Renewed exclusively through the cycle of *evaporation-condensation-precipitation* due to the imbalance between pressure and temperature at two points on the earth. Once fresh water is used, drinking water still reaches the sea and becomes salted; immediately useless.

The human body is mainly made up of water. Between the 75% at birth it falls in adult ages to 60–65% for the elderly.

A homogeneous liquid mixture is called a *solution*. The *solute* is the component that melts. Instead a *solvent* is the component in which the solute is dissolved.

Water is an excellent solvent; it is not the only solvent possible but is definitely a solvent suitable for dissolve everything that originates naturally.

Water in nature becomes a homogeneous mixture of various components; it is a homogeneous mixture because it is simply not possible to separate the phases (liquid, solid or gaseous). A solution of water and sugar: inseparable components and indistinguishable using simple methods.

The fluids don't have rigid bonds and a fixed form: they take the shape based on the container that contains them.

Density (weight of volume) is the ratio between mass and volume.

The density is the weight of a unit volume of matter. Ice has a lower density than water in its liquid state; equal to mass the ice occupies a greater volume than water and therefore at the same volume ice weighs less. Ice has a volume nine times greater than water at the same weight (thus is nine times less dense).

The same weight of water occupies a volume of ice nine times greater destroying, when formed, everything that contains it.

Water is not an organic compound.

The moon causes the daily cyclical tides every six hours, changing the shape and volume of the reservoirs, whether oceans lakes or cells. Cell tides are equivalent to those of small worlds filled with water and therefore they also affect life cycles.

Nature is and remains the overall interaction, the exchange of energy and the continuous formation of new dynamic equilibriums.

A complex organism is the synergistic assemblage of many (hundreds, thousands of billions) of specialized cells, each of which is a unique individual with its needs and its life, structured symbiotically with other individuals of which it enters and becomes a part.

Energy is measured in the *electromagnetic spectrum*: the measurement of available energy in the wavelength and the *frequency*. If the wavelength increases, the frequency decreases (it is inversely proportional). Energy can travel in the form of *waves* in a vacuum and in matter (by changing speed and frequency).

The *cell* is the basic unit, structural and functional of every living organism like the molecule it is and of matter.

Not all cells have microscopic dimensions. Not all have a round shape. Cells carry out transformations of the matter they are made (sugars, phosphates, lipids, proteins).

Photosynthetic transformations that take place using the energy of light or else dark of respiration, fermentation; aerobic (with oxygen) or anaerobic (without oxygen) serve to produce or store energy needed for life. Not many changes but the basic foundation necessary for getting there.

From plants: by day, light + CO2 glucose + E + biomass.

From chlorophyll (green) and anthocyanins (red) during the day (+ E) sugar + O2 + H2O; in any case, they are obtained from a reaction available E. They produce a glucose molecule and one of oxygen. These are products of photosynthesis carried out within the chloroplast, typical of plant cells that take place by day.

If the energy is scarce, at night (- E) then the reaction produces H2O + CO2 (water and carbon dioxide). At night the energy is used for survival (breathing) and to accumulate energy (in the ATP: adenosine triphosphate). Cellular respiration occurs in the mitochondria, organelles in both the animal cell and in the plant; they regulate the exchanges with the external environment.

Production of sugars or destruction of sugars. Going from large molecules to glucose and then the glycolysis, demolition of glucose that produces pyruvate and ATP, substances able to use and store the energy available.

The cell membrane is composed of phospholipids and proteins; allowing cellular respiration. Through the process of cellular respiration molecules of ATP are produced; it occurs in all organisms and in plants, it takes place at night; water, oxygen and carbon dioxide, freely enter the cell, and these are the products, which are then used for photosynthesis in the presence of light.

Inside the cell the endoplasmic network and the Golgi apparatus produce fat, special sugars and proteins to be exported from the cell; enzymes accelerate the biological reactions in respect to the simply chemical.

In any environmental conditions, with or without DNA, in the presence of oxygen or in its absence at the dawn of life, two alternative mechanisms still guarantee the maximum possibility for living nature.

The characteristic of living beings (whether animals, plants, fungi, protists, or Monera) is their ability to respond to stimuli and the fact they have a life cycle. The evolution of living organisms takes place by sum of biological skills, genetically transmitted and adapted to the environment. In animal cells there is no cell wall, which is a characteristic of plant cells.

The organisms of the plant kingdom and the fungi are *autotrophic* organisms (work a little, look for the definition. Okay, I'll tell you, they feed on inorganic substances). The *heterotrophic* eat organic substances produced by the autotrophic.

Again, the viruses are not always living but are activated only under specific conditions otherwise they behave like crystalline minerals.

Coral reefs grow in tropical seas, if they have light, down to about sixty meters: they are of biological origin. They sink under their own weight and become coral rocks, death after sixty meters. Over tens and tens of millions of years like this until they are 10 kilometers thick. Other millions of years and they are found to be known as the Dolomites, and protrude from the surface up to 4 km; not in the Caribbean but in Italy, today in a temperate area. Clownfish and sharks or shellfish don't live on them today but marmots chamois and people. Dynamic equilibrium!

I allowed myself to get carried away but I've given you something to think about. I highly recommend you do it calmly, feed yourself in small bites.

So far I've spoken of nature describing it as a process of interaction, in terms of the available energy for creating a dynamic equilibrium. I've stated that the most stable equilibrium, towards which nature tends, is the most restful (where the expenditure of energy necessary to maintain the least required thus having a higher probability of existence and long-term survival). A system that evolves and is structured as a result of the repetition and multiplication ad infinitum of the simplest forms for maximum efficiency and minimal energy costs; is therefore a system of low energy use is more stable. A chaotic system with E tending to 0 with respect to a system that requires and uses a lot of energy: organized with E tending to 1 (is the theory of chaos).

Man studies natural systems, nature and himself, by applying to ecology, the complex of interacting dynamic equilibrium, the scientific method: observation, deduction, independence of the observer, objectivity, measurement, reproducibility of phenomena, defined for the greatest number of events possible, the space where they take place, the time and the number of interactive parameters involved: who does what, when and where referring them to a certain and shared reference system.

I've defined pollution as one state of alteration, a disease, which coincides with the alteration of the environmental parameters most frequently and statistically known and present. Therefore for the way of life I said that any organism is alive and living, which is able to feed itself on its own and grow, survive as long as possible (putting in place strategies) and reproducing itself (as a species). I affirmed that simple or complex organisms exist unicellular or symbiotic and synergistic aggregates of other organisms and that each and everyone has the same objective, to live.

In the end I decided that the more complex they are, the more developed the simple basic biological skill, choice, in the coordinating organ: the brain. They do this for the purpose of obtaining the conditions to facilitate and allow life, achieving its own pleasure that comprises constantly selecting the most favorable from between two alternative possibilities. Furthermore I've said that life evolves through the random acquisition of new skills and the sum of biological skills, simple and useful, genetically transmitted and adapted to the environment that the most successful will be the simplest with highest yield and lower energy cost. Nevertheless no acquired biological skill is suppressed or lost.

I ask myself what does it mean: To Live according to Nature! Words we fill our mouths with and for which we desperately seek recipes in models that are served up daily by the media.

Humanity is gradually moving away from the natural (as always and more, dominating it and using it, but losing the sense of integrating with it). It is a fact that current lifestyles lead inexorably to disease! But for the rest in all the styles they do and have always done. The difference is, if anything, in the pursued capacity to enjoy life. As long as possible.

Life regime: the words literally mean diets, directly from the Greek!
New proposals every day, year after year confirmed by 'science' and
recommended by the 'scientific community' and regularly contradicted some time later: butter is bad for you, butter is good; meat is bad
for you like chocolate and salami, eggs but the same do good and are
rich in free radicals that prevent (???) aging, etc. etc. The secret is
simply in moderation!
If the weight-loss products and touted diets were effective there
would not be all those people who are too fat, lean or obese, and
everyone would be young and beautiful!
Here we go again with the stimulus for immediate sacrifice for the
promise of a happier life after! Another religion! Eliminate a food they
like too much, with nothing for entire categories of foods, it is simply
wrong: imposes renunciation and sacrifice, not necessary, for living
well and happily and not even to then get to heaven. To avoid getting
fat so as not to have to lose weight the only diet: eat less!
Where do the largest number of fat and obese live in the Italian territory? Where was the famous and 'healthy' Mediterranean diet created
and used! Without calorie control. A diet that is certainly varied and
therefore it is good but the quantities are off balance. Or that fanatical vegan, more ethical than healthy who always asks for artificial integration. I don't know if the salad was treated and how and certainly
don't agree with replacing breast milk with soy! Also in the alternative
diets (an area, only potatoes, onions, bananas, steaks, etc.) alimentation can also be out of balance because of eating too many or too
few of a variety, proteins or carbohydrates or fats.
I am convinced that those who eat well without excess, certainly
won't be safe and live for two hundred years, but those who eat badly, will definitely live what little time they have.
That life is nutrition on the fly with non-food and snacks and then taking medications and supplements, otherwise renouncing the pleasure of the table and of company, which instead is possible without having to exceed or at least not too often? Get it wrong and pay and
fast!

People who can afford it now (not the ones that have to pay attention
to survival) would like a better relationship with other people and a
less stressful life, healthier, those who get closer to Nature (?).

Advertising is the art of telling lies without lying!

For animals living in the wild, good health is taken for granted. Without it, they die! For man it is the same but the oligarchy of financial and productive global economic control, most of its existence is based on this need. Food, water, production, raw materials, labor, agriculture, pharmaceuticals ...
Pharmaceuticals, a multinational industrial source of power and unheard of power on a worldwide basis: perhaps the only one that really trespasses over states and boundaries. Unfortunately or fortunately, epidemics, except for influenza, mainly take place in developing countries, synonymous with the poor and subject to intensive exploitation, economic blackmail since they are without the adequate technological and scientific means to limit its spread. Man but mostly Western women could no longer live without the presence of pharmaceuticals.

Eating patterns sponsored by production companies, imposed by the need to institute consumption and financial yield, high in calories and low in fiber, supplements, are linked to certain chronic diseases; I read about them often: atherosclerosis, hypertension, overweight and obesity, diverticulosis and constipation, etc. The same, I read quite often, are explicable even for jobs and sedentary lifestyles and stressful or that makes one nervous: today one says fatiguing. All these states involve a concrete use of medicines and health facilities for which the pharmaceutical and insurance companies are thanked.

I don't know anyone today, and I believe it's hard to meet someone, who doesn't complain of some disease or disorder: it is considered normal to be affected and conforming to declare it.
Good morning, how are you? you get by, my back pain, my veins, my neck, rheumatism, I had a check-up yesterday, my *heart, diabetes, pressure* ... and so on and so forth ... and again good morning to everyone.
We are constantly bombarded with information that gives us an inside view of new syndromes and diseases (worrying) and the need for research (expensive) for the care needed to combat them but most of the necessary funds, to be allocated after they've been collected with

taxes, for various enterprises and institutions that must carry out such research.

What more do I know and what do I think of the quality of a human organism that lives in the globalized society?

Our organism is a machine: it works with chemical energy provided by the nutrients that we take from the food distributor. Proteins, lipids or fats, carbohydrates or glycides. Fundamental, water! Absolutely primary and indispensable: absolutely the first element needed for humankind and the world itself is perpetually at war over its control, whether locally or globally.

The organism has a natural ecosystem. As with all natural systems, the most durable and stable equilibrium corresponds to the one that uses the system at the lowest possible value. A production cycle at the end has a budget and also our organism has an energy balance. There are entrances and exits. And various items of expenditure or provisions. Incoming energy taken through alimentation. Output energy spending for all biological work. Maybe there could be a balance. In practice there is only a slow, steady, gradual accumulation of losses year after year. The energy balance budget would correspond roughly to an individual's weight and shape with the statistical norm. The energy balance is passive for an underweight individual; it is active for an overweight individual or at least not the norm, always statistics. But it is trivializing. All in all it is less dispersive energy, those who can live better and longer, where you can, if you can happily.

True health is not merely the absence of disease. Health is an interdependent phenomenon of physical energy, mental and spiritual, of the enjoyment and environmental availability for being and staying healthy. In the end health is the pleasure and the opportunity to enjoy it.

Irony of fate: while conquering knowledge and appreciation for good food and cooking, it decreases the ability to enjoy them at will! Aging and death are the normal development of life.

It took me a lifetime to learn how to taste and appreciate foods, wines, combinations etc. and now that I know a little more, I have to eat less. Eating happily in company, what we like the most, appropriately varying and alternating the choice of food is a pleasure. I don't want to give it up if not for urgent reasons. If possible, I want to avoid excessive and self-imposed sacrifice.

Me and my organism often talk, I think it is important to satisfy its requirements therefore I take time to learn. Among the needs of our organism are also and most of all *pleasure* and giving up is just plain stupid. Eating is also a pleasure not only out of necessity. Today we must study in order to select wholesome and healthy foods, distributing them correctly throughout the day. Eating correctly is an undertaking. To provide our body everything it needs: the energy needs but also micronutrients and allow for (lifestyle) of optimizing the use of the environment in which we are living.

What today is natural or natural-like or behaving according to a natural pattern, etc. is at least difficult to define and depends on where, how and when and to what this definition applies (who knows why space-time and interactive parameters).

Enjoying good health corresponds to having a healthy body or an acceptable compromise. A healthy person, physically and mentally the two are inseparable, can do work that provides more satisfaction, have more intense relationships, more varied and rewarding and possibly more time to do everything.

The problem of health, mine and strength and also of all those I meet and they ill-treated me with the explanation of their and the constant media bombardment only matched by foods and drinks, detergents and intimate accessories, palliative medicine and a few cars or mobile phone (the sum of advertising is all here), it prevents me from thinking about it. What do I draw from this? Health is necessary for the management of our own lives so that we can take advantage of the time available and in an economically productive manner. Time and health! In addition to health management, time management: autonomy, self-management, independence (more or less free to choose) a lot of fun to be enjoyed.

Economic development for the following decades includes two main ways that are economically advantageous and profitable for many (consumers) and extremely profitable for a few (the producers).

Words, words, partly true sacrosanct... Healthy mind in a healthy body! Better Lifestyle! Relax! Prevention! Constructive Mental Attitude! Getting closer to nature. A little Physical exercise! Fresh Air and Sun! Save the World!

About nutrition, living in Parma, foodvalley, where the trade fair event Cibus was located and the University of the kitchen, I see that most advertising is based on products in the area. It is very important for the national economy. Unfortunately, I also see we are constantly bombarded by advertisements for all kinds of products e but certainly not food (which is useful and necessary: sufficient and necessary conditions).

'Foods' are not all alike and are seasonal and local; the nutritional elements are normally present in the right place at the right time. It is important to remember that all the useful principles are contained in food, and all are essential but, excess transforms them from useful to harmful, for everyone. 'Foods' may be lacking or overabundant. The best time to eat is when you are hungry; a few hours of fasting in the meantime, is not at all harmful!

The media, and more specifically those in control, do their part! We propose among other supplements of the principle nutrients proposed and provide you whatever they are, necessarily, lacking. They propose alternative foods and palliatives to remedy the faults that these products, healthy, cause every day.

Natural food equals healthy food: this statement is not worth anything. An unbalanced amount of healthy foods does not necessarily create healthy eating and healthy eating still won't cure everything, indeed doesn't cure anything!

The way everyone eats is also the way they all get sick! There are one hundred billion cells of over fifteen billions of different types in the human organism, all to be fed in a different way.

I believe it is commonly known that poor nutrition leads to a condition of poor health but misinformation or rather partial information makes things worse.

Nutrition is passed off as the simple intake of nutrients. As for the ailment, it is passed off as illness, we are told that a homeopathic medicine, that has very little or almost no active substance, the most dilute possible, is an excellent cure and sold in pharmacies.

They sell 'the nothing' at a high price!

If true it would be enough to drink a daily glass of water from the river Po that contains traces and also even more, of every known principle, previously diluted in distilled water tanks, to cure all the world's ills.

Health is also the result of proper nutrition that is the consumption of food (no nutrient mixtures) as natural as possible in correct quantities and combinations, and then also of the possibility for elimination of most of the toxins and unusable materials, gradual and periodically continued detoxification, outside of meals, with as far as possible an appropriate lifestyle.

Proper nutrition is only a prerequisite (one of many) for the equilibrium (dynamic and interactive) between the body chemistry and its functional environment.

But then, I ask myself why eat? How do you eat, how should you eat? What do we really need?

It would be beautiful and this is what the social manipulators tend to do, man could possible live consuming only nutrients, easy to produce and synthesize with low production costs and high profits and not the simple, imperfect, 'food' from the vegetable garden: science fiction nutrition from pills. The usual logic would say that nevertheless a diet made up of only nutrients would be more difficult to design, calculate, plan, manage and maintain, than walking on the moon and returning given the billions of single human individuals present in the world. Paradoxically, this reasoning is also the basis for the success of pre-packaged trendy diets.

Is it possible then, scientifically, to guarantee a balanced diet? Foods contain, to varying degrees but always balanced, nutrients! but when, how much and how nature wants them and not mathematics. A lot of precise nutritional information is provided about food; there are too many, far fewer and obviously less precise about foods. The available information should be transformed into rational choices about food consumption as close as possible to the real needs of our specific organism.

I was given and will give you a tip: eat everything, only a little of everything and as often as you can, at least if you are not athletes.

We always need *water*, in males it makes up between 75% and 60% of our body, more or less, according to age. Water is the environment in which chemical transformations take place, enzymatic and biological indispensible for supporting life. We need *macronutrients*: the *proteins* for the synthesis of cell structures and for the repair and construction of worn out tissues. They are digestible (that is become metabolically usable) only after many transformations, but their use is enduring. *Lipids* are also needed, the fats that transport fat-soluble vi-

tamins and protect, lubricating, all tissues and organs. They are digestible (that is become unusable) with transformation processes and
faster than proteins, but slower than carbohydrates and they have a
vital energetic function for long-term efforts where energy must be
released over longer periods (for example to support pregnancy). Finally certainly carbohydrates are needed for quick to use energy. In
the end all *carbohydrates* become glucose. They are digested very
quickly, but at different times depending on the complexity of the
molecules. *Sugars* (fruits) are burned immediately: give a burst of high
energy, but not lasting, followed by a crises of withdrawal within a
short time (hypoglycemic crises). Pasta and rice starches are burned
and digested more slowly releasing energy continuously over a few
hours.
Carbohydrates are our most common and main source of energy.
Where are they found? A simplification that I like is most indicative of
the lack of information disseminated and yet it is quite simple: all that
is motionless and grows from the earth are carbohydrates, everything
that moves, independently of the earth, are proteins; fats are in both
categories.
Foods: brioches, pasta, bread, pizza, desserts, snacks, the sugars in
coffee, in drinks, worse if carbonated, ice-cream and snacks: better
from cane, who knows. The one selling it will certainly explain why.
Like the salt from the Alps, from India, from mountains, pink black
green and blue. I thought it was the sodium chloride, the principle extract from the sea, fossil or less, with the mixture currently more balanced, of dissolved salts. It is obvious and commonplace to say that
each and every one, can do good.
But can food over time imbalance the chemical basis for our health? I
think so when they are too refined (this means not food but food ingredients, mixtures of simple compounds and well defined) or are full
of additives that aren't necessarily harmful. We forget *micronutrients,
vitamins* and *mineral salts* and the *enzymes* (metal catalysts, the fat-
soluble vitamins that penetrate the cell membranes or the water soluble or those that don't penetrate directly). All of these are involved
as catalysts, activators, integrators, bio-regulators in biological processes; they are essential for life. Other minor components (hormones,
probiotics, amino acids, etc. serve the same purpose).
They sell them all, separately, at the pharmacy.
It is not said then, widely believed, that if we eat carbohydrates the

carbohydrates will be stored and if we eat fat they will necessarily end up as fat: it depends on the conditions and time of energy use.
I remember, also if now they all say that these don't exist any more that once seasons existed in nature that alternated in the various territories where the animals like humans, are a part.
Local foods are seasonal! In season, then they are available and should be used as much as possible. In the production season, the body recognizes the foods because it is in tune with the environment itself.
The winter fruit produced in other countries and climates is fruit, is healthy but does not suit the context of life: therefore it is unnatural. Globalizing in terms of food has become true: there are no more seasons, worse for us, or is it good? It will take time for bodies to get used to the new conditions, in the meantime, some will die, others will get sick, others will adapt: in any case humans and their world will change evolving.

When I was a child they sold the pasta brand 'Gluten Buitoni Pastina'. The gluten was added. Today it is a problem, as established for a few people with celiac disease, but since it is profitable the entire production advertises gluten-free products. Orange juices, milk, meat, polenta, rice, are advertised and labeled as if they were products specifically without gluten. It was not enough to list the very few products containing it and prohibited for them, such as bread and pasta flour and produced especially for them. It was necessary to prove that one even if they are well, if they are not celiac, today, unlike then, perhaps it is true it is better if they don't eat gluten ... maybe it's true, who knows ... They call it prevention and label orange juice or polenta as being without gluten, the gluten free cost and are sold in pharmacies. At this point I cannot fail to evaluate intolerances and allergies. My son is lactose intolerant as is half the world's population; I have become allergic to certain perfumes and mushrooms, which I have always eaten greedily, and with satisfaction.
We are different individuals, unique, all differently sensitive to the side effects that occur in reaction to everything we do.
Tests on intolerances are often quackery with bombastic fantasy names! Food intolerances or they are pathological (illnesses such as celiac disease) and then are cured seriously or are disorders resulting

from metabolic problems in respect to some nutrients that are certainly pharmacologically active and present in food. The effects are always very personal and dose-dependent.

I like grapes and I get stomachache: either I give up the pleasure of grapes or every so often I have a stomachache. I eat fewer and less often but I will not give them up. My body is accustomed to recognizing the disturbing foods and I have no particular problem, sooner or later I will encounter them in any case, in more or less processed and refined foods, one or the other of the principles that bothers me perhaps without knowing it. Each of us must learn to recognize the causes of the illness and to manage the unwanted effects.

The conversation about allergies is totally different, they trigger abnormal and traumatic effects with infinitesimal doses and may occur suddenly even because of something that we have always used with no apparent problem. Our environment sensitizes us, our defenses grow develop and turn against us. They have gone from the war with arrows to nuclear, they make you feel the effects.

Our world is media-induced and controlled; advertising induces illusions and in particular nutrition: promises that are impossible to keep. Often, I think, the exact opposite of what you can really get. Striking examples? Drinks rich in sugar should quench thirst; light products, high-calorie; the advertising of mineral water as if it were simply drinking water without informing you that it is not necessarily drinking water but drinks, soft drinks, with specific characteristics, or without salt or with too many salts, and thus to be used differently in different contexts.

Advertising is the art of falsifying reality without lying. The art of selling products identical or slightly different extolling the minimal merits of one or the other boasting about the quality, (*it is good and better, is new, cheap and does well, is always with you, we ate it all, it makes you hear better*). They are not lies but are not objectively observable or measurable.

All substances in fact, advertised or not whatever they are, liberate and fight the free radicals occupying them. Red wine makes good blood, they said when there was little to eat. Red wine fights free radicals with anthocyanins (true if you drink 50 liters a day). The red wine anyway contains alcohol, which is always toxic. Where is the truth and where is the lie? Whoever drinks beer lives for a hundred years! Whoever manages to scientifically explain how mineral water can fight them more effectively? What does the hardness matter, if you don't suffer from kidney stones or osteoporosis? Or the percentage of sodium if you aren't sick? (It is not that dangerous, if anything it is dangerous to eliminate it). The value indicated as healthy for salt is far less than what is taken in eating and drinking, even a little, without adding any. Apart from the fact that the phenomenon of water retention doesn't depend on sodium alone, because they don't explain that you should drink 50 liters of water with an average normal sodium content to have the same amount of sodium normally found in foods? Save the sodium in the mineral water (choosing water without sodium in respect to the norm) is like hoping to become rich saving 5 cents per day. Someone manages: the bottlers.

Advertising acts deceptively or misleadingly particularly with respect to food information; it is governed by the pharmaceutical and food industries. Using psychological methods of persuasion based on half-truths or exaltation of desires. It invites us to consume foods without fat, but with a lot of carbohydrates.

I have read many nutrition labels: often they have useful comparative information about the components and calories provided. You may discover that they have virtually the same calories as the normal.

I'm watching an American television series about marriages. They only show women who are enormously fat.

The television, newspapers, fashion, in today's world is full of dancers and gymnasts, models, etc. fat is ugly! Thin with a fit body: indispensable.

Yet men, reproductive animals that although they look at and admire them, find and marry strong women with wide hips exactly as they did ten thousand years ago, with an ideal ratio waist–hips of about one to three.

Yet the scientific community (yes even, I admit that there is a serious and impartial scientific community), in this case the part that seems most impartial, says that body fat is essential at the right age, the right amount, for normal health. Without this fat, life is impossible.

One part is actually essential. The average statistical percentage of this fat is different for the two sexes: (Source: Behnke Model) 3% men, 12% women and corresponds to the minimum value compatible with a state of health.

Fat is a reserve of valuable vitamins and trace elements; it comprises an energy reserve for aerobic activities (of a low intensity and prolonged nature) prevent the rapid depletion of energy produced from the sugars. Fat is contained in bone marrow, in the tissues of the heart, lungs, spleen, kidneys, intestines, muscles, in parts of the nervous system; fat makes up a large part of our brain, comprises the myelin sheaths that cover the nerves; form the cell membrane of any cell. The fat deposit is subcutaneous, which covers the viscera and protects them from the mechanical point of view. The percentage is different for the two sexes, but to a lesser extent than for the primary fat: 12% men, 15% women (Source: Behnke Model).

The highest percentage of body fat in women is related to sexual and reproductive functions.

In summary if I understand correctly, it is not mentioned at all, at least for women, that the appearance (big current word) of slender build coincides with having a low percentage of body fat. It is not correlated in any known way (for me).

The human body or living organism generally knows how to turn all foods to its advantage into the components required, with greater or lesser efficiency and production of waste (dross) higher or lower.

The maniacs, fanatics, are not psychologically healthy and balanced. It's called *orthorexia* the obsession with healthy eating. Orthorexic fanatics are convinced that health depends crucially on alimentation. They give up whole categories of foods, reducing the quality of their alimentation, demonize a macronutrient at the same time, usually carbohydrates (but not vegetables...) or meat, cheese, etc. products having an animal origin. They are like the saints and ascetics of a new religion that proposes and imposes sacrifice and abstinence. They impose strict dietary rules, again supported 'by science' and on one side the scientific community forces the individual taking away the pleasure and satisfaction, providing the basis for strong feelings of guilt. In fact their diet deteriorates, it becomes low calorie but inevitably unbalanced. The result is they become ill. Weak people and unable to accept their own physical identity which moreover out of shame they do it themselves without a doctor's advice: increasing the renunciations thus aggravating all possible imbalances and their overall health.

The pleasure of food can only be a further demonstration of the brain
mechanism: combining what is useful for the body to a sense of pleasure; the excesses and deficiencies cause spikes of pleasure and
subsequent withdrawal symptoms, sorrow, pain, malaise: but generally lagging behind the intake.
I bought and ate a cheese with satisfaction at the limit of the use by
date, sold at half price.
I know very few things that actually have an expiry date, most, especially processed foods instead have a recommended use-by date, by
which the manufacturer can guarantee the organoleptic characteristics of the product itself.
It is not discounted at all that going beyond the product date, it will
be harmful to consume it. Possibly it will be different and perhaps
less functional or pleasing; I like to eat mature cheeses so this is an
optimal result.
The true expiry date of foods is a fact certain and verifiable by all such
as the deterioration of health in disease, from the modifications involved; for example you will never buy a swollen tin because it will certainly be altered or rotten fruit or stinking fish.
Margarine in its time was referred to as a dietary alternative to olive
oil and to butter, it is hydrogenated oil that is virtually unusable by
bacteria and therefore is industrially used to extend the date of recommended consumption of foods that might otherwise certainly not
have lasted unalterable so long (try it by leaving a piece in the window
next to butter for a very, very long time). On the recommended date
of consumption, sold in the common information as an expiry date,
they play commercial games and responsibilities in favor of consumerism and therefore of income earnings for the large producers and
sellers at the expense of the poorest.
Enough about eating now I'm hungry!
Throw it out, destroy it, to favor and support price and consumption.
Don't reuse. And tons of oranges and fruits are crushed by bulldozers
and buried in landfills under the eyes of the television cameras. No
one is scandalized: I AM.
Is it possible that even today the concept that recycling and reuse
are different things have not yet taken hold? Many things have beco-

me reusable and in the end recyclable in other different products. It should be destined for disposal or destruction only at the end of the process, obtaining the last remaining energy available. But this doesn't work well in our world. They still make landfills hidden in the mountains and woods, quarries, with the least amount of selection and controls.

I'll retrace my footsteps because they've made me really nervous. But does sport really make you lose weight and keep you fit and healthy? Analyzing using the scientific method: work is the result of the force of displacement. The speed with which the work is done has nothing to do with the total work. Calorie consumption depends only on the duration of the effort that is worked. A slimming sport must exert effort doing the most work possible that is as hard as possible compatible with its uniqueness, variable over time, which allows us to run the longest road possible within a defined time.
What an effort, what sacrifice: then that's great!
You don't need to sweat to lose weight but only to lose water and salts that still must and will be restored by drinking throughout the day. To burn calories you need to work not sweat.
The physical effort is fed into the aerobic environment by the circulation and then with the formation of 36 molecules of ATP (energy) for every two of glucose (1 to 16) that is metabolized).
Under excessive effort you can still work but in an environment without oxygen, anaerobic, with the production (less efficient) of 4 molecules of ATP for every two molecules of glucose metabolized (energy ratio 1 to 2) but with the production of alcohol and lactic acid, and other products that are toxic, which are expelled from the cell causing pain.
Well, I understand this: we live in a social world for a small part real and mostly fake.
At the base of energy use there are three hormonal equilibriums, each dedicated to a specific function: metabolizing the sugars, metabolizing fats, metabolizing proteins.
Diets often act only on one or two of these therefore altering complex equilibriums and they don't do any good over the long term.
To eat only protein is not fattening but the maximum amount of proteins that our body uses to build muscles is low and you cannot force

it to use more for this purpose.

Water retention is not cured by sodium free water. Water will still provide it in a negligible amount. Sodium is essential to life. It is better not to add salt, add little salt, avoid salty foods and ones that don't contain phosphates. You drink also eating, in fact foods are substantially made of water and salts like us. Drinking now and then is certainly fine but drinking 'too much' water, does not conflict with, or favor, water retention!

Free radicals are the normal mechanism of chemical and biochemical molecular actions, parts of negatively charged molecules that tend to bind to hydrogen atoms from other molecules. They are active mainly on fat cell membranes and proteins in the nucleus. Advertising indicating the products one by one, makes it even actually difficult to say what doesn't fight free radicals that is as is logical that they would not otherwise age us, our skin, our organs. Perhaps wine is also good for your heart, but it definitely hurts the liver! In hectoliters it fights free radicals.

A single cigarette introduces up to 10,000 molecules with free radicals to be fought with antioxidants that at the maximum given the disproportion may be poorly efficient.

It is not the food itself but the quantity that creates problems!

Eating is a necessity for the body, everything is necessary, the brain invests the sensation of pleasure if it receives and of pain if it does not.

Eat well, in a balanced way, it coincides with pleasure and satisfaction in the flavor, of the aromatic and optical sensations, the pleasure of the company, the conversation, up to the healthy attainment of satiety; the proof is that to exceed this limit corresponds to a certain and rapid displeasure in respect to the abuse! At the least it will be a pain in the stomach, belly and head or a sense of guilt.

There is nothing permanent or eternal in nature: the woods and forests burn, the rivers, carrying sand and silt, form marshes where there were meadows and forests; bacteria form coal gas and oil; the eroded coasts become eroded plateaus that form new plains; the ice ages follow those that are torrid and again and again. The animal species go extinct all the time and are replaced; life unfolds and evolves; man operates, living one becomes ill and dies; works are developed and then destroyed renewing in a different way until the same man (species) dies, the old always leaves room for the new.

Globalization: always on the increase is the spread of epidemics on farms raising animals and in monoculture agriculture; among the causes are exploitation and intensive treatment and equally intensive raising of livestock in emerging countries that are less controllable. Smuggling and counterfeiting towards the commercial raisers of livestock and Western producers, the absence or scarcity of controls, or embezzlement, increases the risk factors for the health of animals and people. The globalization of livestock raising and of agricultural in respect to the species that are most useful for producing an immediate profit, produces alteration in the environmental parameters and balances, albeit minimal, between the biological systems; in fact, it constitutes a negative pollution; modifies the biodiversity factors, uproots and extinguishes the reservoirs of biological skills present and embedded in local ecosystems of different territories and nations. It is a real threat to the biodiversity available to humankind, to natural variations in environmental conditions. It is a real threat to the agrofood economy in those productive sectors, not only in the countries directly affected but everywhere. It is a real threat to the health of people in the world changing the current equilibrium in which we are immersed.

The intensive use of fertilizers, pesticides, fungicides, herbicides; the implementation of industrial-chemical manipulations, with additives, preservatives, colorings, artificial flavorings, and biochemical, with hormones, antibiotics and medications produces devastating and lasting effects on the biological system to the foundation of agriculture and on the different cultures and eating habits, producing intolerances and allergies in exponential growth in consumer countries.

The transformation of food products into food includes the addition of (overall) large amounts of thickening substances, preservatives, coloring agents, antioxidants, flavor enhancers to improve conservation and adapt to standardized taste that is gradually imposed at the worldwide level with the imposition of new non-native products and the change in locally rooted eating habits.

As always, a minimum alteration in the equilibrium between the interactive biological parameters corresponds to a pollution, which is per-

ceived as negative by the one who suffers from it.
Our organism and that in general of global man has not been able to
develop because of the lack of time possible for adequate defense
mechanisms. Humans have not had time to adapt maybe they will.
The globalization of the system, today you can say world, ever more
manipulated by a dominant oligarchy centralizing financial and production power, cannot fail not to discount populations, on the margins of
the economic globalization of manufacturing and agrifood, the phar-
macological effects derived from the migration of large masses of populations, to the food-related differences to modification within the
context of the territory they belong, to cultural and religious residues
that migrants export, the environmental context in which they developed.

Society, religions and uses also alimentary of those born and genetically imposed for hot climates taking account of the environmental
conditions did not allow them to keep food for long especially meat
or milk; there was the need to drink vasodilators, needed for the conservation of the optimal body temperature (homeostasis).
For populations in cold climates food storage was easy but they needed to eat high-calorie foods and fats.
People now move rapidly, as a result of social changes and of changes imposed by their culture but their eating habits don't change as
quickly: the African forced to emigrate to Germany will have to contend with sausage and pork fat, and probably will feel bad, psychologically and physically and should be cured beforehand, at least in the
West; with great joy I dare say, by the pharmaceutical support of that
same hegemony.

To close the topic definitely I will apply an extreme synthesis maybe it
will be useful if, reading, you jumped over all the didactic part.
The scientific method allows for objective measurement and evalua-
tion, that is, to consolidate the experience (to learn), but this is its limit.
Imagination, intuition and practical intelligence, allow them to break
away from the scientific method and analysis of phenomena, to return to observing the chaos and make inductions as well as deduc-

tions and choices which, while subjective, are not necessarily wrong
or unnecessary but rather, valuable for the rapid advancement of
knowledge and, consequently, on the scale of adaptation and evolution of the species.
Man is not completely free but can increase his freedom and independence, or at least convince himself to do so and be satisfied.
Excuse the technical derivation!

Now that I have summarized things for myself and remembered the
solid foundation of my beliefs I can again think freely. Thoughts start
to flow freely, uncontrolled and not rationally guided they flock to
mind, I return to my memories.
Over time I've collected memories and also impressions that I have
derived from situations and people I've met, behaviors and conversations, observations often collected at the bar, which forced me to see
something teaching me, I believe, that everyone's life is held in a different way that wealth or poverty influences the means but not the
substance and that deep inner loneliness accompanies us always.

I was so immersed in my thoughts, who knows what, that suddenly I
found myself in the middle of the city center, with passersby, black,
red and white, silver cars, yellow busses some green that passed by
gliding and generating a continuous noise alternating, enveloping. I
was passing in front of a lit coffee... attractive. I mad craving for coffee.

Getting up in the morning, I look out the window: its spitting, no there's mist; a shiver. Dress up and drag yourself out in the cold and re-
luctantly go back to work as always, business as usual. A mist to freeze your breath. Smile guy begin again!

Traveling with my daughter, in Sicily near Messina: a random stop, a
small castle apparently abandoned on a hill completely open; within
the walls of a small disused cemetery abandoned since at least 1985,
the last date on the tombstone; ancient tombs or just old, half-open:
in one a small skeleton is visible. Shocking. Silence, an incredible view

that stretches to the sea and around us trees and scents, pomegra-
nates and the lemons rich with flowers, the unmistakable smell of
orange blossoms. When I watch a film located in Sicily I still remember the perfume that alone is enough to describe and speak of Italy,
the south, in the world.

I often like to go to the bar, spending half an hour, have a coffee, take
a look at the headlines strictly standing, watching and capturing pieces of conversations, situations, images. I don't like to sit down and
spend time with friends or chatting: what then? Work, gossip, rubbish.
As a boy of course the places frequented more and rigorously in
company out of necessity, with satisfaction and often very happily.

I remember a New Year's party, now it's morning. In the turmoil of the
party calm took over finally exhaustion. All those remaining with the
same apathetic air, absent. The waitresses are beginning to lift the
chairs onto the tables, to sweep away the streamers and the memories of the past evening. The band still plays the last songs, now enjoying themselves and improvising, maybe jazz. Voices that suddenly
rant: a woman is abruptly woken up, pulled down from her makeshift
bed after a colossal hangover. It is time to go home: Happy New Year
to everyone.

I like to watch people on the street: three young boys with shaved
heads and a kind of protruding ridge, two white one dark, dressed in
practically the same clothes, vest and a pair of pants with sagging lines. The black wears gold-rimmed glasses. Every now and then he
dries the lenses like a tic. They look like beggars but they are obviously well off professional unemployed. They go hand in hand, laughing,
looking at their cell phones, they talk about this and that, probably
like girls.
We were sitting under the arcades of via Mazzini to vote on the girls
who passed. No one ever got more than seven. Even we then could
afford to choose, at least in theory.
I remember one evening, a night actually, I was young. A bar open all
night, towards morning; in the bar room only four of us remained, all

near the counter, drinking the last coffee before we left. Late, almost dawn, there was a strange light. The scene of an unnatural calm even stranger. Two steps, a turn and suddenly collecting myself from momentary contemplation (thinking about it I often get goose bumps) I found myself immersed in the full vitality of the general market on the gravel square, surrounded by the happy confusion of traders who loaded, unloaded, arranged, haggled, joked and teased.
A florist opening up, and cleaned in the front of the store with the broom to arrange the banks of flowers on display.
I saw them dealing with a truck full of onions, nearly an hour, choosing and discarding boxes and crates.
An impressive speed a hundred meters from the quiet, relaxing, silent apathy of the bar and only an hour before. Strange, I realized that the walk into the market was much more enjoyable and relaxing than an evening at the bar.

I still like it today, sometimes in early summer, getting up early in the morning before people go out onto the streets, two street cleaners who wash the pavement, a kiosk and a bar that opens and the shop assistants and employees who slowly arrive. The city begins to come to life, and me with it.

Late July, warm even in the early morning. A man lying on a bench near the station gets up. Had he slept there? With rumpled suit long gray hair, held back in a ponytail. If he had reached out to passersby, probably they would have given him a hand out. Instead he lit a cigarette and stood there, watching the crowd of people flailing around and listening to the different sounds as you might listen to the sea, without asking anything of anyone.
I found out he defined himself as a master of life, he liked to give advice, express opinions and always found someone who stopped to talk to him who practically lived there, on that bench, for the whole summer. Everyone knew him, brought him coffee, a sandwich. He called himself a philosopher and he liked to be at the center of attention. He didn't drink, didn't ask for a hand out didn't sell lighters, towels, or lottery tickets, certainly he didn't wash himself much. In fact he didn't do anything. A human wreck, miserable exploitative, social

parasite or philosopher, purist, psychotherapist of the poor?! Who am I to judge? What right do I have though to judge? Why should I judge? His life takes place and he interacts with others. That is it.
Recently he died, the city bestowed honors and memories with flowers and posters at the bench.

I have a nice photograph, ironic, where I am in the prefecture leaning back in a golden chair, almost a throne, resting my elbows on the armrests, the fingertips making a peak like a small bell tower. From that bell tower I smile at the friends who pay homage to me... but... here is what power could be.

A spectacle of a really angry guy: there were two sitting at the bar, suddenly the hands of one of the two on the chair arms tightening with such force that the knuckles whitened showing the color of bone. Red face red purple: gasping, gurgling no sensible words. Anger evidently had tightened his throat. Eventually he got up and went away, without speaking or doing anything.

The same bar, always in two, probably I believe, a father and daughter evening. She was very chic, thin face, a pointed nose with a mass of red curls, graceful movements, quivering, slender, wearing a sheath dress of black silk; she was ready to go out and leave. I remember the scene of farewell: they came closer he put his hands on her shoulders and kissed the air next to her cheek, on both sides, certainly not to spoil her make up; she leaves with a flourish of her hand and a smile. I remember the wave of perfume, flowers and spices, left as a souvenir.

A mother at school had noticed that her son took drugs and stole. She was forced to make an impossible choice: her precious, obsessively beloved son or the cruel and wicked world. She was angry, she had to turn her anger against herself and suffer, or vent it against the whole world and get away from it all, lose all? Evidently she didn't know how to decide.

We were at Carrara during school time. I know that she lived for years simultaneously doing one thing and then the other: suffering and then drinking, becoming a slave like him to a habit and of the choice of living the solitude selfishly, becoming a brute, detaching becoming distant even from her husband who got tired and left! Understandable? Her son took drugs, her husband left. The failure as a wife, a woman and mother. I believe that as long as she lived she would suffer from this awareness.

Carrara was like this for the people who lived there: not involved, white-collar workers like at Massa; hard and strenuous work in marble, heat and the cold, from morning to night and then to the tavern not to the bar or restaurant like at Massa, a drink and talk about the company's policy of exploitation, to escape to return to the family, to necessary money, everyday problems, moaning; women and strong men who lived, but not egoistically parallel lives, refusing to gratify themselves and choosing to be realized in their children. But not everyone was so strong naturally.
In that environment, you could not but be convinced that the culprits could only be her and her husband, especially her husband, because he had neglected to do something. And maybe it was true.
I bet that the few who have remained close have continued to repeat that it had been society that betrayed her son (in Carrara the common belief that the blame for problems is always society that exploits people: are they wrong?) or that he himself, the boy, was the cause of his own downfall. The pain would certainly not have left him.
Failed as parents? No one had told them what they should do.
Can a parent fail in his or her role? In any case I don't think so!
My father, my mother, my wife and I: the same discussions... You can become anything you want and who can... We are only your parents... Whatever you decide to do in life, maybe at first we will get upset but then we will certainly let you do it.
We will also discuss, wearing you out, because the ideas are not always those that would make us content and happy at least we, can come to terms with you, but without a doubt never question our good intentions... and don't think that your mistakes can make our anger last very long. If you try you will always find us and we will try to be there when needed... without bothering you too much... but don't

make us angry... we are forced to bear with each other because we
have chosen to and put up with you because we have made you but
you also bear with us...

I met a guy at the bar who I later befriended, a little older than me,
polite ways and always quiet. A particular type, he was a watchmaker
in a shop with his mother. Eight, ten hours a day and always alone
and concentrated or with her who was at the desk or chatting outside.
His work was the only thing we spoke about, where he felt safe, everything else embarrassed him. He was shy and reserved.
When they wanted to make fun of him and laugh a little at his expense, they spoke of time clocks, mechanisms: then he started talking
and got excited, launching into long rants. People got bored listening
to him but he didn't notice and the 'friends' laughed, they took advantage of him and he knew it, but basically didn't mind because, perhaps, with his role he felt part of a group of friends.

I was no more than eighteen. I liked a girl at the bar, about 25 years
old, married for three and miserable. She appeared as a sweet and
serene quiet girl, who inspired poems from the boys. She was the
real reason for the many customers at the bar, kind and generous
she saw only the best aspects in others. So it seemed.
She was trying to make everyone happy, to run the house and work in
order to win the praises of her husband and in-laws, the owner of the
bar, of the customers. A job. Actually inside she was an angry, furious
woman. That girl was burning and seething with anger inside. Frustra-
ted, in fact she was eager to betray her husband, hoping to be discovered and make her parents desperate. So simple, so sweet, she
dumped the fault of her frustration on them... and she made many
customers at the bar happy except the owner.
Until I saw, her husband hadn't discovered yet. All had hidden the truth from him.
Lying is the lifeblood of society. The whole world lies constantly.
All of them had lied in their lives... It is a conversation that is often
picked up, especially coming from women who chat: parents, teachers, friends, children, even the husband or they lied or had lied

about what concerned them about some aspect of their existence from the most trivial to the most delicate. In this world you can no longer trust... Is it true?

Trust is necessary we must give it; place it in someone or something, you cannot help it because you cannot live alone and you cannot live without certainty. Trust meets both requirements, eliminates loneliness rendering one participant and provides the certainty of being able to receive disappointments and therefore it is very stimulating. Who does not trust, will certainly not perhaps be cheated, but lives alone and badly.

Good times those at the bar, friends, wasting time: time needed to grow.

Happiness is a sequence of stimulating moments but it is basically a simple emotion identifiable in retrospect: a sense of satiety languid and relaxed, identified with serenity, which is more similar. It is very different from the emotion with the adrenalin of fighting against the everyday, against pain, suffering, the abuse of power or the assertion or the search for that precise state that we often don't know how to recognize, excited and immersed as we are in the emotions that continually envelop us, conflicting and stimulating.

Young people are convinced of power all and mostly of the power to make things go their way. They are full of certainties, sure of knowing the causes and solutions, each of them sadly; and gradually realizing it applies to all, for each individual and thus remains in the end only the best compromise possible. They'll realize that unfortunately none of us is truly free because each is the product of the conditioning received from the society he was born into and where he lives; none of us is truly our own master.

I am aware that my individuality is only an illusion.

I hate social conventions, the need for cordial relations, traditions
that consolidate them like hate for the rules of the road. I don't accept them, don't respect them, it would mean calling out, living outside society, isolating yourself and giving up all that society offers in return for this sacrifice. It's like travelling down the road in a car, I would
like to be able to do it, always at maximum speed compatible with the
means and the structures, if only there were no other motorists on
the same road, but in fact there are, inescapably, and you have to live
with them and thus respect the limits and rules.

The code of laws and rules and regulations are dictated by people in
every age and situation directing and deciding what is best for society, at least at that time; it goes for the sense of decency, for the sense of shame, for the sense of adequacy, for everything.

I have always reserved the right to break any and every social rule
that was opposed to my personal ethics. I was a soldier like many, I
obeyed like everyone but I decided I and I alone, if having to go to
war, if and where necessary to, eventually, direct the barrel of my rifle.
It doesn't exist, there can be no obligation for anyone, not even a regulation that is not accepted and shared!

Normality is not of nature, it is a statistical concept of going by the rules; its definition varies according to the limits of trust imposed by the
society in which we live. Natural phenomena are almost infinite and all
different. Nature creates individuality. Billions of billions of individuals
that are a lot or a little different. Society defines normality and its
laws.
Uniformity, conformity, standardization, social ethics, allows societies
to evolve. There is no room for the individual, in a developed society;
the single ideas are classified, sorted, grouped, united and managed
together and then compulsorily, shared. A developed society cannot
be chaotic.
Nature is chaos, confrontation, conflict continues!

Is the stable society a natural concept?
Individual natural phenomena are in fact only organized chaos, by similarity and clustering of events that are freely interactive but repeated and under certain conditions, predictable. The organization of chaos is essential because the phenomena occur.
Society evolves if it is able to dominate nature. The society of men, a fact, thus comprises only a phenomenon; its existence is guaranteed through the order that allows the phenomena to be such. The phenomenon of society exists because the free interaction, between the unique individuals who compose it, becomes statistically probable under certain conditions. Society being necessarily ordered is then a natural phenomenon but unnaturally, it must continually recreate the order it needs to exist and maintain it.
A paradox? Contradiction? Chaos? All normal?
The order and symmetry are considered and perceived as beautiful, desirable, fundamental; man, however, loves the chaos of the wild, the excitement of the risk of unpredictability, the discovery of the new and the different.

The need for God, instinctive in humans, is derived exclusively from the need to endure and thus to hope for an improvement, whatever that is!

I returned to spend time in my town of origin: that widening and lengthening of time. Virtually every day there is a funeral, the bells ring and at three in the afternoon there are the funerals. Everyone is present or at least many. One leaves the office, work to take part, because the dead have friends or relatives who are also ours; there is participation.
No one has enough time for everything! All things in a small town require more time than is 'outrageously' taken from the 'normal' production.
A friend in Milan refused an excellent job in Parma because he believed it was too slow and boring and so that the offer of fun was too limited.
To go to the cinema in Milan he must come to an agreement and plan for a week, then it takes two hours between transportation and

car to go and two more to return home. Their evening of fun thus includes unavoidably dinner with burgers at shopping centers, connected to the cinema with shopping and bookstores, and more.

He sees his wife at night, unless he makes an appointment and they live totally separate lives but their house is full of antique furniture and luxury fittings. They have no television because they wouldn't use it.

City life is hectic, it is anonymous; my neighbor died in his house, I found out a month later because his daughter was selling the apartment. Individuals are alone or aggregates in places designated for mass amusement gathered in large numbers, among whom they feel even more alone. These places certainly conform to the average, defined normality of their own group. With Internet everything evolves into an even more pronounced form of shared solitude.

Another friend dropped everything and opened an agritourism in the mountains where, except on Sundays and some Saturdays, there's pretty much just him and sometimes family, slowing down to the extreme and isolating themselves from the 'pack' that he meets up with only out of necessity. Where is the norm? That is does it look right? Just explain their choice, no matter how.

I don't know anything about art: about me liking or not a painting or a sculpture, they tell me something right away or leave me indifferent. Only once I accompanied my wife and some friends to an exhibition in Treviso where a dozen paintings were shown by the same author who showed the same subject repeated in the paintings exhibited, the figure of a man in an arid landscape, grayish red. The works reinterpreted the subject approximately every two years. This peculiarity and a kind and prepared guide allowed me to understand that behind the last monstrosity of abstract lines and colors, seemingly random, that intersected and overlapped breaking each other, there was a path, a study, not a random evolution but desired and sought for by the artist who in those ten paintings wanted to document both his own artistic evolution and that of his thought. I realized that an abstract painting is not a random work and I was impressed by my profound ignorance about this topic. In any case, I understood and appreciated the path and the analysis but the final picture and also many of the previous ones, were cataloged under the heading mon-

strosity. The thought then I really hadn't understood. I am therefore
ignorant about matters of art, which is a fact. I felt even more ignorant and marginalized, reading that over a hundred thousand people
had visited the same exhibition, expressing enthusiastic praise. I never imagined there were so many people who were so competent
and involved.
Another time I appreciated the way that another far more famous artist, presented in some paintings exhibited at Amsterdam a rose garden, always the same, as it aged and the degradation of the views as
they advanced. I'm sure you all know who he is. This route of disease
that changes the personal vision of the world instead I understood it
perfectly. It was not necessary to interpret a deep thought, admitting
that there was one.
Still, I see that to admire the 'Girl with Earring' well over a hundred
thousand other people are lined up in Mantua spending € 40 each to
see it, more for the trip, lunch, and for some, the stay. Entire families
parents grandparents and teenagers, even children.
I admit I'm ignorant but wow, how do those hundreds of thousands
of people who don't make a trip without visiting at least two museums and an art gallery, that beam down on all the shows and they
talk of Van Gogh, Gauguin, Rembrandt or Picasso and Dali (I hope I've
written their names correctly) as if they'd known them at school? Ra-
phael, Titian, Giorgione, Mantegna, Michelangelo and Leonardo even
Giotto have exceeded them substantially, now no longer reserve surprises and emotions. They don't even buy the catalog of the exhibition because it is expensive? Oh they already know pretty much everything.
As for the plants, I know a lot of useful properties or medicinal properties of many of them, but I can barely identify them in reality, a
chestnut from a conifer. A beech from a birch. Not to mention the
herbs: I tell you what to pick where and when and how to use them
but I cannot recognize them. I have never been able to. Therefore I
am ignorant and incompetent in this subject.
Now I know how to appreciate the difference in technique between
pointillism, impasto and glazing; I can appreciate the aesthetic result
achieved; I've learned to recognize more or less the paintings of the
1400s and the end of the 1800s; the obsessive attention to detail in
the portraits of the great are useful for understanding how the powerful lived but also the poor in the various eras and how clothing

and furniture evolved. But I am certainly an ignorant incompetent!
In fact colors are more interesting; it is what I find and identify in the
pictures: I found that the art of painting follows hand in hand and
evolves, in the industrial characteristic of the era the paintings were
executed. The red vermilion of cinnabar and the blue of lapis lazuli for
the mantles of saints and kings, blue sulfate and verdigris or arsenic
for the landscape and the skies and the forests and the paintings of
ordinary poor mortals. The gold of the haloes was replaced by cadmium when it was available, the white lead of the white glazing, yellow
ocher and the red of the earth and walls. Pigments derived from
rocks, diluted in the albumin of blood or eggs, gave rise to the cracks
of time and then in oil, marked historical development, the social and
economic integration of Europe. Colors derived from plants for texti-
les and fabrics, from lacquer derived from Robinia, to the indigo of the
textile industry to print cotton. Gesso and vegetable gum for the can-
vases. Colors and pigments based on metal oxides and sulfides when
industry rendered them easily available, up to distempers, and to synthetic azoic pigments and then to the bright, modern indestructible
acrylics, when the synthetic chemistry was developed.
Art has evolved and progressed hand in hand with society and with
technology. Now perhaps I understand how and why it has gone from
concretism of naturalness, to the affirmation and documentation of
aristocratic power, and then to current abstraction to the demented
new trends.
I doubt that all will have realized before me that Guttuso (1912 to
1987) was certainly a master but also a forger who copied, an avid
craftsman, praised by critics and gallery owners soon to be abandoned and neglected after the discovery, impossible to be silenced.
Abandonment by the media aimed at maintaining without diminishing
the value of his paintings that had already been purchased.
They felt bad, they made me recopy his monumental squares when I
was in junior high for art education.
And Fabergé? Who doesn't know those precious eggs? Even sculptors
and architects know so many: David, Moses, La Pietà, Michelangelo?
But Leonardo was he also a sculptor, what did he sculpt? Well? And
even Bernini, that of the coffee maker in majolica, but is it the same
of the fountains and gables of the buildings? And even Palladio, the
one of the villas. I was just a failure at this. I was fascinated even less
by the paintings.

But the Veiled Christ and human machines? Those were fantastic. I seem to have been in Naples in some beautiful, monumental chapel but secondary in respect to the treasure of San Gennaro, I don't remember it well and you? There were very few people when I was there. It must have been chance.
I am doubtful that maybe I'm obviously different: less intelligent, less informed, less interested, less cultured than all of them and, therefore, might as well give up, on going to see exhibitions and museums just to fill an apparently unbridgeable gap. I'll be at home, in the garden, I will rest, read as I like to do and also save a little, for hard times, as my mother and father taught me. You never know!

Ignorance advances in the society I know, more and more educated but less cultured. Always more rapid and fragmented information, supported by the increasingly universally adopted dogmatism, the Montessori method of education; increasingly less investigation, always more available to the conditioning work of the media, from advertising, from the creators of artificial situations, from the inductors of non-basic consumer needs.
Who governs today's society? Who carefully avoids and silently, to the least nonconformity, individualism and free thought? Who requires and imposes conformity at any cost? Suffering social isolation, social enslavement. The financial oligarchies, economic, scientific production. Be quiet and obey without question, but whom? Free choice? In the name of a social prize, of a symbolic gratification socially presentable, of social ethics at the expense of your own individual ethics? It's right for the common good!
The good of the State, of society, is greater than that of the individual! The state may send you to die at war, then can condemn you to rot in prison, can even take your life for its sake. But wasn't the state the expression of the individual, a simple service for the protection of rights and duties, an association to regulate social relations guaranteeing individual freedoms and avoiding or at least reducing the clash of liberties that touched superimposing them?

The system works by funding either a scientific community which does not allow replications and autonomies, which expresses the thought of one or two or ten scientists, salaried; opinions expressed and strongly amplified in a particular time and place and customized in the two common dogmatic and demagogic phrases: science affirms, the scientific community confirms; whoever doubts is a conceited ignoramus. You naturally need an information system that supports them.

Oligarchies (the secret government of the few who carry out their own interests regardless of the people's) always manipulate and control society by inducing secondary needs and proposing solutions to their own satisfaction. Who doesn't need a fungicide for toenails to be shown in the summer? Who doesn't dream, while happily eating his single portion of pre-cooked ready for the table or *quattrosalti* pasta in the pan, to participate in a Master Chef in competition including, and this if it is not absurd and outrageous, the children, who indeed they even make them sing like adults? Who doesn't follow the Sunday cooks in the race between their dreaming of cooking with plenty of seeds and palm hearts or creating huge dishes based on grass peas and carob?

The media spread the tempting image of a fantasy world, communication communicates nothing more petty and complete.

People will provide football stadiums for matches as a corrupt place for the controlled release of violent instincts, musical concerts for hundreds of thousands of people, music and reality shows, soap opera trivially predictable with continuous re-mixing of four ingredients: all the protagonists meet, fall in love, quarrel, are reconciled, they leave, go away; sometimes the villain dies; they get together and live happily, in dream environments and in economic and social success. In this context, the current moral is being elaborated on!

I remember when I was a young man that I took part in the presentation of a Swedish project, and I was asked to actively take part in the development of San Domingo, which was still not very civilized and very natural: it was to provide an abundance of toilet paper and to stigmatize its need and convenience.

It was understood but no one mentioned that the indigenous people were not used to using paper, which until then had not been or had been used very little, its use would create the need for drains and sewers of bath systems and water treatment plants and waste disposal, and then, perfumes and soaps and any other kind of so-called comfort of a truly civilized life.

I went out shocked, it was contrary to my conception of the ethics of assistance, but only I was out while the project continued. And I, an individual who didn't comply, what role would I have had positive or negative? None! We take everything too seriously!!! We all believe that there is only one right way of doing things... it's the way we're used to.

There is only one logic that I respect: that of endless possibilities, freedom and opportunity, not that of prohibitions and taboos, judgments and prejudices. I was blessed to have met some, a few, brilliant teachers, many capable and interesting people, to have read and had interesting and instructive experiences but mostly, of having given myself the permission to try to learn as much as possible, without setting a limit, without getting tired of doing it; it is something I continue to do today. I'm happy when I go to bed and I can say: today I saw, understood, learned something new, something I didn't know before.

Earth, the mother of us all, the patient fertile virgin and generous with her children, if you don't take too much advantage of her! Start and end of a circle where everything moves back to its place, at the start. An endless cycle of concentric circles called nature.

I noticed casually, listening once to the litanies linked to the recitation of the rosary and recited in Italian (in Latin they were a song, a rhythmic sequence of sounds, enveloping but incomprehensible) that the Catholic Church defines among so many titles to the Virgin as Always Virgin Mother and not only virgin mother as she is normally and popularly known.

The Catholic Church, therefore, to commit its cult to the dogma of the virginity of the Mother of God doesn't question the possibility at all of a completely normal earthly life with other children besides Jesus, while never taking away the title of Mother of God, that is of the human Son of God who is the icon of human aspiration similar to the imagined God. A God who is capable of assuming human form and of exerting power on earth, recognizable in his image and likeness.

The man feels instinctively, for the dependency that the environment has and the variability of natural phenomena, the need to get in touch with the uncontrollable world, therefore, the spirit, of the invisible, the destiny of the gods. The innate desire to dominate his environment necessarily leads him to want to see, shape it, in order to take part and not simply submit.

The modus operandi of the Roman Empire comes to mind, which didn't conflict with and destroy but absorbed the pagan cults that it encountered during its territorial expansion, and under which, originated by Constantine onwards, from the start of Christianity to codified Catholicism, assuming temporal, social and economic relevance that negatively characterized, at least in the last millennium; absolute power, indeed imperial even superior to that which remains today a minimal legacy. It seems (to me at least) clear that the statement Always Virgin Mother absorbs and incorporates the ancient cult, indeed extremely ancient almost as much as man, of the earth mother, always the ever-virgin mother in an infinite cycle, eternal. The Madonna therefore represents the maternal principle, fertility, eternal renewal, independently of the story.
The symbols are the basis of religiosity applied to religion and that in particular doesn't seem to be a coincidence: Mother, Mary, Madonna. The downwards-pointing triangle M is the symbol of woman, that pointing up W of man, the opposite. Insert them, trace them and see if you recognize the central diamond evolution of the symbol of the initial Marian that you see in many churches. The triangle has three sides and three is the number that symbolically represents the possibility of generation. It is sacred.

It is strange to find that others often have a problematic if not unhappy family life. It is strange how this finding is common and it is strange that no one even talks about it, this I say, while it makes up the main topic of the conversations of others. It seems to be an exorcism.

The Montessori method of education was created to shape people to enslave them to the ruling regime; for this reason it is more than ever appreciated and has spread throughout the entire world: in the twenties the motto was to *Believe, Obey, Fight*; today it has been changed to *Believe, Obey, Compete.*

If you teach from primary school that Napoleon was a crazy egomaniac you will grow up with this certainty. Only much later in life, and only when someone asks if it was really like that.

The school has assumed scientific guidelines everywhere, with the de facto abolition of the willingness to access knowledge and free and creative thought in favor of easier and widespread knowledge, made up of notions, faith and certainty.

Believing: why think, discuss, opine, criticize? *Obeying*: in the name of a greater good or recognized ignorance. *Competing*: always compete, at all costs in life, work, fun, success, social survival and then to use and exploit the excess of vital energy that cannot be used otherwise, of the individual. Compete for glory, rather than to live longer healthier... better one day like a lion...

I feel that I should propose, every so often, reduced working hours. No matter how many hours you work, once the problem was to eat, sleep, make love a couple of times a year and produce children, it was necessary to engage in twenty hours of work; per day, now eight if they can waste two or three and get infinitely better results but the issue became what to do with the so-called remaining free time.

If you work hard five hours you have three more free to be committed: where and how? Who can profit? Society is not currently ready to respond adequately.

Even if your personal conviction gives you something to do to respect, satisfy, assist, your neighbor, to act honestly and not to take advantage, at times indeed you place yourself at their service, don't make the mistake of thinking that your fellow human will do the same for you.

Debts make friends treacherous and debts of gratitude even more so, because they are materially inextinguishable. Friends will turn against you at the first opportunity to escape the debt that you remember.

Man is an animal that behaves like an animal; he survives in every way
and to do so he cheats, lies, steals, kills the first time that he has to
choose whether his survival, his well-being, his status is at stake. And
not for this, in general, man is a wicked animal.
When I was in the military during the long nights on guard in the gun-
powder magazine, and in the nothingness and darkness of nature, superficially and apparently empty, made up of meadows and three-me-
ter fences, they had taught me to place snares to catch rabbits. We
needed to supplement the rations that always arrived late, cold and
not always attractive. Rabbits forced and pressed act instinctively: ir-
rationally they run away and run along the free pathway. They don't
see the snare. They put their head in without realizing it. The noose
tightens around its neck and as it wriggles frightened and desperate,
the noose tightens more. It is rapid. I never wanted to do it again, I
found it horrible but remembered it as useful, you never know. Today
I remember it in connection with many human behaviors. How many
times I've seen it happen around me, even if only in the figurative
sense but however equally destructive.
The need for having to rely solely on their ability to survive has become impossible.
Still today, within certain strict limits and conditions of being young,
healthy, strong and fit, it is proposed like a challenge to reality to
sprawl on the couch. Have you never seen 'Naked and Raw'? At least
'The Island of the Famous'? 'Wild' something?
A man alone, even if well-equipped, in any place, a forest a mountain
a river, a sea or lake shore, especially in our forests, would survive for
a very short time. Fortunately there are no longer the conditions of
really having to do it.

I've often wondered why the prehistoric statuette of a woman is por-
trayed as fat and round. I was always told that it represented fertility
and the ability to procreate.
I believe that perhaps it is so, but that what was worshiped and de-
picted in this way because the state of fatness and therefore abundance, at the time would have only been wishful thinking.

Men belonging to a community, either of two people or a thousand or

a million, will always find a way to create a hierarchy. It is the natural instinct of belonging to a pack. The condition is implied and usually is not, politely, carried out. It is efficient!
In a modern community, Western, prosperous and peaceful, individuals are not very bound; in the dynamic and continuous evolution of the balances, they enjoy a certain freedom and independence, in that they must give up a little for the good of the community. In other conditions individual freedom is much reduced and the sacrifice is imposed in the name of the common good and can be very high.

Man is not the result of evolution from the 'monkeys' but rather a new species of monkey in the course of evolution.

What a wonderful moment to remember the one when, for a moment, we fell into an awkward silence, and no one knew what to say. An eternal moment as long as one decides not to break it, in some way, that silence restores the atmosphere!

Sometimes mistakes are made, if you pay the consequences. Making a mistake is normal and even to commit another. Instead it is foolish to commit the same mistake twice.

There are those who firmly believe in predestination, entire religions proclaim it. It doesn't exist! Everyone creates their destiny on the basis of the natural gifts at their disposal, adaptability, intelligence, his or her ability to dare to go towards new and different risks and sometimes, just sometimes, winning.

Wishes unfortunately do not make things come true but certainly push toward that end. To make a lot of effort to reach an objective and then when the goal is almost reached you realize that its achievement will seem inconclusive.

Intimacy is not a question of numbers, closed doors, of shadows and lonely or separate places; intimacy is a matter of mutual respect and tolerance, always reciprocal, being close at all times. This is the foundation of a marriage and this strengthens over time while its lack will bury it.

There are two categories of persons to which 5% of the population can, wants and must belong: those that are popular known and admired by all or those who are powerful, practically known only to those who should know them: I think I belong to the latter. Popularity is not that important, it comes and goes but the recognition of ability remains.

Anger, determination, commitment, concentration, satisfaction, gratification, dissatisfaction, withdrawal, shame, humiliation, depression... reaction... these terms remind me of something, but what? We have to get used to new ideas to see the facts in the right perspective. What can I do to convince you that I'm telling the truth? Good question! It would be nice to be sure about knowing what we are going to do, whatever it is. It needs time and encouragement, but mostly time. Sometimes you look at a distant mountain view. You wonder what you're really looking at, if they are really the gigantic structures, full of details that you know but you can't see or are they a mirage, you see gigantic mountains that are incredibly close and detailed; you know they can't be there, and that you don't even know them. Everything seems so distant or so close and unreal.

A friend died yesterday; one among many who preceded him. I don't feel pain, only bitterness: we are all just like islands, separated, in a unique archipelago. In suspense: hit enter and turn on the video!

Nature is important it is linked to us and we are part or it; we must respect it but we can't reduce ourselves to living with the least of our needs, which would be enough for a person in the same condition as Robinson Crusoe: we cannot all retire to a hermitage to live 'comple-

tely alone; we can't all, reduce ourselves to the exclusive consumption of certain plants, in so far as when in need it may be possible to
do so; we are not able to, none of us can, do without society and its
constraints, nor completely escape it; we need to pollute.
Ecology encompasses us, of course, within the active parameters but
also can't do less. It would be enough, maybe, just a little moderation
in each; it can be done; and the application of common sense, to limit
the damage by increasing the benefits: maybe even this could be
done; and these could be shared with all humanity. Share benefits?
Equal for all? Free? .You don't say!!
Who knows if one day you will be able to produce what you need, or-
ganically 'in the world for the world'. A world state, the land of men;
pure science fiction, at least for now and whatever is pushing the
most.

Thoughts about Women's Day, commercial event, slogans, universal
manifesto of social hypocrisy! It seems strange that the cult of the
Virgin Mary, that is of the Mother in the various senses, up to Mother
Earth, to the 'fertile structure' is necessarily feminine, what is not represented is no longer as it was in ancient times, universally present
in the various and different religions, large or small that were or have
been.
Mother inviolate, ever renewed, ready for any cycle of rebirth and the
source of ever-new life.
It was certainly the first cult of humanity, even predominant to the
sun, because it bore with immediate effects on life and survival. It
could withstand even though it was raining, cold or with mist and
even at night, thanks to 'Mother' Earth. The sun was managed by the
matriarchy Gea-Gaia coming together with her own majesty and divinity, the other, the biological community but in the specific case of
the human children of the earth, with the power of prayers, sacrifices,
tolerance required to convince him, he, the Sun to participate actively
every day.
Willing sometimes shrewish and capricious 'Mother' at times angry
and sullen, always, in the end, sweet and generous with her children
has been the 'law' for millennia that has guided men in the use of her
'gifts'.
Yet it should be a natural thing for humanity to honor and venerate

the Mother and what she represents, either your own mother or nature.

Cultures and mostly ancient religions, tend to put on an equal plane
the reverence for the male and female principles; natural phenomena
are considered to be direct emanations and therefore also these are
deified.
It was necessary to also place man, to declare that he was higher, at
least, than the animals. This was achieved by associating the divine
principle of nature, as beloved children of the earth (men).
Once the secondary male and female gods were wiped out, the natural phenomena became increasingly controllable and more easily explained. Generally it passed from paganism to monotheism returning
to the basic principle and unifying everything.
A hierarchy was set up with the sons of the earth, plants herbivores
or carnivores, prey or predators up to the son of man, and then
among them: whites, people of color or blacks, the first-born and brothers and finally women. A fundamental step in historical development took place in the management and preservation of power.
The man who wants to rule his world, adapt it, force it to fit himself
and his needs. It seems that the exclusive male principle is now reve-
red, absolutely current and dominant, at least in the most backward,
least emancipated cultures.
In these cultures dominated by force and violence they don't exalt, or
revere the two principles but submit to the male principle, the Sun,
Energy, brute force, the masculine male, however all femininity is still
represented.
To the principles, male and female, was joined and was added, the ve-
neration of the children (the first born male of man was elevated to
divinity); children who appropriate the inheritance. And the legacy is
power.
Spiritual power is acquired with the deity and derived from it, but above all real power is that derived from material heredity, which is consecrated by it. In the great religions with social value, at the most femininity is recognized as existing and is respected for what it is, but
more easily, since it is useful to the woman, physical representation
of femininity, animals vegetation and altogether natural, it is considered for the most practical of uses. It becomes the object, property,

instrument for the affirmation, reproduction and preservation of male power.

Almost no religion venerates femininity and woman as its expression any more. Outside modern Catholicism (and also here for dogma, affirmation of an undeniable and unquestionable principle, but that then is really applied and respected with great difficulty, perhaps because while easily understandable and, having been imposed rebellion is generated).

I believe that people, especially males, presume too often that they are omniscient and omnipotent, because of their physical strength, convinced of their power. A serious mistake that places them into women's hands, vulnerable to a song or a sad story, idiots faced with a smile full of promise and an exposed breast.

Easily manipulated.

I'm afraid of getting old, because I am afraid of not being able to see, to understand, to think; I'm also afraid of dying but only because I am not ready to stop living.

What is worse than death? I believe it is to live outside of the senses, unable to be, to want, to remember, staring into the void!

I remember a love affair: when? How? I don't deceive myself enough! To be involved it is not that important to have the certainty of love, but it counts more to have the illusion of being loved.

I found old scattered papers, I was 16 or 17 years old I think; how beautiful the little poems I could write once were.

Autumn: leaves in the road, black hands against a gray background!
Skeletal trees pointing to the sky: hope!

How stupid and useless it is to live sick or unfortunate before the illness or misfortune hits us. Diminish the constant fear: it gives power to others!

When there is no obvious alternative, hesitation is always only a mistake! You can always decide to do something or not to do something, but to decide not to decide is unacceptable!

How many times am I angry particularly with myself: it's time to learn to forgive myself for not being perfect.

There is always an excuse for everything... or nevertheless it can be found!

You cannot reason and do everything only in terms of the 'principle'! It is *a matter of principle*... these statements are heard constantly justify any actions carried out or requested, solutions often in contrast to those suggested by simple common sense.
The 'principle' is related to morality, the moral to the social situation of the moment. The principle, thus, which inspires many when with scarce or few reasons argue positions they don't know how else to justify, it is a variable; anything but a reliable reference. Their (own) positions at all costs are the real matter of principle! Right or wrong, rational or emotional, comprehensive or minimally thought out it isn't important; they are ours and need to be supported, raising the voice or repeating three times as though the others, hard of hearing and savvy, weren't listening at first... it is a matter of principle!

Humans are the only animal that cannot see or feel anything if they don't want to! At any cost.

I wanted to be an adventurer. I loved anything I've done that would allow me briefly, to go away. Away from myself and from the world or maybe just away from my responsibilities, from my overwhelming responsibilities even though, however, more or less freely accepted. In practice I found that just reading, a little solitary wandering in the woods or fishing in the canals and streams, very few other activities don't involve the assumption of additional, new or different obligations and responsibilities. Over time I simply chose always to use and consistently more and only the mind, to reduce the effort required for escaping! I have understood what the crazies do and those who are out of their minds.

In the end it all comes down to deciding which category of use the things in the world belong, nothing excluded: legitimate or illicit uses. Which of the two the majority in power decides at that particular moment in history.

The statistics are the key with which you try to interpret and make sense of a series of data collected on a computer screen. Most often they are unreliable, however, the exercise is still useful, to pass the time and to find new reasons to generate chatter.

There are dozens if not thousands of faiths in the world. Maybe even one for every man woman and child. They are dynamic evolutions of thought, even rational, influenced by the need to know, to hope, to react to society and the current state of things that closely concern us. I believe (I have faith) that no faith is negative if it presupposes respect for other human beings, in a general sense.
The consciousness of being in the right cannot be separated from the certainty that others can, at least in part, also be.
Right or wrong (moral or immoral?) how is it possible to define these concepts outside of the context of the study? Time, space and interactive parameters!
To have a conscience assumes that it will be used. Unfortunately it is not a dogma, as demonstrated by human behavior during a war.
An error that I find in the faiths that originated from the Bible is that not everyone has the same chance of being saved, forever, by the so-called mercy of the God referred to.
In fact it will be only the righteous, and the same God already knows them and will save them anyway sacrificing the others, regardless of their behavior. Or is it a race and thus still is and always will be a com-

petition, so those arriving in the first places win the award and for everyone else there is eternal oblivion? Let's hope for the best.

I believe it is impossible for me to do only what I don't know how to do! But that is just for me. I would like to do something else, I would like time to learn how to do it; I would like to get and achieve other objectives and possibly for what they are, with what I know how to do; possibly without getting anything from others or deceiving them or flattering.

I went on a trip to the bar, to the local market, I went to the hyper-market, I walked on the street; I had a coffee, I watched television and looked at people: talking constantly. But what was everyone talking about? Basic discussions, about important decisions, to chat to be part of the world, just empty words spoken to be heard? *I will chatter, ergo sum!*

The priests? They are only teachers! Officials of a school and a method that has been persevered for thousands of years wherever and in every culture and they still do it. Without a school we cannot talk about religion. It remains religiosity, an individual matter, in an embryonic state.
Doubt, the hunger for knowledge, the search for answers to questions not yet asked, it would put any system of government or existing or potential organization into a crises. Original sin!

Twists and turns: In five hundred years Rome went from being a small agricultural settlement to becoming one of the largest cities in the world and in another five hundred, returned to being an agricultural town of 20,000 inhabitants, full of ruins but with a Pope; to start over again from there.

Good and evil? They are just opinions that are intertwined in the evolution of history, you influence it and in doing so it influences you.

Physical laws? Govern all of nature: the world as it is; the galaxy, galaxies; the whole universe, and perhaps all interfering universes. Perhaps, perhaps.... or at least we call reality a part of these. Inertia, gravitation, electromagnetic spectrum and measurements. *Everything is relative!* – great affirmation of a madman named Einstein – and *everything evolves...* continued the other not very normal: Darwin.

The result of ignorance is fanatical acceptance or fanatical rejection; to believe or not to believe; an unequivocal choice; from time to time, absolute faith or its absolute negation and this only in function of what each one knows, believes they know or that has been presented as known. Maybe I really know or think I know but probably usually, simply suppose.

Who knows if one day I will really decide to gather up and who knows, maybe publish these thoughts. The question is: will they be interesting or will someone find them useful? On the other hand, this is more or less my life experience.

They tell me, why are you never satisfied? Why should I be satisfied? If I die today, the objectives I've achieved in my life will have been what they are now and only those; if I live longer then there will be others to do, to accomplish, to see, to understand, to learn.

CHAOS AND THANKSGIVING
Chaos contains within itself and spontaneously generates order which again spontaneously tends towards chaos by continually using and dissipating the immense energy it seethes with.
So, what is Chaos? Perhaps the tendency of the universe to stabilize in a state of absolute rest, to use as little energy as possible. A definitive form of order. Order requires energy. Every equilibrium sustains

itself with the effort of its use. Chaos is the anagram of Case! Each variation of energy alters the balance and generates new changes and new chaos and from chaos new changes and new orderly points. Textures, proposal networks and response nodes. Environmental action and response, whatever the environment intended as a context. Chaos is life, it is mutation, it is evolution. Slowly the particles move away, the interactions fade, the universe or their whole if there are others, tends to the stillness in which everything is equilibrium just like the mind, a place that slowly becomes still, full of memories, memories of life, memories of energy interactions, substituting actions for emotions until finally the chill arrives, the absolute immobility, the expectation of a new beginning, of a new infinitesimal spark that returns to generate chaos and the notes will spread again. A new melody and then another and a new symphony will fill the space.

The scientific method teaches us to observe without intervening, to consider, to take note, to evaluate the indications, to start deductions for new in-depth research, to learn as much as possible unfortunately man's desire for control leads him to continually seek answers. Okay, let's look for the answer, but what question? No answer has meaning if the question is not first and foremost identified.

The oldest and most widespread because it is human is the one on the meaning of life. For thousands of years man has been asking himself the question and has arrived, has arrived thousands of times at the same conclusion: life is a random phenomenon, it has no meaning outside the context in which it exists. Action, reaction, proposal and environmental response that selects the winning response for a short moment. But the question persists until it becomes a boring but shared routine at the base of every existing or existing religion and the answer continues to be that. It should be noted.

Try to imagine life limited to a grain of sand, even two, three, a hundred, even a thousand. Imagine dropping them from high, very high, from the sky and watching them fall and evolve, roll, hop until they reach kilometers of sandy beaches made up of billions of billions of similar but sterile grains. Insignificant episodes if not for those who live on the grains deliberately ignoring being part of the beach.

But also, something bigger if you will, not a speck but a big rock, big enough to support a castle a rock full of life. Do the same experiment, take it to the upper atmosphere and drop it to the earth. You will get the exact same result, a grain, a rock among billions of rocks.

Even more, lift a mountain, Mont Blanc, is it big enough? It will fall making a loud noise, upsetting its surroundings for a limited time, then it will be a mountain among thousands of others as big as it, a little more, a little less. Once again: think of being a giant, big enough to use the earth, the planet as a marble and launch it with an immense slingshot into space. Something will happen, certainly all around its passage, at its point of arrival, like the grain of sand, finally, a little hopping, a little rolling, will find its place among billions of billions of similar marbles while the beach undergoes the action of the sea waves that lap it, mixing it, redesigning it, grain by grain.

So maybe the question is wrong, the answer is useless, senseless. But what other question is left for us to finalize the search for the conclusive answer? The fundamental answer? Perhaps that if there is a beginning to the chaos that determines and has determined our existence. A point, where? When? What value can we attribute to it? If the universe follows physical laws and so does chaos, mathematics is the only science capable of describing reality even beyond our ability to see. Mathematics describes or approaches to do the existing and even the chaos and at least the mechanism of its possible consequences: interaction and interaction and interaction in an infinite loop. The whole interacts with the whole in an infinite number of ways of points, of moments. Mathematics is expressed in numbers, perhaps then the answer is a number. Yes, but which one? In the beautiful crazy book 'The Hitchhiker's Guide to the Galaxy' crazy, demented, cheerful, irreverent, not by chance the final answer it's a number, a random number. I am not the only one who has perceived this need, to find the answer to the main question. Why do we exist? And if we exist, what do we do with our lives? Attention, it is not the same as what is the meaning of our life!

If there is a need for a number perhaps infinite is the right one but too vast, indeterminate, there must be a more precise answer that includes the possibility of infinity. I believe there is: my answer is '0'. Why zero? Because everything that exists and can exist unravels from him, infinite values greater than him and as many infinite values less than him. $-\infty - 0- +\infty$. Here then is my answer which contains every other answer, every other search, every other question: '0'

END

Acknowledgements

A book is written because it will be read and therefore. I thank the readers and the kind and competent Doctor Pamela Michelis who edited the Italian version of this book.
Again, thanks to the patience, competence and dedication devoted by Rosemary Dawn Allison to the translation, the book will be available to more of the world.

www.ingramcontent.com/pod-product-compliance
Lightning Source LLC
Chambersburg PA
CBHW061323250726
48657CB00016B/19